How God Became God

How God Became God

What Scholars Are Really Saying
About God and the Bible

✳

Richard Smoley

A TarcherPerigee Book

tarcherperigee
An imprint of Penguin Random House LLC
375 Hudson Street
New York, New York 10014

Most Tarcher/Penguin books are available at special quantity discounts for
bulk purchase for sales promotions, premiums, fund-raising, and
educational needs. Special books or book excerpts also can be
created to fit specific needs. For details, write:
SpecialMarkets@penguinrandomhouse.com.

Library of Congress Cataloging-in-Publication Data
Names: Smoley, Richard, 1956– author.
Title: How God became God : what scholars are really saying about God and the
Bible / by Richard Smoley.
Description: New York City : Tarcher, 2016. | Includes bibliographical references.
Identifiers: LCCN 2015046609 | ISBN 9780399185557
Subjects: LCSH: God—Biblical teaching.
Classification: LCC BS544 .S64 2016 | DDC 231—dc23

Printed in the United States of America
1   3   5   7   9   10   8   6   4   2

BOOK DESIGN BY KATY RIEGEL

*For
Nicole, Robert,
and William*

Contents

Acknowledgments   *xi*

Chronology   *xiii*

Introduction   *xvii*

Part One

1. Groundwater: The Problem of God   3
2. The Defective Scripture:
   What We Now Know About the Bible   13

Part Two

3. The Haze of Legend: From the Flood to the Judges   35
4. Monarchy, United and Divided:
   From Saul to the Fall of Israel   50
5. Who Was Yahweh?   60
6. Fall and Return: The Exile and Its Aftermath   74

Part Three

7. Jesus in His Context   93
8. The Life of Jesus: Origins   109
9. What Jesus Taught   124
10. The Life of Jesus: The Public Career   145
11. The Birth of the Church   166
12. Paul: The Great Apostle   184
13. Revelation: The Overthrow of the Wicked Angels   199
14. The Master and Two Marys   211

Part Four

15. Practical Mysticism   241

Coda   261
Further Reading   267
Notes   271

Maps

The Near East in the First Millennium BC   33
Israel and Judah During the Divided Monarchy   49
Palestine in the Time of Christ   91

ACKNOWLEDGMENTS

Like any such effort, this one owes debts to countless people and sources that have informed my thinking over the decades, and it would be impossible to think of, much less list, them all. First and foremost I'm grateful to my wife, Nicole, and to our sons, Robert and William, for the loving home that they have provided for me during the writing of this book.

I would like to thank my agent, Laurie Fox, for her help and support in this process. She dealt skillfully with a difficult prospect: a fully completed manuscript that I wrote out of my own head without a contract and without consulting her or, for that matter, anyone else.

A similar debt of gratitude is owed to Mitch Horowitz, my editor at TarcherPerigee, who took on this project with tremendous enthusiasm and who, moreover, has shown tremendous faith in me and my work over the past decade. He is an old-fashioned editor in the best sense of that term.

Drew Stevens, art director of *Quest: Journal of the Theosophical Society in America*, very graciously designed the maps and diagram for this book. I really appreciate his kind and enthusiastic help.

I would also like to thank Michael Burke, my copy editor, for his careful attention to the manuscript, which has been of great benefit both to me and to the final state of this book.

Richard Smoley
Winfield, Illinois
January 2016

Chronology

BC

c.2250–c.1500. Middle Bronze Age.

c.1900. Traditional date of Abraham.

c.1800–c.1550. Hyksos period in Egypt.

c.1500–c.1200. Late Bronze Age.

c.1300. Traditional date of the Exodus.

1207. Merneptah Stele: first mention of Israel.

c.1000. Reign of Saul.

c.1000–920. Reigns of David and Solomon.

c.940–586. First Temple period.

c.920. Conventional date of invasion of Israel by Sheshonq I, pharaoh of Egypt.

c.920–722. The divided monarchy: Israel in the north, Judah in the south.

c.858–824. Shalmaneser Stele.

c.850. Tel Dan Stele, mentioning "the house of David." Reign of the house of Omri in the northern kingdom of Israel. Building of Samaria.

c.760. Time of the prophet Amos.

722.	Conquest of northern kingdom of Israel by Assyrians under Shalmaneser V.
700.	Jerusalem, under Hezekiah, besieged unsuccessfully by the Assyrians.
697–642.	Reign of Menasseh, king of Judah.
640–609.	Reign of Josiah.
c.620.	Reformation of the Temple cult. First version of the Deuteronomic history.
586.	Sack of the First Temple by the Babylonians under Nebuchadnezzar.
586–539.	Babylonian Exile of the Jews. Revision of Deuteronomic history.
539.	Jews return from Babylonian Exile, begin to rebuild Temple.
539–AD 70.	Second Temple period.
521 BC–485 BC.	Reign of Darius, king of Persia.
167.	Antiochus IV Epiphanes sets up altar to Zeus in Jerusalem Temple. Jews revolt.
c.165.	Date of the book of Daniel.
164.	Antiochus defeated and expelled from Judea.
c.140.	Maccabees establish Hasmonean dynasty in Judea.
63.	Pompey conquers Judea, enters the Temple.
49–46; 44–31.	Roman Civil War.
37.	Herod the Great takes the throne of Judea.
27.	Establishment of the Roman Empire under Augustus.
23.	Herod begins restoring the Temple.
c.8–5.	Probable date of the birth of Christ.
4.	Death of Herod.

AD

6. Birth of Christ according to Luke. Quirinius governor of Syria.

26–36. Pontius Pilate governor of Judea.

29. Beginning of Jesus's public career according to Luke.

30–33. Approximate date of Jesus's crucifixion.

62. James the brother of Jesus stoned to death.

64. Persecution of the Christians in Rome under Nero.

66. The Jews in Judea revolt against Rome.

68. Nero toppled from power as emperor of Rome.

70. Sack of the Temple by the Romans under Titus.

81–96. Reign of the emperor Domitian.

313. Edict of Milan issued by the emperor Constantine, granting freedom of religion to all sects, including Christianity.

325. First Council of Nicaea.

367. Athanasius establishes New Testament canon.

391. Pagan temples closed in the Roman Empire.

395. Christianity made official religion of the Roman Empire.

431. Mary the mother of Christ proclaimed *Theotókos*, Mother of God.

476. Fall of the western Roman Empire.

Introduction

TODAY THERE ARE many books about God on the market. Histories of God, analyses of God, biographies of God—all that's left, it seems, is to splash the innermost secrets of the Supreme Being on the cover of a tabloid.

A number of these works are sincere, thoughtful, and learned. They tell us how the idea of God arose and grew into what it is today. But I've come away from all of them wondering where this leaves us. Are we supposed to believe in this God whose history we've just read? Or should we toss him away? I usually go away concluding that somehow we are still supposed to believe in him, even though we can believe practically nothing that people have been saying about him for thousands of years. Maybe we're just expected to believe out of habit. It has been done.

We could, of course, approach the problem of God from any number of angles. For us in the West, it is intertwined with Christianity. It can't be answered without reference to Christianity.

Not that Christianity has any privileged position among the world religions. It is, to my mind, neither more nor less complete or true than the others. In fact, I think other religions have much to offer that Christianity has never given. Buddhism has developed the art and science of cognitive awareness to a very high level; the West has yet to digest all of its insights. Hindu metaphysics and epistemology—the philosophies of being and knowledge—far outstrip their Western counterparts. The religions of China—Taoism and Confucianism—seem the sanest of all, because they emphasize living in harmony with the way things are rather than fighting against them. And so on.

But our culture is Christian, or post-Christian. Our language, our morals, our ideals all come out of Christianity. Of course Christianity has very often failed to live up to these ideals. But the ideals that it has failed to live up to are Christian ones.

The same is true with God. Can you be an atheist in the West today? Certainly. But it will be the Christian God that you don't believe in.

The twentieth-century philosopher Martin Heidegger had a word for this situation. In its original German, it is quite a mouthful: *Geworfenheit*. The usual English translation is "thrownness." It means this: We have been thrown into this world without knowing why or how. As people sometimes say, "I didn't ask to be born." And you didn't (at least as far as you can remember). But you are here, and you have to deal with it.

For us in the West, Christianity is part of our thrownness. Even those who were raised without religion, or in another religion, have had Christianity in their cultural background. Like it or not, we have to come to terms with this heritage.

Some writers use the term "Judeo-Christian tradition." I will avoid it for two reasons. First, Jews sometimes resent being lumped together with a religion that has long been alien and hostile to them. Second, I am not a Jew and I don't see it as my business to say what Judaism should or might mean today. So I will speak of Christianity rather than the Judeo-Christian tradition.

Nevertheless, I have the highest respect for the Jewish tradition and will often make use of its insights in this book. In fact Part Two is devoted to some of the issues that come up in regard to the Hebrew Bible. Besides, a great deal of early Christianity makes no sense unless you have some grasp of Jewish mysticism.

To go further: In America the problem of Christianity is inseparable from the problem of the Bible. America is a Protestant nation, and Protestantism in one way or another has affected practically everyone who was born here. As its fundamental stance, Protestantism holds that there is no intermediary between man and God. Nothing should or can stand between us and the ultimate Source of being. Not even, and especially not, the church.

Protestantism started as a revolt against the arrogance and hypocrisy of the Catholic church. Rejecting the church's authority, it needed another authority to stand in its place. It turned to the doctrine of *Scriptura sola*, "Scripture alone," as the source of spiritual truth. (By contrast, the Catholic church has always held that the church's own traditions and teachings have an authority equal to that of Scripture.)

This fact makes the Bible a much hotter topic in America than it is in western Europe, where the influences both of Catholicism and twentieth-century secularism have diminished its importance. In the United States, on the other hand, there is much controversy about the Bible—and that controversy touches the nerves of our society at the deepest level.

But as many people have heard, modern scholarship has made the Bible seem a lot more shaky as an authority, much less as a sole authority.

So we are left with these questions: What is scholarship telling us about the Bible? And in the face of these findings—which by no means always confirm the Bible's literal truth—what new meaning can be found in it?

These are the questions I will try to address in this book.

To begin with, although an incredible amount of work and thought has gone into the historical background of the Bible, it hasn't had much impact on the general public.

Here is one reason, as stated in 2006 by author John Dart, addressing the Society for Biblical Literature (the foremost scholarly body on the subject): "Unfortunately, there is built-in resistance to popularizing biblical research findings for the general public. . . . It is believed that complex, nuanced scholarly arguments tend to get 'lost in translation' to readers and audiences unfamiliar with the terminology and background."

True, but there's more to it than that. I look back to a 1998 *Time* magazine feature about Moses ("In Search of Moses," by David Van Biema). It's a pretty typical treatment of a biblical subject by a newsmagazine. Strictly speaking, there is nothing wrong or inaccurate about it (at least as far as I can see). But it is a bit slippery. On the one hand, it does discuss what modern scholarship says about Moses. On the other hand, having sketched out in the briefest possible terms the very small amount that scholars actually know about Moses, the article goes on to retell the story in Exodus, complete with golden calf and the giving of the Law on Sinai. Overall you are left with the impression that these things actually, literally happened, when they almost certainly did not. At the end, the article says, "Archaeology and scholarly speculation can take us only so far. It can be argued that even the holiest of texts cannot do Moses justice."

This is meant, of course, to leave us with questions. Because if the *Time* article had said outright what scholars really believe—that much if not all of the story of Moses and the Exodus is mythical and has little if any historical value—the publishers would be flooded with mail from outraged believers. The same would happen with their stories about Jesus. (Jesus is not quite as shadowy a figure as Moses, but there are serious questions about who he really was as well.)

A later story—"How Moses Shaped America" by Bruce Feiler, in *Time*, October 12, 2009—avoids this topic altogether. Instead it is about Moses as conceived in the American political imagination.

Why do journalists write these stories? Because religious covers sell. In the early 1990s, a reporter *for U.S. News & World Report* told me that her magazine's religious covers outsold all others, except for those about major disasters. Unfortunately for publishers (though fortunately for the rest of us), events like 9/11 don't happen every week. So, especially at holiday time, Jesus and Moses are regularly unearthed, and the reader is enticed with promises of amazing new discoveries about them. But there are no amazing new discoveries. In fact the magazines don't even want to tell us about the old discoveries.

Some news sources do try to get closer to the truth. But even here journalists are hamstrung by the real or supposed need for objectivity. It usually means that the reporter offers both sides of the issue, shrugs her shoulders, and leaves people to make up their own minds.

Biblical documentaries—or pseudodocumentaries—on television are another matter. There is an endless number of these. You could probably watch them on a twenty-four-hour basis if you wanted to. The format is pretty standard. It consists of bits of interviews with scholars (some of them mainstream, some from the fringe) interspersed with scenic footage of the Holy Land and reenactments abounding in fake beards and costumes that have not been updated since Charlton Heston received the Law on Sinai in 1956.

These shows can be ingenious. I watched one recently on King Herod the Great and the slaughter of the innocents in Bethlehem after the birth of Christ. The show was a kind of psychobiography trying to determine whether Herod was capable of such a horrible deed. In the end, it concluded that he was.

Which is certainly true. Herod committed any number of atrocities. But scholars almost unanimously doubt that he carried out the slaughter of the innocents, which is unknown and unheard of outside of Matthew's Gospel. Even the other Gospels make no mention of it. The show said almost nothing about that.

Such programs try to have it both ways. There is some lip service to scholarship, and even quite a bit of actual historical information (in this case, about Herod's reign, his construction programs, and so on). But the main point—whether the slaughter of the innocents actually took place—is pushed to the background or ignored entirely.

Many, even most, biblical documentaries on TV take the same tack. Why? The biggest audience for these shows is people who believe quite literally in the Bible. No producer with any sense is going to alienate his main audience.

Some documentaries, by contrast, have gone into these controversies, often capably. Of those that I've seen, the best is probably a 2008 program from the PBS series *NOVA* entitled "The Bible's Buried Secrets," which does try to do justice to many of the real issues at stake.

Admittedly, times are changing. The culture wars in the United States have gotten so acute that more and more of these facts are entering into the debate. In a 2013 article for *The Huffington Post*, Episcopal bishop John Shelby Spong writes about the Gospel of John: "There is probably not a single word attributed to Jesus in this book that the Jesus of history actually spoke." Furthermore, "not one of the signs (the Fourth Gospel's word for miracles) recorded in this book was, in all probability, something that actually happened."

Spong is one of the foremost spokesmen in liberal Christianity against fundamentalism. He is stating mainstream scholarly opinion. And he has a wide readership, meaning that some of the findings of scholarship are now trickling out to a mass audience.

Not all clergymen are able to go as far as Spong. On the one hand, there are the evangelical and fundamentalist Protestants. They make much about the literal truth of the Bible, so what they say and what they believe (or are supposed to believe) are more or less the same. On the other hand, there are the mainstream and liberal Protestants as well as the Catholics. Their ministers and priests are well educated. They know the problems about the historical Moses and the historical Jesus, and everything in between; they learned all this in seminary. But they balk at sharing this information with their flocks.

Many mainstream scholars, for example, do not believe that Jesus rose from the dead. They believe this was a myth that grew up around him after his death. (I don't agree, for reasons I will get to later.) And the ministers know this. Some of them believe the same thing.

I was having lunch recently with a good friend of mine, a pastor in a mainstream Protestant denomination. We got around to the subject of the resurrection. He said to me, "I think Jesus just died." He's in line with a great deal of scholarly opinion. The distinguished New Testament scholar John Dominic Crossan has gone even further and said—no doubt with some intent to shock—that not only did Jesus die (permanently) but his body was eaten by dogs. (There is actually no evidence for this claim.)

What's a minister to do with these things? They would hardly make an inspiring subject for an Easter sermon.

Another time I was talking to my friend about the afterlife. He seemed to believe less in it than I do. So I said, "Well, what do you tell people at funerals?" He replied sheepishly that he generally phrased it in terms of "Christian hope."

Another friend, a minister in another mainstream Protestant denomination, is based in Dallas. When he was in our town recently, my wife and I had him over for dinner. While we were talking after the meal, I said, "You know all this stuff about the scholarship and so on. Have you tried to tell your congregations about any of this?"

"No."

"Why not?"

His answer was characteristically frank: "I chickened out."

I don't mean to sneer at clergy who are in this position. They are in a tight spot. They have felt a calling to their profession—to serve God and their fellow humans. They went to seminary, where they learned that much of what they believed is, from a historical point of view, simply untrue. Were they taught what to do with this, how to take this knowledge and turn it into something that has genuine power and comfort? It doesn't seem so.

At this point, someone may say, "Well, the Bible wasn't *meant* to be literally true." As a matter of fact, I agree—and I will talk much more about this later. But over the centuries Christianity has sold itself on the fact that the Bible *is* literally true. In the centuries when Christianity was young, the Greeks and Romans (at any rate the educated ones) had lost faith in their gods. They no longer believed stories about Zeus changing himself into a swan, hell being guarded by a three-headed dog, and so on.

Then Christianity appeared, offering all the answers. Of course, they said, the pagan myths weren't true. The truth was in the Bible. God had created heaven and earth; God gave the Law to Moses; and Jesus, God incarnate, came down to save us from ourselves. The Christians insisted that these were all solid historical facts. They may not seem quite so easy to believe today, but they were undoubtedly more plausible than gods changing into swans.

Then as now, not all Christians believed literally in the Bible. But most of them did, and soon practically everybody followed suit. Western civilization was given a new sacred history—the story of human sin and fall and redemption, first through the Law of Moses, and finally in the death and atonement of Christ.

But ever since the Enlightenment in the eighteenth century, when the Bible began to be seriously evaluated as a historical source, its credibility has continued to erode. On the scientific side, this process started in earnest in the early 1830s, when Charles Lyell published his *Principles of Geology*. Lyell argued, on the basis of geological evidence, that the earth had to be much older than the six thousand years allocated to it by Genesis. About twenty-five years later, Darwin and the theory of evolution took this claim further.

Soon Noah and his Flood were tossed out as well. By the middle of the twentieth century, doubts extended to the patriarchs Abraham, Isaac, and Jacob, who are conventionally dated to the early second millennium BC. The narratives about them were written (at the very earliest) a thousand years after their time, so scholars no longer believe that these contain anything but possibly the faintest hint of authentic history. The Exodus (often dated to around 1300 BC) came next.

The march continues. In 1976, when I was at Harvard, I took a course with the great Old Testament scholar Frank Moore Cross. At that point scholars generally believed that the biblical accounts of David and Solomon (who are dated to the tenth century BC) were more or less historical, and that was what I learned in the class.

That is no longer true. Archaeologists have done a lot of digging in Israel, and they have found nothing of the glories of David and Solomon. Many of them have concluded that Solomon's supposedly magnificent Jerusalem was an unremarkable hill town numbering maybe 250 people. Some scholars even doubt that David and Solomon ever lived. At most they were chieftains who, through personal charisma, managed to more or less unite the Israelite tribes for a couple of generations.

What about Solomon's great Temple in Jerusalem, the most famous holy site in the world? We don't know anything about it archaeologically, and we won't anytime soon. Its site is occupied by the Muslim Dome of the Rock, and it is impossible to conduct archaeological digs there. While Solomon could have built, and probably did build, a temple of some kind, in all likelihood it had nothing like the magnificence the Bible says it had.

Let me put the matter more concretely. I take the copy of the Bible I have closest to hand. It is a fine old edition of the King James Version from Cambridge University Press, with gilt-edged pages, bound in brown calfskin, worn from honorable service. In this Bible, the first eleven chapters of Genesis—dealing with the creation and the Flood and so on—take up thirteen pages. Over the past two hundred years, because of science and other advances in knowledge, biblical scholars came to accept that this section was mythical.

I move ahead to page 465, the passage in 1 Kings which describes the rise of the house of Omri in the northern kingdom of Israel, every last one of whom "wrought evil in the eyes of the Lord." (Biblical quotations in this book, unless otherwise noted, are from the King James Version.) Omri's son, Ahab, is better known, and Ahab's wife, Jezebel, is more famous still.

Why do I bring this up? The Omrid dynasty, as it is called, is the period when the Old Testament begins to be verified in the archaeological record. We don't have any remains of Solomon's Temple, but we do have remains of the stables of wicked King Ahab in Samaria. He lived in the ninth century BC. Here the Bible starts to become historical. Even so the picture is still blurry. It comes into sharper focus only two hundred years later, after 620 BC.

To illustrate the point, in December 2015 the imprint of a seal was discovered in Israel bearing the name of Hezekiah, king of Judah. It has a winged solar disk (an emblem of the Judahite kings) and, surprisingly, perhaps, an ankh, the Egyptian symbol of life. Eilat Mazar, an archaeologist on the excavation, suggested that the imprint might have been made by Hezekiah himself, "since it's hard to believe that anyone else had permission to use the seal." And Hezekiah is discussed at length in the Bible, particularly in 2 Kings 16:20–20:21.

There you have it. Proof positive that Hezekiah was a real king. This fits perfectly into the picture I've just drawn. The dates of Hezekiah's reign are placed between 715 and 686 BC. He lived over a hundred years after Ahab. He is in the part of the Bible that is historical.

But no such seals have been found for David or Solomon, despite the alleged breadth and magnificence of their kingdoms. They lived in the tenth century BC, and much of what the Bible says about them is likely either legend or fiction.

In my edition, the Old Testament takes up 1109 pages. Thus almost half of it—covering the years from the foundation of the world to, say, 850 BC—is either mythical or only dimly reflects historical truth. Practically all the rest of those 1109 pages is taken up with the "Writings" (texts such as Psalms and Proverbs), and the utterances of the prophets, which are not historical accounts. Much of what the prophets predicted didn't come true either.

I might interrupt myself here to make an important point. As far as I can tell, the historical facts I'm stating in this book agree, at least in general, with the views of the most reputable scholars in universities and divinity schools, whose works I have done my best to study. When I write, "Scholars say . . ."—and I often will—this is what I mean. Of course there are areas where they disagree, and I will also make this clear to the best of my ability. There are some areas where I disagree with them, and again, when I do, I will say so and why.

There are other instances where I will make speculations of my own or mention those of others. *Speculate* here means that what is said is consistent with known evidence, but in order to be proved it would require evidence that we do not have and may never have.

Let's take Moses. His name means "son" in ancient Egyptian. We see this in some names of the pharaohs: *Thutmose* means "son of [the god] Tut" or Thoth. *Rameses* means "son of [the god] Ra."

All of this is well accepted. But let us go on to speculate about something, as some scholars have done. When you think about it, "Son" is a curious name. We have many Johnsons and Richardsons, but practically nobody has the surname "Son." This suggests that Moses too, raised as an Egyptian, may have originally had the name of an Egyptian god in his own name. Possibly he discarded this god name when he chose to follow Yahweh, the God we know from the Old Testament. Or maybe later generations found this awkward fact embarrassing and shortened the name to obscure it.

I find this idea fascinating and plausible, but there is absolutely no proof of it, nor, I imagine, will there ever be. Thus this claim is speculative. When I'm making claims like this in the course of this book, I will take every pain to say so clearly.

Another point: the scholars of the last two centuries—biblical experts, archaeologists, theologians—have put an almost inconceivable amount of work into searching out the historical truth of the Bible. Few of these individuals were skeptics or debunkers. They were not setting out to prove the Bible wrong. Many of them were clergymen themselves. To look at the literal claims of your own faith, to scrutinize the evidence down to the tiniest jot, and to face results squarely and honestly? As Albert Schweitzer wrote in his classic study *The Quest of the Historical Jesus,* "it is a uniquely great expression of sincerity, one of the most significant events in the whole mental and spiritual life of humanity."

This book is in part about what the scholars found. But it will also attempt to suggest what may take us past these factual problems.

FINALLY, THERE IS the personal question. Who am I, the author of this book? What gives me the authority to speak on this subject? In the end, it's you who give me the authority. It's you who decide whether what I say makes sense to you. Even if you judge me on the basis of whatever credentials I may have, this still remains the case. The same holds true, as a matter of fact, for any authority you trust in.

That much said, it's fair to expect me to talk a bit about myself. I have published eight books on religion and spirituality. One of my most successful is *Inner Christianity: A Guide to the Esoteric Tradition,* published in 2002. It has made its way into some unusual places, and it has touched a number of lives. A number of people have told me that they've read it over and over.

Another book of mine, *Forbidden Faith: The Secret History of Gnosticism,* traces the heritage of Gnosticism (an early Christian "heresy") and other esoteric paths throughout Western history. *Conscious Love: Insights from Mystical Christianity*, tries to look at the Christian concept of love from a deeper level than usual. My latest book, *The Deal: A Guide to Radical and Complete Forgiveness*, discusses how to forgive from a practical angle.

So I have thought about, and studied, these subjects for quite some time—forty years—and my views have touched some readers deeply. During the course of this period I have found myself coming back to the Bible over and over again, sometimes in a devotional way, sometimes from a scholarly perspective. When I was at Oxford in the late 1970s, studying—or as they say there, "reading"—classics and philosophy, I made time to attend a course on biblical Hebrew. (The instructor was an affable Baptist minister who pointed out that the word *ohel* means "tent." He said it pretty much summed up his feelings about camping.)

Issues such as the historical Jesus and the history of Israel in biblical times have continued to fascinate me in the years since, and I've approached them from any number of angles. One project I've worked on over the past decade has been to annotate *Secrets of Heaven*, a verse-by-verse commentary on Genesis and Exodus by the eighteenth-century Swedish savant Emanuel Swedenborg that amounts to more than two million words.

Some may ask if I am a Christian. Recently I got an e-mail from a woman who said, "I grew up among fundamentalist Christians, who would say, 'Have you been born again?' before they would ask your name." To me, anyone who jabbers on like a salesman about being "born again" has no idea of what that really means. (What it does mean, or may mean, is yet another thing I will go into.) And I am not a church member or a churchgoer, not out of any ideological conviction, but simply because I prefer to stay at home drinking coffee on Sunday mornings. When my sons, who are six and seven, have asked me about Jesus, I've replied, "He was a good man who lived a long time ago."

Nevertheless, I try to live by the teachings of Christ as set out in the

Gospels. Although these texts are not historically accurate in every detail, the basic message is clear. And as I will try to show, beyond this basic message are layers of deeper meanings that may help us escape from the trap of biblical literalism.

As for the rest of the Christian tradition—the epistles of Paul and the others, the teachings of the church, and so on—I take them as advisory *only*. I don't feel any obligation to believe them or follow them unless they make sense to me.

Well, then, you may ask, "Do you believe in God?"

Read on.

Part One

Groundwater: The Problem of God

DOES GOD EXIST? Often when this subject comes up, people start talking about science or reason or revelation as authorities.

Science is not much help. Because, in the end, science is a method and not a body of doctrine. It is a very narrow and specialized way of investigating physical reality. Any and all of its findings are subject to refutation at any point, and that is the way it should be.

Here's an example. Over the last generation or two, the educated world has come to believe in the Big Bang as the origin of the universe, much as our ancestors believed in Genesis. There have even been efforts (though not very inspiring ones) to turn the story of the universe, starting with this Big Bang, into a new myth for our time.

In September 2014 a news item announced that a physics professor at the University of North Carolina, Laura Mersini-Houghton, has proved mathematically that "singularities" don't exist. Since the Big Bang would have been a singularity, there was no Big Bang. So we will have to rethink our theories about the origins of the universe.

Will Mersini-Houghton's work stand up to scrutiny? I have no idea.

But I do know that if science decides there was no Big Bang, many people's views of the history of the universe will come crashing down. Science is entitled to—obliged to—change its mind when the facts so dictate. It is not a reliable source of timeless truths.

Then there is reason. Briefly, during the French Revolution, reason was worshipped as a goddess. With the God of Christianity supposedly overthrown, it must have looked like a worthy substitute. It doesn't look so appealing today. Why? Because it's all too clear that reason can be used to prove almost anything. Ordinary language even has a word pointing to this fact: *rationalization*. When you rationalize, you are making up a reasonable excuse for something, wrong or right, that you had already decided to do to begin with. Your reason is not the master; it is the servant of your wishes. It is easily led.

I taught philosophy at a community college for several years, and among the subjects I covered were the philosophical proofs of the existence of God. They have been widely discussed, and I won't go into them here. The upshot, however, is that you will find them persuasive to the exact degree that you wanted to believe them in the first place.

Finally, there is revelation. The summit of Roman Catholic theology, the Scholasticism of Thomas Aquinas, says that revelation (along with reason) is the great foundation for our belief in God.

Is this so? It depends on what you mean. If you have a direct experience of revelation, there is nothing to debate. If the Lord himself appears to you out of a fiery bush, you are not going to doubt. You will be on your knees before you have even thought about whether to doubt or not.

Most of us aren't in this position. We haven't been struck down by visions on the road to Damascus. Instead we're expected to believe in the revelations of the past, revelations that occurred to somebody else, thousands of years ago, offered to us in fine calfskin Bibles. We are expected to put faith in them.

But as the kid says in the joke, "Faith is believin' what you know ain't so."

Nevertheless, there may be a bit more to this revelation business than it seems.

A good place to begin would be with this quote from Thornton Wilder's play *Our Town*: "Everybody knows in their bones that *something* is eternal, and that something has to do with human beings. All the greatest people ever lived have been telling us that for five thousand years and yet you'd be surprised how people are always losing hold of it. There's something way down deep that's eternal about every human being."

Here, in this stale old play, rarely performed outside of high-school auditoriums, is the central truth of our existence, stated plainly and nakedly. There is no need to elaborate on it.

But is it true? I strongly suspect that you know it's true. For one thing, you are reading this book. Whether you have bought it, are browsing through it in a store, or had it forced on you unwillingly, you would not have opened it if you did not sense this truth, however differently you might state it and whether or not you end up agreeing with what this book says.

I could come in here, as if on cue, with rhetoric about sensing God in magnificent sunsets, the starry sky above, and so on. But I will approach the subject of the eternal from another angle that, if nothing else, may seem a little fresher.

When I think about—or, rather, try to sense—this "something eternal," one image that comes to me is that of a water table. Somewhere under me is a table of water that sits beneath the ground. Most places on earth, as far as I know, have this water below.

I would say that this something eternal is like a water table underlying everything that we call reality. It is a living, vibrant, moving presence, and it is there whether we know it or not. The world of the five senses—everything from your coffee cup to the submolecular particles and remote galaxies proffered to us by science—is simply a crust that floats on this eternal presence. And it is this eternal presence that gives life to this crust that we call reality, and this reality would not exist without it.

What name shall we give this underlying presence? Some people, possibly thinking of an image like the one above, have called it the Ground of Being. Another common term is Spirit. (We have not gotten to the point where we can talk about God yet.)

I could take my water table metaphor a little further. There are areas where it does not rain or hardly rains at all. If people live there, they have to rely on the water table for their water supply.

Let's say that our physical reality is like a region of this kind. It has no life, no energy of its own. All the life it has is drawn from this Ground of Being, this Spirit.

What, you may ask, about the forms of energy described by science? They are not what we are talking about here. Those energies are the operations and reactions of things on the crust—no matter how small and subtle, or how large, they may be.

To live, in any true sense, is to have a connection with this Spirit. The Spirit must "water" the surface crust of physical reality. We can imagine this process as involving wells, or springs, that connect the two levels of being.

Given this much, we can say that there are points in this crust of reality where the water of the Spirit breaks through, or where the crust is thinner and it is easier to dig down and draw up this water.

These "wells," shall we say, are moments of encounter with the sacred. They are described in many places. If you want to turn to books, you can read *The Varieties of Religious Experience* by William James, or *Mysticism* by Evelyn Underhill, or *The Perennial Philosophy* by Aldous Huxley. These are all classic studies with many firsthand descriptions of such encounters. But it would probably be better if you looked back on your own experience to see if you find anything that resembles what I'm talking about.

Sometimes the word *revelation* is used to describe these encounters. As I said before, if you have such an experience, all the doubts will go out of your head. You will not be bothered about creationism versus evolution or why God isn't always a nice guy. You will believe. Or rather, you will not believe. You will *know*.

Encounters with the sacred have many features in common, but they also vary wildly. I have known people who have had these experiences while walking down the street on an ordinary day. One of the most famous of these revelations came to a shoemaker who happened once to glance at a glint of light coming off a pewter dish. Entranced, he stared at it for some time. It seemed to him, he said later, that he could see into the heart of things.

This happened in the year 1600. The man was a German named Jacob Boehme. He had a similar experience ten years later, about which he said, "The gate was opened to me that in one quarter of an hour I saw and knew more than if I had been many years together at a university. . . . For I saw and knew the being of all beings."

Boehme wrote down his insights in books that still echo today. He is considered one of the great mystics of the West.

To take the groundwater analogy a step further, let's say that there are places where it seems to arise more often. People are attracted to these places. They come repeatedly, and the place starts to become famous. More people come. Hotels and other accommodations are built for them. Someone notices that this water seems to surface more often at one time of the year than others, so the place attracts even more people then. These become regular occurrences, and, like everything else in human activity, they become somewhat formalized.

This groundwater does not belong to anybody. It cannot be owned. It comes and goes as it will, sometimes in a more or less predictable pattern, often unexpectedly. But the land around the spots where the water comes up can be owned; it is real estate just like anything else. The property is bought up, by the devout and by the shrewd, and they start to limit people's access to the water. These owners set themselves on high. They say the water rises because of certain things that they themselves do. They will let others take part—if these others will do exactly what they say and pay them a price for the privilege.

This is a capsule summary of the history of religion.

One thing you may have noticed about my description so far is that this Spirit, this Ground of Being, does not sound very *personal*. In fact I feel more comfortable speaking of it in the neuter gender, rather than as *he* or *she*. Many sacred traditions do the same thing. The American Indians speak of the Great Spirit (Wakan Tanka in the language of the Lakota Sioux), the Chinese of the Tao (or "Way"), the Hindus of Brahman. These are not gods; they are ways of speaking of this Ground of Being.

Maybe we can see this Ground of Being from a wider angle still. Let's look at one of the most famous mystical journeys of recent times: the near-death experience recounted by Eben Alexander in his bestselling book *Proof of Heaven*. In 2008 Alexander, a neurosurgeon, came down with a violent case of bacterial meningitis that put him in a coma for seven days. During this time (when, according to standard neurology, he should have been experiencing nothing at all), he had an elaborate and beautiful vision of worlds above our own. This is how he describes his experience of the deepest level:

> I continued forward and found myself entering an immense void, completely dark, infinite in size, yet also infinitely comforting. . . . The "voice" of this Being was warm and—odd as I know this may sound—personal. It understood humans, and it possessed the qualities we possess, only in infinitely greater measure. It knew me deeply and overflowed with qualities that all my life I've associated with human beings, and human beings alone: warmth, compassion, pathos . . . even irony and humor.

I've interviewed Alexander myself, and I have no doubt of his sincerity and integrity. His vision has resonated so deeply with the American public partly because of its deep and intuitive truth. Alexander's experience points to a Ground of Being that is both personal and impersonal.

Of course it is impersonal. How could it be otherwise? Do you really believe that God has an ego like ours to be vexed or coddled?

But I believe, precisely because this Spirit is infinite and has, for reasons of its own, generated beings like us who are persons, it can also understand and address us personally.

All of this may help us understand how our idea of a personal God comes out of a profound, universal, and *true* intuition.

Some will balk at using the word *God*, having all kinds of unpleasant associations with it. This is understandable, given what religion has become. They may call it Spirit, as I have above, or Mind, or Nature, or something completely different. It comes to much the same thing.

Clearly, then, some people do experience a transcendent reality that they equate with God. Boehme and Eben Alexander are two examples. In fact, I think religious experience is far more common than people generally believe. Sometimes it passes through so quickly that the mind does not grasp it. Sometimes it is so baffling, and so contrary to everything else we believe, that the mind forgets it. In other instances, the mind, unstable to begin with, distorts the experience and is distorted by it. Hence people may believe that they are God themselves. These cases, pathetic or grotesque, are common enough to give spiritual experience a bad name.

At any rate, for most of us these tastes of revelation are very fleeting, and we simply don't know what to do with them. They are not enough to give us a coherent and meaningful worldview. In fact they're just as likely to disturb the mind as to enlighten it. But still people need concepts and images that will enable them to conceive of this transcendent reality and integrate it into their daily lives. And here is where revelation as commonly understood comes in.

To go back to my earlier metaphor, let's say that this groundwater of the Spirit erupts in an especially powerful way at a particular place in time. These are the revelations known to world history. Those who experience them have not only seen—and seen in a very powerful way—but they often believe that they are inspired to guide humanity in the right path.

Usually one individual encounters this eruption most directly and powerfully. He becomes the founder, the lawgiver. We could cite Moses on the mount, the coming of Christ, and the Prophet Muhammad's encounters with the angel Gabriel, who gave him the Qur'an, as familiar examples. The lawgiver gives commandments about how to pray and how to live with your fellow humans in a decent and responsible way.

This eruption of the groundwater of the Spirit revives and nourishes the land around it for many years. Life becomes possible there. And the water continues to bubble up from time to time in varying quantities—sometimes enough for an individual only, sometimes for a group. But it bubbles up less and less over the centuries. Soon the land is all but dry again. Only the tiniest trickles of water appear from time to time, faint and perfunctory. But people still live on the land, remembering a time when the water was abundant. Some even eat dirt and tell themselves they are drinking water.

This could be said of all world civilizations, because all of them have been inspired by a religious impulse of one kind or another. The impulse comes with great force, then over the centuries it weakens. Its truths are diluted, its ideas are subtly changed, until it has only the faintest resemblance to what it originally was.

The spiritual teacher G. I. Gurdjieff, speaking to some students in Russia during World War I, put the matter this way:

Imagine that we are sitting here talking of religions and that the maid Masha hears our conversation. She, of course, understands it in her own way and she repeats what she has understood to the porter Ivan. The porter Ivan again understands it in his own way and he repeats what he has understood to the coachman Peter next door. The coachman Peter goes to the country and recounts in the village what the gentry talk about in town. Do you think that what he recounts will at all resemble what we said? This is precisely the relation between existing religions and that which was their basis. You get teachings, traditions, prayers, rites, not at fifth but at twenty-fifth hand, and, of course, almost everything has been distorted beyond recognition and everything essential forgotten long ago.

That this has happened to Christianity is beyond question. Much of contemporary scholarship is devoted to discussing these distortions over the centuries. The basic outlines are clear enough. But eventually we are led back to the question of what Christianity originally was and was meant to be. Unfortunately, here the details are very vague and the documentation very thin. The scholars then create an "original" or "primitive" Christianity that is based on their own preconceptions of what Christianity should be. The liberals paint a politically correct and socially conscious Jesus. The conservatives create a Jesus who upholds a moral order like that of the United States in, say, the mid-twentieth century. Few of these pictures can be taken seriously.

So we are very far from revelation, even though believers are told that what they are getting is pure revelation, faithful to the original, and that they dismiss it only with grave peril to their souls.

Such is the message; such are the advertisements. But people today are gorged on advertisements, so they stop believing and drop away. The only ones left are bigots and fanatics. This, too, tells us a great deal about the present state of religion.

In 1922 T. S. Eliot published his great poem *The Waste Land*. Most obviously it is about the spiritual and moral desolation of Europe after the catastrophe of World War I. But in its own way it is also about the desolation of Christianity. It too uses the metaphors of water and dryness to talk about this spiritual emptiness: "I will show you fear / In a handful of dust."

The Waste Land was written almost a hundred years ago, but the situation today is the same. The desolation that Eliot speaks of is still here. It is part of the thrownness both of Christianity and of us.

To see where it might be possible to go from here, many starting points can be chosen. But one of the most useful may be to look at the central religious artifact of Christianity in the United States today: the Bible.

The Defective Scripture: What We Now Know About the Bible

To travel without it I never would try;
We keep close together, my Bible and I.

TWO LINES OF this corny old poem are quite enough. (It's entitled "My Bible and I," author unknown.) But it points to something that is often overlooked. Many people are attached to the Bible—in fact, they are attached to *their* Bibles.

In his book *The American Religion*, critic Harold Bloom says that the "limp leather Bible," hoisted aloft by a charismatic preacher, is the chief sacred artifact of fundamentalist religion. It is so. No matter what the census says, at heart America is a Protestant country. And since Protestantism discarded the accoutrements of the Catholic church—its statues, its vestments, its rosaries—the Bible alone is left.

I can understand why. I have a number of religious objects of one sort or another, but in a curious way the limp leather Bible is probably the thing I most regard as a sacred artifact—both the one in brown calfskin that I mentioned earlier and another one, virtually identical except that it's bound in red morocco, that I keep at the office. When my sons were born, I tried to buy equally beautiful Bibles for them. I didn't succeed. I bought the best ones I could find, but the standards of Bible manufacture seem to have fallen over the last forty years, even in the august precincts of Cambridge University Press.

I have others, of course. There is the small American Bible Society copy, bound in blue cloth, which my father got while he was serving in the Second World War. He wrote some details of family history in it (for some reason, he got his parents' birthdays wrong). There is the Lithuanian Bible from 1915, whose flyleaf my great-grandmother used to practice her handwriting. Perhaps the strangest is Kittel's *Biblia Hebraica*, third edition. It is a large, handsome volume, bound in sand-colored cloth. It was the standard scholarly version of the Hebrew Bible until it was replaced in 1977 by the *Biblia Hebraica Stuttgartensia*, which is essentially just an update of Kittel.

What makes Kittel's *Biblia Hebraica* so strange? It was first published in Leipzig in 1937. So the best and most authoritative edition of the Hebrew Bible for much of the twentieth century was first published in Nazi Germany.

All of these Bibles appear seamless. The texts follow one another in an orderly fashion, with no breaks or interruptions. This format, along with fine bindings, leaves us with the impression of the Bible as a single, mono-lithic book.

Which it is not. Even its name proves as much. It is derived from the Greek *biblía*, meaning "books." In the plural. These books vary greatly. There is Leviticus, with its meticulous details about animal sacrifice; the Song of Solomon, enigmatic poetry that is half mystical, half erotic; Jonah, which is placed among the Prophets, although it is actually a sat-ire about prophecy.

Dates? Some parts of the Old Testament are quite old. One of the oldest is probably the Song of Deborah in Judges 5, which may date as far back as the twelfth century BC. The earliest of the prophets was Amos, who was active around 760 BC. But most of the Hebrew Bible was written in the period from 620 to 450 BC. The latest was probably the book of Daniel, which can be dated with some certainty to c.165 BC.

The problems of authorship are enormous, and there is no way that I can do justice to them here. One of the most perplexing involves the first four books: Genesis, Exodus, Leviticus, and Numbers. Read as a single unit, they contain any number of contradictions. In some places the name of the mountain on which Moses received the Law is Sinai; in others it is Horeb. Moses's father-in-law is named Jethro and Reuel in different passages.

Over the past century, scholars have dealt with this difficulty by saying that there are four primary texts that underlie this part of the Bible. They are known by initials: J (for "Jahwist" or "Yahwist") is so called because it calls God Yahweh; E ("Elohist") calls God Elohim; P, the Priestly source, is, as its name suggests, mostly about priestly matters. At some point (probably in the fifth century BC) somebody put these texts—which no longer exist in their original forms—together and added some material to make them flow better: he is called R ("Redactor").

This theory (called the Documentary Hypothesis) has been widely accepted by scholars. In recent years, it has come under attack, and there have been scholarly debates back and forth about it, with no clear resolution. I only offer this short account to give some idea of how complex and difficult the problem of biblical authorship is.

Another source is D, for the Deuteronomist. This is a bit different from the others. It is a coherent, unified source, as is obvious from the prose style and the dominant themes. The Deuteronomic history, as it is called, begins with Deuteronomy. The word means "second law" in Greek, and it is so called because Deuteronomy to a great extent restates the Law that has already been described in Exodus and Leviticus. The Deuteronomic history continues into Joshua, Judges, 1 and 2 Samuel, and 1 and 2 Kings. It tells the story of the Israelite people, how they came into the Promised Land, and the fates of the two kingdoms, called Israel and Judah, up to 586 BC. So the Deuteronomist is covering a span between 1300 (the supposed date of the Exodus) and 586 BC.

The Deuteronomic work is the first known history in world civilization. When I say "history" I do not mean that it is historically accurate in all, or even most, of its narrative. But it is the first work to give some kind of structure and meaning to the period it covers. While there are enormous numbers of chronicles of the deeds of the pharaohs and the rulers of Mesopotamia, they are just that: they are lists of facts, usually adorned with boasting and exaggeration, and they don't try to be anything else.

Deuteronomy tries to do more. It is not only about the deeds of judges and kings; it is the story of Israel's covenant with Yahweh, and it states its moral consistently, even redundantly: Yahweh brings good fortune on his people when they follow his laws, and ruination upon them when they do not. While it often massages the historical facts to fit into this framework, the meaning of the Deuteronomic work is clear. For the first time in history, a text has tried to impart meaning and shape to the past.

We can date the Deuteronomic history fairly precisely. It was first written in the reign of King Josiah of Judah, in the period between 620 and 609 BC. It was later revised and updated shortly after the Babylonian Exile, which began in 586 BC. Thus there must have been at least two authors who wrote this work. But for the sake of convenience, I will speak of the author simply as the Deuteronomist.

As a factual record, the Deuteronomist's history is open to dispute. While it does incorporate some genuine older material (such as the Song of Deborah), the farther back it goes from the date of composition, the less we can take it at face value historically. To judge from archaeology and extrabiblical sources from the period, it wildly overstates the power and wealth of David and Solomon, and its stories of the judges before them are in all likelihood mostly legends.

To put it bluntly, *it is not true that archaeology confirms the literal truth of the Hebrew Bible. In many ways the archaeological record contradicts the Bible.* This is one of the uncomfortable facts that are acknowledged in the university and the seminary, but have been held back from the public, or stated in only very muted and equivocal ways.

Then there is the New Testament. This is quite a different matter. These texts fit in well with what secular history and archaeology have to tell us. At one point some scholars doubted that Pontius Pilate ever existed, but in 1961 a stone was unearthed from that period that mentions him along with the Roman emperor Tiberius. In short, there is no real argument about the context of the New Testament. It makes perfect sense in the light of Judea and the Roman Empire of the first century AD.

The problems with the New Testament lie elsewhere.

To begin with, there is no archaeological record of Jesus Christ. This is not surprising. Jesus was not a king or a priest, and the historical accounts of those days focus very much on kings and priests. But it means that the archaeological record is not going to tell us much more about Jesus than do the written texts.

As for the written texts, here is another awkward truth: *nothing in the New Testament was written by any of the twelve apostles or by anyone who knew Jesus personally.* This is standard scholarly opinion, but again it has been obscured and shunted aside because of its sheer awkwardness.

Where, after all, in the New Testament does anyone say, "I was there with Jesus and I saw these things myself"? The closest we get is at the end of John. It is an odd statement: "This is the disciple which testifieth these things, and wrote these things: and we know his testimony is true" (John 21:24).

What could this possibly mean? If Jesus's beloved disciple had actually written these things, he would not have said, "And we know that his testimony is true." Clearly this text was written by somebody else—we don't know who. Scholars call him John because they have nothing else to call him. Maybe, as some have suggested, this passage is a coda tacked on to the rest of the text. But this doesn't change the situation. The Gospel of John, exalted and mystical as it is, reads much less like a first-person account than the other Gospels, which don't even mention eyewitnesses.

Mark and Luke were not apostles by any account, and scholars again do not believe that Matthew was written by the tax collector whom Jesus called as a disciple (Matthew 9:9). Why? For many reasons, although the most obvious one is that the Gospel itself speaks of Matthew in the third person and makes no attempt to identify him as the author.

Then there is the apostle Paul. He did write many, though not all, of the epistles attributed to him. The ones that are acknowledged as genuine are Romans, 1 and 2 Corinthians, Galatians, Philippians, 1 Thessalonians, and Philemon. Scholars on the whole do not believe that he wrote the other epistles, no matter what the epistles themselves claim.

Paul, then, is a flesh-and-blood figure, the man in the New Testament whom we see and know most intimately. We have more than a glimpse of his personality; we see his moods, his hobbyhorses, even his way of reasoning, as in Romans, where he sometimes seems to be thinking aloud on paper. But Paul did not know Jesus personally.

Nevertheless, he gives us the closest thing we have to an eyewitness account of Jesus. Paul says:

For I delivered unto you first of all that which I received, how that Christ died for our sins according to the scriptures;

And that he was buried, and that he rose again the third day according to the scriptures:

And that he was seen of Cephas, then of the twelve:

After that, he was seen of above five hundred brethren at once; of whom the greater part remain unto this present, but some are fallen asleep.

After that, he was seen of James; then of all the apostles.

And last of all he was seen of me also, as of one born out of due time.

(1 Corinthians 15:3–7)

Paul is saying that he has had a vision of the risen Christ like those of the apostles. He would have been in a position to hear about their own experiences, since he knew them personally. The Bible even tells us about his arguments with James, the brother of Jesus, and Peter (also known as Cephas). So there were indeed people who had visions of the risen Jesus. What this means remains to be seen.

On the other hand, Paul in his letters says almost nothing about Jesus the man. There are no reminiscences of him, even secondhand ones; no anecdotes; almost no quotations. Paul does not seem to be interested in the personal Jesus. Instead he focuses on Christ, who is in Paul's eyes a cosmic being.

Certainly I could say more about the historical Jesus versus the Christ of faith, and I will. My goal here is simply to show that there are some very basic difficulties about the literal truth of both the Old and New Testaments.

We don't know much more about how these texts were put together. Let's take the first four books of the Bible: Genesis, Exodus, Leviticus, Numbers. According to the Documentary Hypothesis, they are a stitched-together collection of earlier texts. A standard date for this final redaction (i.e., edit) is the fifth century BC. Who did it? Again we don't know. Richard Elliott Friedman, a professor of Jewish studies at the University of Georgia, wrote a book called *Who Wrote the Bible?* He argued that the man who did this redaction was Ezra the scribe, who lived around 450 BC. The Jewish tradition hints at this possibility. A line in the Talmud says, "Had Moses not preceded him, Ezra would have been worthy of having the Torah given to Israel through him." But there is no concrete evidence. Friedman's is an attractive theory, but again a speculative one.

Scholars do not agree about when the canon of the Hebrew Bible—what Christians call the Old Testament—was finally fixed. Some say it happened in the first century BC; some say it was not until the second century AD or later. Most would probably agree, though, that the Hebrew Bible had taken more or less its present form by AD 100.

There is another collection of works called the Apocrypha. It includes books such as Tobit, Judith, and 1 and 2 Maccabees. These texts were included in the oldest and most influential translation of the Hebrew Bible ever made—the Greek Septuagint, translated probably in the third century BC. The Septuagint was the official Bible for the early Catholic church, so Catholic and Orthodox Christians regard the Apocryphal texts as Scripture. But the Apocrypha was never included in the original Hebrew Bible, so Jews and Protestants do *not* regard it as Scripture. In any case, these texts have nothing like the resonance or authority of the books universally accepted as canonical, and I won't say anything more about them here.

If the creation of the Old Testament is a subject laced with question marks, the creation of the New Testament is a subject laced with misinformation. Much of this occurs in popular contexts—bestsellers and the like. In his novel *The Da Vinci Code*, Dan Brown writes, "The Bible, as we know it today, was collated by the pagan Roman emperor Constantine the Great." Others say that Christianity originally taught mystical doctrines such as reincarnation, but that the books mentioning these things were taken out of the Bible by the Council of Nicaea in AD 325.

None of these statements is true. The mainstream Christian church has never taught reincarnation, either before the Council of Nicaea or after. Constantine, who reigned from AD 306 to 337, was not exactly a pagan and not exactly a Christian. He proclaimed an edict of toleration that included Christianity in 313, and he supported the Christian church financially and in other ways. But he kept much of the regalia of the pagan emperors and was not baptized until he was near death. He may have postponed his baptism because Christians believed (as they still do) that the sacrament wipes away all sins, but at that time there was no consensus in the church about what to do about sins that were committed *after* baptism. (The Catholic sacrament of confession, today called the sacrament of penance and reconciliation, was not created until the Middle Ages.)

Another matter that had not been settled in Constantine's time was exactly who Christ was supposed to be. The main body of the church—the ancestor of the Catholic and Orthodox churches—believed he was much more than human, but the bishops argued about his status in relation to God. Was Jesus, the Son, a little lower than God himself, as some claimed, or was he fully equal? Had he existed, like God, from eternity, or had he been created at some point? The fight was a bitter one, and Constantine called the Council of Nicaea in 325 to settle it. The council consisted of the bishops of the Christian church throughout the Roman Empire (although many of them did not come). They, and not Constantine, decided that Jesus Christ was fully equal to God—a ruling that led to the doctrine of the Trinity.

As we'll see, this is almost certainly not what the early Christians—including those who wrote the New Testament—believed.

That was what the Council of Nicaea did: it defined the status of Jesus as equal to God. It did not talk about reincarnation. It did not say anything about the canon of the New Testament. Constantine did not have anything to do with the creation of the New Testament either.

The New Testament grew up organically, along with the mainstream Christian church that in the second century AD started to call itself the "catholic"—meaning "universal"—church. By the end of the second century, the canon of the four Gospels was beginning to form. Around AD 180 the church father Irenaeus wrote, "It is not possible that there be more Gospels in number than these, or fewer. By way of illustration, since there are four zones in the world in which we live, and four cardinal winds, and since the Church is spread over the whole earth, and since the pillar and bulwark of the Church is the Gospel and the Spirit of life, consequently she has four pillars, blowing imperishability from all sides and giving life to men." These four Gospels were the ones in the New Testament today: Matthew, Mark, Luke, and John.

Other books were added to the New Testament, including the epistles of Paul, as well as others (such as 1 and 2 Timothy, Titus, and Ephesians) that he was believed, incorrectly, to have written. Epistles attributed to other apostles, such as James, Peter, and John, came to be accepted as well. Last of all was the difficult and ambiguous book of Revelation.

If you want to set a date for the establishment of the New Testament canon, you can pick AD 367. In this year Athanasius, bishop of Alexandria, sent out an Easter letter to his diocese. Athanasius, the great champion of the doctrine of the Trinity, was one of the most influential Christian theologians of all time. (The Athanasian Creed is named after him, although he almost certainly did not write it.) In this Easter letter, Athanasius lists the books of the New Testament that are actually Scripture. Athanasius writes, "These are fountains of salvation, that they who thirst may be satisfied with the living words they contain. In these alone is proclaimed the doctrine of godliness." These are the same as the twenty-seven books in the New Testament today. So this is the first recorded description of the New Testament canon as we now know it.

Many other works were thereby excluded. They include Gospels attributed to just about every one of the twelve apostles (including the recently discovered *Gospel of Judas*); Acts of various apostles; epistles written by early Christian leaders; and *The Shepherd of Hermas*, an inspirational allegory that was much esteemed in the early Christian church but today is mostly forgotten.

Practically all of these apocryphal texts, as they are called, are later than the books that made it into the New Testament. All the apocryphal

Gospels—the *Gospel of Peter*, the *Gospel of Philip*; there is even a *Gospel of Nicodemus*, also known as the *Acts of Pilate*—were later than Matthew, Mark, Luke, and John. With one possible exception: the mysterious *Gospel of Thomas*, about which I will have more to say later.

Were there any texts older than these that didn't make it into the New Testament? Yes, but we no longer have them. There is an ancient tradition of a Gospel written in Aramaic, the language that Jesus spoke, by Matthew, but nothing of it has survived. It is very far from clear how this text might have related to the Gospel of Matthew as it now exists.

Scholars believe that the earliest writings about Jesus were collections of sayings. The most famous is simply called Q (from the German *Quelle*, meaning "source"). This book has never been found. It is a hypothetical text, reconstructed from similar passages in Matthew and Luke.

The standard view is that Mark is the earliest Gospel, and that Matthew and Luke used it in writing their own. But Matthew and Luke also use common material that does not appear in Mark. So scholars have argued that they both used a common source that is now lost—the sayings collection called Q.

Here is one example. Matthew 6:24 reads, "No man can serve two masters: for either he will hate the one, and love the other; or else he will hold to the one, and despise the other. Ye cannot serve God and mammon." Luke 16:13 is identical. This verse, then, according to the theory, came from Q.

Q was a collection of sayings *only*. It did not contain anything of the deeds of Jesus, the story of the crucifixion or the resurrection, or any other narrative elements. Not all scholars believe that there was a Q document, though most of them do.

So here is the story: Around the time that Jesus's original disciples started to die off (in the middle of the first century AD), people began writing down collections of his sayings as remembered in the oral tradition. Slightly later, other men took these sayings collections and combined them with what was recollected of the Jesus story to write the Gospels. The earliest, Mark, probably dates to around 70. The latest, John, may be as late as AD 95 or 100.

This dating is significant, because it means that these books were written just as Jesus was beginning to slip out of living memory.

To sum up: The New Testament canon grew up along with the Catholic church in the first four centuries after the time of Christ. By and large it contains the oldest texts we have about Jesus and Christianity, though there may have been, and probably were, older texts that have been lost. This may have happened partly because the contents of these older texts were included more or less completely in the biblical Gospels.

The *Gospel of Thomas*, which I mentioned earlier, is an exception. Like Q and the other earliest texts, it is a sayings collection. Thus *Thomas* may be older than the canonical Gospels, possibly going as far back as AD 50—but this is a matter of great dispute.

Corrupted Texts

What I have given above is a rough capsule description of the history of the canon of the Bible. At this point I need to say something about the *text* of the Bible. What is the relation of the contents of the Bible today—I mean the texts in the original languages: Hebrew, Aramaic, and Greek—to what the authors originally wrote?

Here is another fact that is little known to the public: *The biblical texts we have now are not the way they were originally written. They have been changed, in some ways significantly.* We know about some of these changes, but we do not know and will probably never know about many of the others.

Some, no doubt most, of the alterations were accidental. After all, we are dealing with manuscripts copied by hand—a laborious and often boring job. Sometimes, for example, a scribe would lose his place and he would leave out a line, or more.

Could this have really happened with the sacred text of the Bible? It could, and did. Here is one example. If you look at 1 Samuel 11, you will see that it starts with a campaign of the Ammonite king Nahash against the Israelites of a town called Jabesh-Gilead. The Israelites are ready to surrender and ask for terms. Nahash's are harsh: "On this condition will I make a covenant with you, that I may thrust out all your right eyes, and lay it for a reproach against all Israel."

This passage starts abruptly. It is also curious because Jabesh-Gilead is far north of the Ammonites' territory. What's going on here? How did the Ammonites get so far into Israel?

The answers are found in the Dead Sea Scrolls, discovered starting in 1947. Among them is a fragment of 1 Samuel that includes a missing portion of this passage. It turns out that Nahash had previously overcome the tribes of Gad and Reuben, which occupied outlying territories (he gouged out their right eyes too). This fact explains how Nahash got so far into Israelite territory.

How was this passage lost? By far the most likely answer is "a scribal lapse—the scribe's eye jumped from one line break to the other, both beginning with Nahash as subject."

Here I am quoting Frank Moore Cross, whose course on the Old Testament, as you'll remember, I took at Harvard in the seventies. The quote comes from his article "Light on the Bible from the Dead Sea Caves," in a book called *Understanding the Dead Sea Scrolls*, edited by Hershel Shanks. You can read it if you want a more complete discussion of this matter, or if you want to read the missing passage. (If you want to know how the story ends, which does appear in the Bible, King Saul mobilizes the Israelites against Nahash and crushes his army.)

There is no evidence that this omission was intentional. The missing lines contain no controversial or doctrinal material, and the omission makes the story harder to understand. A scribe simply made a mistake.

Sometimes, however, the changes are not so innocent. Look at Deuteronomy 32:8 in the King James Version: "When the Most High divided to the nations their inheritance, when he separated the sons of Adam, he set the bounds of the people according to the number of the children of Israel."

This is an accurate translation of the Masoretic Text, the standard text of the Hebrew Bible. Unfortunately it makes no sense. God set the bounds of the people according to the number of the children of Israel? What does that mean? That God made as many nations as there were children of Israel (traditionally 600,000)? There never have been and never will be 600,000 nations on earth.

Now look at the New Revised Standard Version, probably the best and most authoritative of the twentieth-century translations. It reads: "When the Most High gave to the nations their inheritance, when he separated the sons of men, he fixed the bounds of the peoples according to the number of *the sons of God*" (my emphasis).

This is a little easier to understand. The verse in the Greek Septuagint, the first translation of the Hebrew Bible, made in the third century BC, is even clearer: it ends the verse with "... according to *the angels of God.*"

Now we can make sense of this verse. It is saying that when God created the nations, he created as many as there were "sons of God," a common Old Testament way of saying "angels."

Meaning that each nation was given a ruling angel.

This idea was extremely important, and I will have more to say about it.

But why was the verse changed? Because the idea that each nation had a ruling angel had become a secret teaching. Even much later it is still found in the Kabbalah, the mystical tradition of Judaism. The Italian Kabbalist Giovanni Pico della Mirandola alluded to it in 1486: "No king is punished on earth unless the celestial militia is humiliated in heaven." This means that the fate of a king on earth depends on the fate of the nation's ruling angels in heaven. If they are humiliated, the earthly king is punished.

Like many of the most ancient teachings, this doctrine survived in the Kabbalah, but the Kabbalah was not taught to everyone. As for this verse, it was thought prudent to hide its meaning from the people. To say that each nation has its own ruling angel—or "god"—sounded too much like polytheism. And in a way it was. So the verse had been changed by the time the Masoretes, a school of Jewish scribes active in the late first millennium AD, created the text that is standard today. But when the Septuagint was translated, over a thousand years earlier, the verse had not been changed yet. In this case, a translation preserves the correct reading, whereas the supposedly original Hebrew text doesn't.

Other textual problems aren't so easy. If you look through a modern Bible, you will see many footnotes that say "meaning uncertain" or "meaning unknown." For one example, turning to Job 34 in the New Oxford Annotated Bible, I find a little note in the lower right-hand corner: "Meaning of Heb of verses 29–33 uncertain." This note is telling us that for these four verses, the most dedicated scholars, who know the languages and manuscripts in great depth, still can't quite figure out what the text is saying. There are many passages like this.

Such cases are common—more in the Old Testament than in the New, partly because the surviving manuscripts of the Old Testament are much further from the originals than are those of the New Testament texts.

The New Testament text has difficulties of its own. Probably the biggest is the ending of the Gospel of Mark. As it is now, the Gospel ends with Mark 16:8: "And [the women] went out quickly, and fled from the sepulchre; for they trembled and were amazed; and they were affrighted."

This ending is extremely abrupt. The women have gone to Jesus's tomb, found it empty, and have met a young man (no doubt an angel) who has told them that Jesus is risen. Then they are frightened and run away. That is all.

A few scholars believe that this is really the way Mark meant to end his Gospel, but they are in a minority, and their views seem to me unconvincing. The resurrection of Jesus is the climax of the whole story, but we have been told nothing about it yet. Thinking that Mark meant to end his Gospel this way is like thinking that Shakespeare could have ended *Hamlet* with the fourth act. It makes no sense.

No one has ever solved the mystery of the ending of Mark, and no one will unless some new manuscript is discovered. But very few Bibles let the Gospel end this way. The King James Version has a passage (Mark 16:9–20) that does provide a more or less satisfactory ending. But it is not in all the manuscripts; more importantly, it is not in the oldest ones; and there is an alternative shorter ending as well. (Most modern Bibles include both.) Scholars conclude that somebody who was familiar with all four Gospels concocted these endings later on from similar passages in Matthew, Luke, and John.

Such is the standard view. But it does not tell us why or how the original ending was lost. Was it simply another honest mistake, a page or two falling off the end of a book, or torn off the edge of a scroll? Did some bishop later on disagree with Mark's view of the resurrection, take it out, and replace it with something safer? Again, we probably will never know.

Personally I think the simplest and most obvious answer is that Mark did not finish the Gospel. Of course we don't know why. We know little or nothing about the conditions in which it was written, and equally little about the author. One ancient tradition says that Mark was martyred in Alexandria. But it could simply have happened that he fell ill and died before he could finish his book. After all, life in those times was much shorter and more uncertain than it is today.

My idea is, of course, speculative. But many great works of classical antiquity are also unfinished. Thucydides's *Peloponnesian War*, Lucretius's *On the Nature of Things*, and Vergil's *Aeneid* are only some of the most famous examples.

I'm arguing, then, that Mark is missing its ending for completely innocent reasons. But there are other changes that may have been less honest.

One case appears in Luke 3:22, in a scene about Jesus's baptism. Early manuscripts of Luke have the voice from heaven say, "You are my Son, today I have begotten you" (quoting Psalm 2:7). But later manuscripts have this line as it is translated in the King James Version: "Thou art my beloved Son; in thee I am well pleased."

New Testament scholar Bart D. Ehrman argues that the first version—"You are my Son, today I have begotten you"—is probably the original reading. It was changed because it seemed to support a position called *adoptionism*, according to which Jesus became the Son of God by "adoption" at his baptism. Some early Christians believed this, but the Catholic church did not. Ehrman is saying that this line may have been changed for this reason. As church doctrine developed, it became expedient to alter biblical verses that might lead believers to heresy.

The verdict isn't clear, but it *is* clear that here, as with many other disputed verses, the minute you start to explore the issue, you have strayed into a forest of enigmas and agendas and speculations. It would take the work of a lifetime—more than a lifetime—to sort through them.

All of the examples above have this in common: scholars are able to figure out the true (or at any rate the most likely) reading because it was preserved somewhere or another—in ancient translations, in some manuscripts, in the Dead Sea Scrolls. There are undoubtedly many others that we will never and can never know about, because no manuscripts with those readings have survived.

The Curated Artifact

The centerpiece of a Jewish synagogue is the *sefer Torah* or Torah scroll. The rules for making these scrolls are rigorous. They must be handwritten. And if the scribe leaves out even one letter, he may make the entire book worthless for sacred purposes.

This procedure certainly has an austere beauty, but it belies the text's actual history. Fifteen hundred years ago, a scribe loses his place on the page and leaves out a couple of lines about Nahash the Ammonite. Today everything must be accurate to the letter.

The archaeologist William G. Dever has called the Bible a "curated artifact." Meaning that the history of the text shows this: if the Gospel of Mark is missing an ending, you write one. Meaning that you might change the reading of a line if you don't want the people to hear about the pernicious idea of ruling angels or the idea that Jesus was adopted at his baptism.

Visiting the JewishKids Web site, created by a Hasidic Jewish group called Chabad, I learn: "The first Torah scroll in history was dictated by G-d [*sic*] verbatim and written by Moses, just before his passing."

The Hasidim are an ultratraditional sect. They are the men you see on New York subways wearing black suits, long beards, and broad black hats. Clearly they still hold to the idea that the Torah as we have it was dictated word for word by God to Moses. But any biblical scholar who believed this would be unable to get a position in any mainstream seminary or divinity school, Jewish or otherwise.

So I turn back and look at my limp leather Bibles, one in brown calfskin, one in red morocco, both with worn covers after forty years. And I look at my sons' Bibles, bound in black leather, with gilt lettering on the covers that is just the slightest bit blurred. These copies are not nearly as nice, though they cost much more. Partly with Harold Bloom's image in mind, I bought ones with limp leather covers, but I bought them online, and when they arrived, I found that the covers were not limp, and the books are hard to keep open. I could have sent them back, but I probably wouldn't have gotten anything else that was much better.

Perhaps this loss in workmanship is a sign, not just of the relentless march of commercial culture, but of a reduced valuation of the Bible itself.

In any event, let's move on to look at what scholars currently believe about the Bible as history.

Part Two

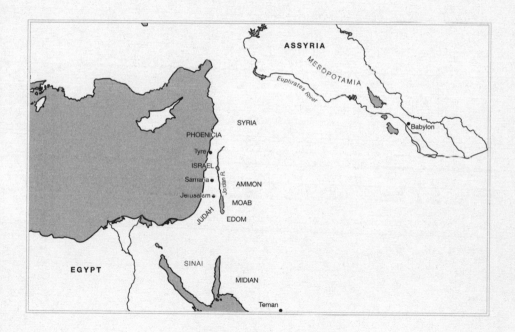

The Near East in the First Millennium BC

The Haze of Legend:
From the Flood
to the Judges

USUALLY YOU'RE SUPPOSED to begin at the beginning.

But I'm not going to do that here.

When you are talking about the Bible, the beginning means the creation story in Genesis, followed by the tale of the Fall of man. As most people know, these things did not literally happen. They did not take place within the time frame of history.

Yet in another sense these stories are profoundly true—more true, in a way, than a mere collection of facts about the past could be. But to look at them takes us into the realm of metaphysics, and we are not ready to go there yet. I'll take this subject up in chapter 15.

The Universal Myth

So let's flip a few pages forward and begin with Noah's Flood. The story is so familiar that I'm not going to retell it here.

Again, how true could this myth be? Was the entire earth flooded with water, leaving only one man in a boat with his family and a collection of animals?

But before we toss this story aside, let's look into it a bit further. The facts behind it are stranger than you may think.

Long ago scholars deciphered the ancient Sumerian epic *Gilgamesh*, written down around 2000 BC—although how much further back it goes in oral form is anyone's guess. *Gilgamesh* contains a story of the Flood in which the hero's name is not Noah but Utnapishtim. Sumeria, in present-day Iraq, is not far from Israel. Originally written in Sumerian, the *Gilgamesh* epic was translated into Babylonian, which is, like Hebrew, a Semitic language. It's natural to suppose that *Gilgamesh* is somewhere in the background of the story of Noah.

But the Flood story extends across a much wider range. It is found among Australian aborigines, the Pygmies of Africa, and South American Indians, as well as in Ireland, China, and Siberia. The ancient Greeks had the same myth: the Noah figure was named Deucalion. The motif is so widespread that the Harvard scholar E. J. Michael Witzel, in his book *The Origins of the World's Mythologies*, argues that this myth goes back to the time, perhaps as long as 100,000 years ago, when the whole human species still lived in east Africa.

If this story is so ancient, we can see how it might have a kernel of truth. It's much easier to imagine a flood wiping out almost all of humanity when humanity was still located in a small part of the world.

But why did the story prove so durable? There may be a clue in Plato's dialogue the *Timaeus*. In it an Egyptian priest tells the Greek sage Solon, "There have been, and will be again, many episodes of destruction for humanity. They have come about for many reasons. The worst have been by fire and water, others of lesser extent from any number of other causes."

Without going into the story of the *Timaeus* (fascinating though it is), we can see why a Flood myth might have been preserved. There was a remote time when the whole human race, small as it then was, was almost annihilated by a flood. Later floods and other cataclysms happened to people in later ages. In their recollections they merged the story of these disasters with the tale of the original Flood.

If we grant this much, it certainly explains a great deal.

But not everything.

Another element to this myth is almost as universal (it's missing, for example, from the Pygmy version, but it's found in most of the others). This part says that the Flood came as a retribution by God or the gods for human wrongdoing.

In Genesis, God devises the Flood because he "saw that the wickedness of man was great in the earth, and that every imagination of the thoughts of his heart was only evil continually" (Genesis 6:5).

We need to consider this aspect of the Flood myth as well. It says there is a relation between human behavior—that is, moral behavior—and the state of the earth, even the weather.

This is another more or less universal theme. It appears often in Shakespeare, for example in the first act of *Julius Caesar*, where portents and strange weather foreshadow Caesar's murder. At one point the Roman senator Casca says to Cassius, the ringleader of Caesar's assassination, "Who ever knew the heavens menace so?" Cassius replies, "Those that have known the earth so full of faults."

Is there a relation between human wickedness and natural disasters? I can't even imagine what kind of meteorological study would try to answer such a question. But the instinct to believe that there *is* such a connection runs deep.

Sophisticates may laugh—and rightly—at fundamentalists who rail that AIDS and the Ebola virus are signs of the wrath of God. But in a strange way we see the same theme in the argument about global warming: human evil, especially greed, is causing environmental disaster.

I wouldn't try to explain away concerns about global warming and other environmental menaces by saying that they are just an old mythic mind-set cropping up again. I am willing to take the scientists' warnings at face value. But it is curious to see how this, perhaps the oldest myth in the human race, continues to echo today. Maybe this idea has proved to be so long-lived because it contains some truth.

Noah's Rest

Thus there is probably a kernel of fact to the story of the Flood, even if it is surrounded by layer upon layer of mythic elements. The kernel of fact may be small or even infinitesimal: a long time ago there was a big flood that killed many or most people. The mythic layers consist of everything from memories of later events that got mixed up with the first to other legends that are vaguely connected.

Most importantly, there is a moral lesson to the story. It is telling us that human wickedness will bring on evil consequences—even natural disasters.

Is this as far as it goes?

I don't think so, and here I am parting ways with conventional scholarship. There are also hints of deeper, inner meanings, probably more than one and perhaps an indefinite number.

In the Kabbalistic tradition, it has been said that the Flood is a story about meditation. With your meditative practice, you build an "ark" in which your consciousness can float upon the floodwaters of the psyche (water is an almost universal symbol for the psyche). Eventually these emotional waters subside, and the ark of the spirit touches upon land again—giving new life to your earthly reality.

This symbolism I've just described is not exactly well known, but it does appear in esoteric Christianity—the more mystical version that serves as a guide to inner awakening. Geoffrey Hodson, author of *Hidden*

Wisdom in the Holy Bible, writes that in biblical symbolism "ships, arks, and cradles represent vessels, whether of containment or conveyance, whether physical, spiritual, superhuman or divine. The element of water symbolizes the realm of emotion and the feelings of man."

What I have just given is a very simple version of this view. But it is enough to show what may be going on in the Bible—and what the most learned and profound commentators have always said is going on. There is a deeper meaning to the Bible. It is deeper than even the moral lessons, and it has to do with inner experience and awakening.

You may think that the idea of the Flood as a meditation story is far-fetched. It seems less so if you realize that the name *Noah* in Hebrew means "rest." Is this an accident? Probably not. The Flood story uses words with this same root twice: once in Genesis 8:4: "And the ark *rested*..." and the other in Genesis 8:9: "But the dove found no *rest*..." This root does not occur that often in the Bible, and to have it show up twice in an extremely terse story about a man named "Rest" is striking.

When I was first told this interpretation of the story, I had not read it in the Hebrew, and no one had told me that the word *rest* recurs. But when I did read this passage in Hebrew later on, this motif leaped out at me.

I am making this aside here to suggest new (or rather, extremely old) ways of making sense out of the Bible that go far past its surface meaning. For the time being, I will say no more about this matter. Let's go back to the Bible as history.

Babel and Babylon

We can see similar factual kernels and moral lessons in the rest of Genesis. In the story of the tower of Babel, for example. First, there is the name, Babel, which sounds like "Babylon," one of the great capitals of the world of the Old Testament. Then there is the tower, which brings to mind the great stepped pyramids of ancient Mesopotamia—the ziggurats. These towers were built for religious reasons, to serve as bridges between heaven and earth.

Thus there may be a core of fact within the story of the tower of Babel. Babylon was a good choice for the location. Its king Nebuchadnezzar II (more correctly Nebuchadrezzar) destroyed the Temple of Jerusalem in 586 BC,* so the Jews were not disposed to look kindly upon Babylon. He also restored Babylon's great ziggurat, destroyed a century before, known today as Etemenanki. Scholars believe that this ziggurat, seen by Jewish captives in Babylon in the sixth century BC, inspired or shaped the biblical story.

The moral meaning: if man tries to build a bridge from earth to heaven of his own devising, without the help of God, he is doomed to confusion, symbolized by the confounding of tongues.

Bronze Age Patriarchs

Let's go then to the patriarchs Abraham, Isaac, and Jacob. Today only the most conservative scholars try to find any connection between these figures and the historical realities of the era when they are supposed to have lived: the early second millennium BC.

Scholars do admit that again, there are shreds and fragments of historical truths in the stories of the patriarchs. For example, the names found there—Ishmael, Isaac, Israel, Joseph, and Jacob, and so on—are characteristic of the Middle Bronze Age (generally placed between 2250 and 1500 BC; dates of this kind are highly approximate). Beyond that, scholars have given up trying to sort out legend from fact.

In other cases, the biblical account reflects known facts from other

---

*The exact year is a matter of dispute, for various technical reasons. It is often given as 587 BC.

sources, but in strange and distorted ways. Around 1800 BC, for example, mysterious "shepherd kings" from Canaan known as the Hyksos invaded Egypt and ruled it for around two centuries. This certainly evokes the story of the descent of Joseph and his brothers into Egypt, which was supposed to have taken place in this period. Astonishingly, seals have been found bearing the name of one of these Hyksos kings, who ruled sometime in the seventeenth century BC: Yaqub-Har, which looks very much like "Jacob."

What are we to do with this fact when we compare it with the Bible? Jacob in Genesis is not a pharaoh. He is an old man whose son brings him down to Egypt, much as a successful son today might transplant his aged father to a retirement community.

Should we, despite the Genesis story, believe that the biblical Jacob was really a pharaoh? Or did the name of Jacob—said to be the common ancestor of the tribes of Israel—somehow become confused with that of a Canaanite king of Egypt? Were the Israelites descended from this king but forgot about it? Or was it simply that there were any number of Canaanites named Jacob (it was a common name in that period) and that one Jacob had nothing to do with the other?

We have to remember that if people come from royal or noble ancestry, they tend to make as much of it as possible. If they come from low origins, they try to hide the fact. So if the Israelites were descended from a royal dynasty of Egypt, why would they have distorted the historical memory to turn their ancestors into slaves?

Nonetheless, there was a great deal of trade between Egypt and Canaan in the middle of the second millennium BC. In times of famine, Canaanites would go down to Egypt and sell their families into slavery in exchange for food. This may not have been quite as cruel as it sounds. A father might well have decided that it would be better for his children to live as slaves than die of starvation.

And there were also Canaanite settlements in the eastern part of the

Egyptian delta (known as Goshen in the Bible). So there is some basic truth to the general setting of the beginning of the Exodus story.

About the rest of the story of the bondage in Egypt, there is nothing.

The Elusive Exodus

Nor is there any reference to anything like the Exodus in Egyptian records of the period, which are numerous and detailed. There is no archaeological evidence that a population of 600,000 men (plus women and children) moved from Egypt to Canaan in this period. In fact, Canaan was an Egyptian province at that time. To say that you had escaped from Egypt to Canaan in those days would be like saying you had fled the United States by going to Alaska.

At what point do we start to find references to Israel outside the Bible itself?

In 1207 BC.

There is a black granite slab about seven and a half feet high, found at the site of the ancient Egyptian capital of Thebes, which is covered with hieroglyphic writing. It tells of a military expedition by Pharaoh Merneptah. Here is part of what it says:

> Canaan has been plundered into every sort of woe;
> Ashkelon has been overcome;
> Gezer has been captured.
> Yanoam was made nonexistent;
> Israel is laid waste; his seed is not.

Archaeologists have dated the Merneptah Stele—as it is called, a stele being a large standing stone—with confidence to 1207 BC. The inscription cannot be taken at face value, since it implies that the people called

Israel were exterminated. Obviously that didn't happen. Inscriptions of this kind, meant to glorify kings, tend to exaggerate greatly.

What this *does* tell us, however, is that there was a people identified as Israel in the land of Canaan by 1207 BC. This is one of the few solid facts in the early history of Israel.

Of course, this still doesn't tell us much. Archaeologists have tried to fill in some of the details with what they know of excavations from this period, known to scholars as Iron I: the first part of the Iron Age, when iron implements begin to be found. The beginning of the Iron Age in Canaan dates to just about exactly the time of the stele: 1200 BC.

The scholars do not all agree about what the archaeological digs are telling us. They have found certain details that *some* scholars link to the Israelites or proto-Israelites. These include the "four-roomed house," a particular type of house style that begins to appear around this time. It is U-shaped with a large open courtyard, and it would have been big enough to house a large extended family, with stables for animals on the ground floor. These houses are found only in the hill country in this period.

At this point I need to say something about the geography of the land of Canaan—today mostly occupied by present-day Israel. It consists of three vertical bands. The westernmost, which is found alongside the Mediterranean, is a wide coastal plain. East of that is hill country that is sometimes called the Central Highlands. Finally, there is the Jordan River valley, which forms the eastern boundary of Canaan proper.

The coastal plain alongside the Mediterranean is the most desirable place to live, because agriculture is comparatively easy there (as it tends to be when the land is flat). The hill country is less desirable, and up until the Iron Age it was very lightly populated.

After this point, starting around 1200 BC, the population of the hill country jumps rapidly over the next couple of centuries. Starting from an estimated twelve thousand for the whole region, it went up to perhaps seventy thousand by the year 1000 BC. Four-roomed houses began to appear. They are usually grouped into villages of four or five, each one housing a large extended family. These villages were not defended: there are no walls around them. Nor, as a matter of fact, are there any temples or shrines—only, occasionally, a flat stone altar on the top of a hill, used for animal sacrifice. These are probably what the Bible calls the "high places."

Most scholars equate these villages with the beginnings of Israel. In the Bible, this time corresponds to the era of the Judges—charismatic leaders who rose up from time to time to save the nation from its enemies. The Bible discusses this period in the book of Judges. Scholars do not believe in the specifics of these stories, because they were written down after hundreds of years of oral transmission. The period of the Judges runs from between approximately 1200 and 1000 BC. The *book* of Judges, however, was written sometime after 620 BC (it is part of the Deuteronomic history, which, as we've seen, dates from this time).

The general scholarly view is that so much legend and folklore are attached to these accounts in the oral tradition that it is very hard to sort out the truth. Scholars, rightly or wrongly, tend to take a minimalistic view of history that was written after so much time has passed. Unless the history can be verified by outside texts or artifacts, it is usually dismissed as more or less legendary.

But how do we know that these people were Israelites? One thing is strikingly absent from the archaeological remains of these villages: pork bones. Because pigs are adaptable creatures and can live well in many climates, scholars tend to think that there must have been some kind of taboo against these animals. And as everyone knows, the Law of Moses forbids the children of Israel from eating pork.

Can we shape these details into some sort of meaningful history of Moses and the Exodus? I think we can, although I have to stress that it is a highly speculative picture, taken from this kind of archaeological evidence plus what we can read in (and in between the lines of) the Bible.

We go back to Moses. The only solid fact about him is his name, which, as we've seen, is Egyptian and means "son." Baruch Halpern of the University of Georgia suggests that this may have been some sort of nickname, so that the name of the great lawgiver of Sinai would have meant something like "Sonny." Perhaps, as I suggested earlier, his name originally included the name of an Egyptian god that he stopped believing in. In any event, Moses is an Egyptian name, so it makes sense to assume that he was either an Egyptian or raised as an Egyptian.

The Bible says Moses had to flee from Egypt after killing a man, and that he went to a country called Midian. Midian was located in what is today southern Jordan and northwestern Saudi Arabia. Here Moses was taken in by a chieftain named Jethro (or possibly Reuel), whose daughter he married. He started to work in the family business, meaning that he "kept the flock of Jethro his father in law" (Exodus 3:1).

While engaged in this profession, Moses went to a mountain called Horeb. Again the Bible is not consistent; sometimes the mountain is called Horeb, sometimes Sinai. Very likely this is *not* the Mount Sinai as identified today. The present Mount Sinai was identified as Moses's mountain only thousands of years later. Where the mountain really was is unclear, but there are reasons for believing it was elsewhere—confusingly, not even in what is today called the Sinai peninsula. We shall see why.

On this mountain, Moses has an encounter with "the angel of the Lord," who in a curious way seems to be the Lord himself (again, more about this later). This "Lord" identifies himself by a new name. Most translations, the King James, for example, render this as "I am that I am" or something similar. Later on, the Lord identifies himself by another name: Yahweh. What this name really meant, and who Yahweh really was, are extremely important questions, and I will dedicate chapter 5 to answering them.

The Missing Pork Bones

To boil this all down to a simple theory, let me say this. There was a man named Moses, who was raised as an Egyptian but fled into Midian, probably because of some crime. While he was there, on a certain mountain, he had what he experienced as an encounter with Yahweh, the god of the Midianites.

In his encounters with Yahweh, Moses was told to lead a certain group of people from slavery in Egypt to a new country. He was also given a law code for these people to live by. Some of what is called the Mosaic Law may really go back to Moses—perhaps the ban on eating pork, as well as circumcision. They both show Egyptian influence.

Circumcision was practiced by the Egyptians, and, according to the Greek historian Herodotus, the people of Phoenicia (present-day Lebanon) and Syria learned it from them. The Jewish historian Flavius Josephus, writing in the first century AD, also says that the Jews learned it from the Egyptians.

The Bible does not agree. The Bible implies that it was Moses's wife Zipporah, a Midianite, who introduced him to the practice of circumcision (Exodus 4:25). Does this reflect actual history? It may well not. The biblical authors were by and large prejudiced against Egypt and downplayed its influence whenever and wherever they could.

The ban on eating pork could possibly be traced back to Egypt as well. The priests of the Egyptian goddess Isis were forbidden to eat pork. Did Moses learn this practice, too, from Egypt—perhaps from his own upbringing as a priest?

It is tempting, though certainly speculative, to say so. As for the Exodus itself, it could not have happened on the scale that the Bible says. There could have been, and probably was, a charismatic figure named Moses who had what he experienced as a revelation from the Midianite god Yahweh, and who led some number of Canaanite slaves out of Egypt.

But if there is any truth to this story, Moses led out hundreds, not hundreds of thousands.

Why? Because a migration of hundreds of thousands would have left archaeological remains of some sort, and there are none. Nor is there any mention of such a migration in the Egyptian chronicles. But if the migration took place on a small scale, it could have happened without leaving behind any evidence that we can find today.

It's certainly possible that these escaped slaves, under Moses's leadership, went first to Midian and then wandered about for a certain period of time (forty years, according to the Bible) before entering the hill country of Canaan, which, as we've seen, was lightly populated at the time.

I seem to be contradicting myself. Didn't I say earlier that Canaan was an Egyptian province in those days?

It certainly was. But the Egyptians focused on the coastal plain, the richest and most civilized part of the region. They mostly ignored the poor and lightly populated hill country, where chariots, the mainstay of the Egyptian army, would have hindered rather than helped them. Thus a small group could possibly have come into the hill country and established itself there without attracting much attention from the Egyptian overlords. Again, however, it could never have been the million or so people proposed by the biblical account.

I mentioned a population explosion in this hill country between 1200 and 1000 BC. Where did these extra people come from?

Scholars do not agree. Their disputes about this matter often grow bitter and personal. Here are the most popular theories:

1. They were people fleeing from the coastal plain. The time of the rise of Israel was also a time when Egypt was losing control of Canaan. The whole region—Canaan as well as Egypt itself—was suffering from the attacks of what the Egyptians called the "Sea Peoples," the period's equivalent of the Vikings. These attacks destabilized the city-states of the

coastal plain. So this theory says that the hill country was populated by people fleeing from the decaying urban coastal centers.

2. These people were nomads who had moved in from the desert east of the Jordan and settled down.

3. They consisted of peasants from the coastal plain who, fed up with the oppression of their lords, revolted and removed themselves to the hill country.

As a matter of fact, these theories aren't contradictory. The newly forming nation of Israel could well have been made up of people from all three categories. Later parts of the Bible hint at this diversity—for example, Ezekiel 16:3: "Thy birth and thy nativity is of the land of Canaan; thy father was an Amorite, and thy mother was a Hittite." Possibly, too, the idea of the twelve tribes of Israel comes from the same fact.

If the Israelites were so diverse, what basis for unity did they have? The covenant of Moses and allegiance to Yahweh. The people under this covenant were called the "people of Yahweh." At this time there were several other such leagues in that area: in Ammon, the league offered allegiance to the god Milkom; in Edom, to Qos; in Moab, to Chemosh. These peoples, too, were united by allegiance to a common god.

Thus let's say that a small group of people, led perhaps by Joshua (Moses, says the Bible, never entered the Promised Land), established itself in the hill country sometime before 1207 BC. These people of Yahweh lived in this region, accepting outsiders who were willing to obey their Law and worship Yahweh. They lived in small, family-based villages that were more or less autonomous, only uniting from time to time under a charismatic "judge" to face a common threat. "In those days there was no king in Israel: every man did that which was right in his own eyes" (Judges 21:25). That was the situation in the early Iron Age, from around 1200 to 1000 BC. It would soon change dramatically.

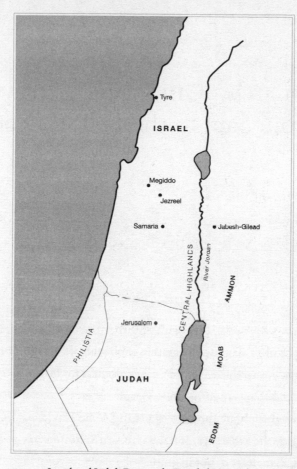

Israel and Judah During the Divided Monarchy

4.

Monarchy, United and Divided: From Saul to the Fall of Israel

THE YEARS BETWEEN 1000 and 850 BC (the dates are approximate) are by far the most disputed period in biblical history. World-renowned scholars, who know the texts and archaeological finds intimately, simply can't agree on what was going on in Israel.

They disagree about almost everything. Who David was, whether he was as great as the Bible says, and who his son Solomon was and if he ever existed are all matters of hot dispute.

Let's begin with King Saul, the first ruler of a unified Israel. He probably lived around 1000 BC. Saul has sometimes been called the only truly tragic figure in the Bible—with good reason. Everyone else is either wicked or just; everyone else receives what he deserves of the Lord's hand. Saul is somewhere in between. A great military hero, he is also moody, suspicious, and half mad. He is paranoid about the loyalty of his henchman David—but then he is not entirely wrong: the Bible also tells us that David unites with the Philistines against him. (The Philistines were probably descendants of the Sea Peoples who settled on the coast of Canaan.)

Anointed by the Lord to be king, Saul has his kingship taken from him—for a very curious reason. He failed to carry out the Lord's command to exterminate a tribe known as the Amalekites. In an eerie scene before a crucial battle, Saul desperately turns to a witch to call up the shade of the prophet Samuel to advise him. Samuel says that Saul's throne will be taken from him: "Because thou obeyedst not the voice of the Lord, nor executedst his fierce wrath upon Amalek, therefore hath the Lord done this thing unto thee this day" (1 Samuel 28:18). The first king of Israel falls into the Lord's disfavor because he has failed to carry out an act of genocide.

How much of this is historical, how much of it later embellishment? There is no consensus. Saul is a shadowy figure. Even the part of the biblical text that talks about him is in bad shape. You may remember that the missing passage in 1 Samuel about Nahash the Ammonite, mentioned in chapter 1, falls during the reign of Saul. Another line, which gives the time frame of Saul's reign, is also damaged. In one reconstruction it says, "Saul was . . . years old when he began to reign; and he reigned . . . and two years over Israel" (1 Samuel 13:1).

But it is reasonable to suppose that there really was a King Saul, and that he managed to unite many of the tribes of the Israelites into something like a coherent nation, even if this coherence lay only in personal loyalty to Saul. Even here, though, evidence suggests that his reign was more or less limited to the northern highlands and did not reach to the southern highlands in the vicinity of Jerusalem.

The Invisible Empire

As for David, there is one, and only one, reference to him in any source outside the Bible that is even close to his time. It is found on what is called the Tel Dan Stele, discovered in 1993–94. Like the Merneptah Stele, it consists largely of a series of boasts by a king, in this case probably Hazael, king of Aram, in present-day Syria. The text is fragmentary. Here is part of it:

[And I killed . . .]ram son of [. . .] the king of Israel, and I killed [. . .]
yahu son of [. . . the ki]ng of the House of David.

As usual, the parts in square brackets are supplied by scholars to make up missing bits of the text.

The stele probably dates to the mid-ninth century BC—thus around 850. You will notice that it mentions an unnamed king of the "house of David," that is, the dynasty of David. It also mentions a king of Israel, because by that time Israel and Judah, its southern neighbor, were divided nations ruled by two different kings. Judah was ruled by the house of David.

That is all the evidence we have of David from a period even close to the time he lived—and this is a hundred years later. It means that there was a dynasty at this time that traced itself back to David.

That is all we can say from the archaeological evidence.

So why is this a problem? We have the Bible as evidence for the greatness of David.

So it would seem. The boundaries of David's empire are outlined in 2 Samuel 8. If you look at maps of this empire, you will see that it included all of present-day Israel, Jordan, and a large portion of Syria extending to the Euphrates River, and went into the Sinai peninsula as well. Some maps include a chunk of western Iraq to boot.

Solomon's empire was just as extensive and far more magnificent, says the book of 1 Kings. His own house was lavish, as was the one he built for Pharaoh's daughter, one of his wives. His crowning achievement was the Temple in Jerusalem, with its cherubs ten cubits high, overlaid with gold (1 Kings 6:26–28).

Of none of these wonders do we have any remains. As I've said, the site of the Temple can't be excavated at any time in the foreseeable future, so it is anyone's guess what you might find there. But there is no external evidence, textual or archaeological, for anything like the buildings that the Bible describes, or for an empire of the kind that David and Solomon were supposed to have. None. No records, no mentions in any texts from Egypt or Mesopotamia, the neighbors of this supposedly mighty kingdom. No inscriptions. No artifacts, not one ivory comb from even one of Solomon's thousand wives.

Instead the evidence suggests this: At the time of David and Solomon in the tenth century BC, Jerusalem was a remote hill town. David and Solomon were chieftains who no doubt ruled the southern part of the land of Canaan—what would soon become the kingdom of Judah—but perhaps not even the northern part of the hill country.

All this is controversial to the point of being explosive. One article on the subject, in the December 2010 issue of *National Geographic*, observes, "In no other part of the world does archaeology so closely resemble a contact sport."

Above I am for the most part restating the views of archaeologist Israel Finkelstein of Tel Aviv University, whose work has attracted much attention and much criticism. But his views overall make the most sense to me. Other archaeologists, such as Eilat Mazar and Yosef Garfinkel, claim to have found buildings that *do* go back to the century of David and Solomon. Finkelstein claims that they date from the ninth century BC—a century *after* David and Solomon. The argument hinges on how you date these buildings—which can only be done through highly technical analyses of pottery shards and similar finds. (The *National Geographic* article mentioned above, available online, would be a good place to start if you want to look further into this matter.)

There's no certain way for a layman to decide who's right. I don't have the technical knowledge to judge one way or the other. But in the end, I tend to agree with Finkelstein: if David and Solomon had anything like an empire of the size and magnificence the Bible says it had, there would have to be more—much more—evidence for it in the archaeological remains.

It's also wise to remember that there is a huge amount of preconceived belief in the reigns of David and Solomon as described in the Bible. It is further overlaid with the political implications of who has the right to be in Palestine today, which make some archaeologists desperate to find the remains of the great Davidic kingdom.

All in all, however, the arguments in favor of the greatness of these kings seem hollow to me. Even the great Frank Moore Cross sounds a bit desperate when he offers a possible reason for the lack of inscriptions from the time of David and Solomon: they were written on plaster overlaid on stone, and the writing washed off or the plaster flaked off.

The Glories of the Temple

Before we move on, let's look at another odd little piece of evidence that suggests the Bible is not trustworthy as history—at least for this period.

The Bible is unsparing in its praises of the richness and magnificence of Solomon's Temple, "overlaid ... within with pure gold" (1 Kings 6:22). But, it admits, the Temple didn't look like this for long. After Solomon's death, in the reign of his son Rehoboam, "Shishak king of Egypt came up against Jerusalem: And he took away the treasures of the house of the Lord, and the treasures of the king's house: he even took away all: and he took away all the shields of gold which Solomon had made" (1 Kings 14:25–26).

By the chronology suggested by the Bible itself, Solomon would have dedicated the Temple around 940 BC. Shishak would have taken the furnishings away around 920 BC—leaving only twenty years for the Temple to enjoy its full-blown magnificence.

As a matter of fact, Sheshonq I, pharaoh of Egypt—identified with the biblical Shishak—*did* invade Canaan. Of this we have a record. It is another stele, found in the temple of Amun at the great site of Karnak in Egypt. It shows a gigantic Sheshonq smiting his enemies, along with columns of hieroglyphs describing his campaign and the damage he has wreaked. The details are so specific that scholars can map Sheshonq's route.

There is one little peculiarity here—Sheshonq didn't go to Jerusalem. There is no mention of Jerusalem or Judah or Rehoboam or anything of the kind on his stele. We have already seen that this kind of stele usually includes a great deal of boasting and exaggeration, so it's not likely that Sheshonq would have kept from mentioning these facts out of modesty— particularly if the booty from the Temple had been anything like what the Bible suggests.

To put it more starkly: *the Bible is saying exactly the opposite of what the evidence from the period says.* This evidence says that Sheshonq invaded and destroyed many places in Canaan, but not Jerusalem. The Bible mentions only Jerusalem.

Two options are left: (1) the kingdom that Solomon left, although weakened under Rehoboam, was too strong for Sheshonq to attack; or (2) it was too insignificant to bother with. The second possibility is by far the more likely, especially since archaeology shows layers of destruction at that period in the cities that Sheshonq actually mentions.

Besides, if Sheshonq had actually plundered such rich booty from the Temple, he would have made sure to boast of it on his stele.

Partly because of the evidence of the Bible, most scholars believe that Sheshonq's invasion took place in the late tenth century—around 920 BC. But Finkelstein argues that Sheshonq's invasion happened much earlier—in Saul's time, at the beginning of the tenth century. Finkelstein points out that the places that Sheshonq attacked were places where Saul was most active—in the northern hill country, rather than in the south, where David and Solomon were headquartered. In this case, the Philistines—who the Bible says destroyed Saul—would have been Sheshonq's allies and vassals. The southern kingdom of Judah under David would have stood aside, watched this happen (if it did not actually help Sheshonq too), and hoped to reap some benefits.

As you see, the arguments become very intricate. But to sum this all up, the evidence for the reigns of Saul, David, and Solomon is paltry. The

Bible account contains much exaggeration and outright fabrication, whether by the writers themselves or through the legends that grew up in the centuries between the time of David (c.980 BC) and the time the Deuteronomic history was first written (after 620 BC).

The Divided Monarchy

There is one other sure thing we know both from the Bible and from the external evidence. By the ninth century BC, Israel was divided into two kingdoms. The northern portion, by far the larger and richer and more powerful of the two, is simply called Israel. The smaller and poorer kingdom in the south is called Judah, because it mostly consisted of the land and people of the tribe of Judah.

As we shall see, these two kingdoms had extremely different fates.

They differed in other ways as well. Scholars can even find differences in dialect in the inscriptions from the following centuries. For our purposes, the greatest difference lay in this: the southern kingdom of Judah was ruled by kings of the house of David, and its worship was centralized in the Temple of Jerusalem. The northern kingdom of Israel never had such a centralized place of worship and was ruled by a series of dynasties, all of whom "did that which was evil in the eyes of the Lord."

Here it's useful to remember that the Deuteronomic history—the chief biblical source for this period—was written in Judah. So the historian was naturally inclined to have some prejudice against the northern kingdom. Furthermore, it is talking mostly about two issues. In the first place, the kings of Israel did not recognize the Temple in Jerusalem. They continued to allow people to use the old, local sites of worship called the "high places." What was still worse, the rulers of the northern kingdom tolerated foreign gods—gods other than Yahweh.

We have taken the story now up to the middle of the ninth century— around 850 BC. You may remember an earlier remark of mine that this is the period at which history starts to come into focus. At this point the external evidence from archaeology starts to fit in much more closely with the biblical account.

Which brings up the topic of Samaria. Samaria was the capital of the northern kingdom of Israel. It is one site at which we start to find archaeological remains of a great kingdom; others nearby include Jezreel and Megiddo. This kingdom was ruled by Omri and his successors. By far the best-known of these was Omri's son Ahab. Ahab's Phoenician queen, Jezebel, is more famous—or more notorious—still.

"Ahab did more to provoke the Lord God of Israel to anger than all the kings of Israel that were before him," says the Bible (1 Kings 16:33). Perhaps. But Ahab did another thing: he brought Israel into greater international prominence than any king did before or after him.

Again the archaeology speaks. Again it is a stele, this one erected by Shalmaneser III, king of Assyria between 858 and 824 BC. It tells of Shalmaneser's attempt to invade Syria, Phoenicia, and Israel. It also says that he was opposed by a coalition that included "Ahab the Israelite," whose force included "10,000 foot soldiers" and "2,000 chariots." Ahab was by far the most powerful member of this coalition.

The outcome? Shalmaneser, of course, said he had won. But he may have been lying, because after this battle he went back to Assyria and did not bother those nations again.

To put this in context, Assyria at the time was the most powerful nation in the region, and probably in the world as then known. Turning its forces back was no small accomplishment for the ruler of a much smaller kingdom.

The dynasty of Omri eventually fell from power. At one point a prophet predicts that "the whole house of Ahab shall perish: and [the Lord] will cut off from Ahab him that pisseth against a wall"—a salty Hebrew idiom, translated literally in the King James Version, meaning all male offspring. And the prophecy is fulfilled (1 Kings 10:11).

Nevertheless, the kingdom of Israel continues for another century or so, marked by huge inequalities in wealth. In the early eighth century the prophet Amos rails against the "kine of Bashan, which are in the mountain of Samaria, which oppress the poor, which crush the needy" (Amos 4:1)—a passage that a modern American minister could apply to the rich today. To express Yahweh's fury with wayward Israel, the prophet Hosea marries a whore and has children that he names Loruhamah and Loammi, meaning "No mercy" and "Not my people" (Hosea 1:2–29), possibly making Hosea the first conceptual artist in world history.

These prophecies came true. Ahab may have driven the Assyrians away for his lifetime, but eventually they came back. In 722 BC, the Assyrian king Shalmaneser V conquered Israel, destroyed Samaria, and deported a huge part of the population.

These people, by the way, were the Ten Lost Tribes of Israel. While the lists of the twelve tribes don't always agree (sometimes, for example, Levi is counted, sometimes not), the northern kingdom of Israel comprised ten tribes, while the southern kingdom of Judah included only two—Judah itself and Benjamin.

The lore about the Ten Lost Tribes is elaborate and alluring—for example, legends about a "Land of the Red Jews" that was "far beyond the Mountains of Darkness, beyond the restless river Sambatyon, beyond the peaceful River of Youth," as Joseph Gaer puts it in his delightful book *The Lore of the Old Testament*. The Mormons say that the tribes came to the New World and became the American Indians. In the palmy days of nineteenth-century Britain, a movement called Anglo-Israelism tried to prove that the descendants of the Ten Lost Tribes were nothing other than the Anglo-Saxons.

The truth, alas, is probably more humdrum. The Assyrians deported conquered peoples, believing (no doubt correctly) that, thus disoriented, they were less likely to rebel. Hence the Ten Lost Tribes probably mixed into the general population of Mesopotamia. Their descendants may well still be there today, indistinguishable from everyone else. It is sobering to think that both the lunatic who blows himself up in Iraq today and the victims that he blows up may be the offspring of old Israel.

Assyria also tried to conquer the southern kingdom of Judah, but, as we shall see, it did not succeed. Judah survived as an independent nation for almost 140 years after the fall of Israel in 722. Even afterward, it preserved its identity and gave rise to the people now called the Jews—from the name Judah.

At this point the center of the biblical story shifts to the south, ruled by the line of David. Before we go into this story, however, we will have to say a little more about the god called Yahweh, the hero of the Hebrew Bible.

5.

Who Was Yahweh?

MANY, PERHAPS MOST, polytheistic religions have a similar structure. At the top is a creator god, a superior deity who produced heaven and earth and all that is in them. But often this creator god is inaccessible. In the religions of the African diaspora, for example—Voudun, Santería, and so on—this god is Olodumare, the king supreme. But Olodumare is old and no longer interested in his creation. If you pray to him, you will not get any results. You have to pray to one of the intermediate gods if you want to have anything done.

The Canaanite religions were similar. There was a supreme being called El, a word that means both "above" and "god." Under him are any number of other gods. As mentioned earlier, some of these were gods of nations. If you were an Ammonite, you worshipped one god; if you were an Edomite, you worshipped another. The people of Israel worshipped Yahweh. As I've said, I believe that allegiance to Yahweh was the thing that unified the peoples in the Canaanite hill country into the nation called Israel.

Who, then, was Yahweh? He may have started as a kind of representation or manifestation of El, the high, universal god, in a particular time and place and to a particular people—first the Midianite league, and then the Israelites.

To clarify what he may mean, I could turn to Hinduism. Hinduism has innumerable gods—hundreds of millions by some counts. But the Hindu sages have always insisted on one central truth: these countless gods are all manifestations of Brahman, of the One.

In this sense Yahweh was a manifestation of El, the One, to the Israelites.

Was he, then, just a national god among many other national gods? Or was he the one Supreme Being, the only God that exists?

To answer these questions, we can start by looking at the meaning of his name.

He Who Causes to Be

The meaning of Yahweh's name has been widely disputed. Scholars have come up with any number of fanciful origins for it. But to me the most persuasive one comes from Frank Moore Cross. To get technical for a moment, he suggests that it is a causative imperfect form of a verb meaning "to be."

To go into this a bit, Hebrew does not, strictly speaking, have tenses as English does. Instead it has *aspects*. Aspects do not so much say *when* an action happened, but *whether* it is completed or not. (Modern Russian has something similar.) The imperfect aspect simply means that the action is not completed. It is often, though not always, translated with the English future tense.

A causative form is what its name implies. A causative form of "to be" would mean "to cause to be." In Exodus 3:14, God identifies himself to

Moses by saying, "I am that I am." At least this is how this sentence is translated. Originally, however, it probably meant something different—something like "I am causing to be what I am causing to be"—or, as it were, "I create what I create."

Where does the name *Yahweh* come in? That's simple. It is merely a third-person form of the same verb: "he is causing to be"; "he is creating."

Causing to be? Causing *what* to be? There's an answer for this as well. You may have come across a mysterious phrase in the Bible: "the Lord of hosts" or "Yahweh of hosts." In Hebrew it is *Yahweh ts'va'oth* (admittedly a bit awkward for English speakers to pronounce). This phrase probably doesn't mean "Yahweh of hosts," if only for grammatical reasons (these particular noun forms can't be used in a possessive relationship in the original language). Instead it means—or originally meant—"he who is causing the hosts to be." Frank Moore Cross suggests that his full name was originally *'el du yahweh ts'va'oth*: "El who is causing the hosts to be." Eventually it was shortened to *Yahweh ts'va'oth* and finally just to Yahweh.

To get technical again, *Yahweh ts'va'oth* is what is called a *hypostasis*. The closest English equivalent is "personification," although this is not exact. Basically it is an attribute (usually of God) that takes on a life of its own and becomes a kind of independent entity, even a person.

In this case, *Yahweh ts'va'oth* is a hypostasis of El. Yahweh was originally a kind of personification of the creative power of El ("he who causes the hosts to be"). Then Yahweh came to take on an independent existence, as the god of the Midianite league and then of Israel. As we will soon see, Yahweh was also seen as an angel.

Who are the "hosts"? Very likely the "hosts of heaven," the "sons of God," what were later known as angels. Cross concludes that Yahweh was "a cultic name of 'El, perhaps the epithet of 'El as patron deity of the Midianite League."

Scholars do not, by the way, know exactly how Yahweh's name was pronounced, because Hebrew did not and does not write most of its vowels. After a certain point in Jewish history, it was considered sacrilegious even to speak the name aloud, so the pronunciation was lost, or at any rate concealed. *Yahweh* is the best pronunciation that today's scholars have come up with.

That, it would seem, is the meaning of the name *Yahweh*. What else do we know about him?

Scholars have identified some passages in the Bible that are older than others (based on the language, poetic form, and other such considerations). These include passages in Judges 5 and Habakkuk 3. Judges 5:4 says, "Lord [i.e., Yahweh], when thou wentest out of Seir, when thou marchedst out of the field of Edom . . ." Edom is the country southeast of Judah, in the south of present-day Jordan. Habakkuk 3:3 says, "God came from Teman." Teman was in what is today northwestern Saudi Arabia. This is exactly the territory of Midian. Thus according to the oldest traditions, Yahweh came from Midian, and that is where he first appears to Moses in the book of Exodus. The mount "Sinai" on which Moses saw the Lord was not, then, on the Sinai peninsula, but in northwestern Arabia.

The Great Angel

Did the earliest Israelites believe that Yahweh was the only God, or only one out of many? It's not entirely clear. In the Bible, when Jethro (a Midianite and Moses's father-in-law) hears of the miracle of the Red Sea, he exclaims, "Now I know that [Yahweh] is greater than all the gods" (Exodus 18:11). Jethro is not denying that the other gods exist. He is simply saying that Yahweh is the strongest.

Is this, then, what the Israelites themselves believed at the outset—that there were many gods, and that Yahweh just happened to be theirs? There are reasons for thinking so.

Let's go back to a passage that we've already looked at: Deuteronomy 32:8–9. I will give it in the New Revised Standard Version, substituting the original Hebrew God names for the English ones.

> When [Elyon] apportioned the nations,
> when he divided humankind,
> he fixed the boundaries of the peoples
> according to the number of the gods;
> [Yahweh's] portion was his people,
> Jacob his allotted share.

In light of what I've said above, this passage now becomes very interesting. Elyon is another name for the high god, El. It now looks very much as if Elyon, or El, is assigning Israel to Yahweh much as he has assigned other nations to other gods. Yahweh, then, is special to Israel. It is Yahweh that Israel is supposed to worship and Yahweh's law that Israel is supposed to obey. But the passage does not say that other nations should not worship other gods. They have their own gods and it is their own business whom they worship.

That may have been the faith of Israel in its earliest days. El was the high god; Yahweh was the god of Israel.

In her book *The Great Angel: A Study of Israel's Second God*, the British biblical scholar Margaret Barker offers some fascinating ideas about this matter. She says that Yahweh started as an angel—the ruling angel of Israel.

You will remember that the above passage in Deuteronomy was changed because it made somebody nervous—particularly this idea of "ruling angels." You now know why. Later Judaism said that there was only one God; all others were false. This God was the Yahweh of the Bible. It would be a bit disappointing if Yahweh were just another angel in the heavenly court along with all the others. So the Hebrew text was changed to obscure this point. The Greek Septuagint was translated in the third century BC, before this change had been made. So it preserves the true, original text, and that's why present-day scholars have been able to correct the reading.

If you look at a number of biblical passages, you will see that the line between Yahweh and the angel of Yahweh is rather blurry. Here is one example, from Exodus 3:2–4: "And the angel of [Yahweh]* appeared unto [Moses] in a flame of fire out of the midst of a bush; and he looked, and behold, the bush burned with fire, and the bush was not consumed. And Moses said, I will now turn aside, and see this great sight, why the bush is not burnt. And when [Yahweh] saw that he turned aside to see, God called unto him out of the midst of the bush."

Notice that the passage slips from Moses dealing with the angel of Yahweh to Yahweh himself.

Here is another one, Genesis 18:1–2: "And [Yahweh] appeared unto [Abraham] in the plains of Mamre; and he sat in the tent door in the heat of the day; And he lift up his eyes and, lo, three men stood by him: and when he saw them, he ran to meet them from the tent door, and bowed himself toward the ground."

It helps to know that in the Hebrew Bible, angels are sometimes (confusingly) known as "men." Yahweh appeared to Abraham. Yahweh was one of the three men. Thus Yahweh was a "man"—an angel.

After the men have been entertained and are about to leave, the passage says: "And the men turned their faces from thence, and went toward Sodom: but Abraham remained standing before [Yahweh]." This verse has also been changed. Originally it read, "... but Yahweh remained standing before Abraham." This reading makes it much clearer that Yahweh is an angel—in fact, one of Abraham's visitors.

You can now see why this text too was altered. The idea that Yahweh

---

*The King James Version usually translates *Yahweh* as "the LORD" (in small capitals). In these passages I have replaced this rendition with the actual name *Yahweh*.

was an angel did not fit the theology of later Judaism. And the idea that God himself would do something as mundane as stopping to talk to Abraham seemed irreverent.

Still not convinced that Yahweh may have been an angel? Look at Genesis 48:15–16: "And [Jacob] blessed Joseph, and said, God, before whom my fathers Abraham and Isaac did walk, the God which fed me all my life long to this day, *The Angel* which redeemed me from all evil, bless the lads" (emphasis mine).

Here is one possibility that would explain these verses. Originally Yahweh, the god of Israel, was one and only one more angel in the heavenly court of the "sons of God," as the Hebrew Bible calls them. But later Judaism changed this to make Yahweh the one, sole, universal God. Yahweh came to be seen as identical with El.

Someone going through the Bible today comes across Joshua 22:22, reads, "The Lord God of gods, the Lord God of gods," and thinks nothing of it. In English it is unremarkable and even redundant. Not in the Hebrew: *"Yahweh 'el 'elohim:"* "Yahweh is El of the gods." The god of one nation had become identified with the God of all.

This statement appears in the Deuteronomic history, written around the turn of the sixth century BC. By this time the change had been made: El was identified with Yahweh.

The Great Mistake

Thus Yahweh was originally a kind of manifestation of the high god, El, worshipped first by the Midianites and later by Israel.

In all likelihood he was also seen as an angel—one of many "sons of God" in the heavenly court. He just happened to be the one assigned to Israel. As the Israelite religion evolved, Yahweh came to be identified more and more with El until Yahweh and El were seen as one and the same—and indeed the only—God.

In this situation we're not dealing with a time when learned scholars were quibbling over theological intricacies. The people who held these beliefs, especially at first, were nomads or farmers in a hill country. In all likelihood they did not draw such sharp lines and it never occurred to them to try.

Thus it became all the easier to say that Yahweh was El and El was Yahweh. The God of Israel was the one, sole, and ultimate God.

All of this helps us understand how God—the God we believe in today, or do not believe in—came to be God.

There is a fatal error here—so fatal that I could hardly overstate its consequences.

There is the Ground of Being, the ineffable, unnamable Reality that gives rise to everything. This Reality can never be understood or expressed in ordinary terms, because ordinary terms are limited and this Reality is not. But we ourselves think in limited ways, so we represent this Reality in limited ways—the only ones meaningful to us.

There is nothing wrong in this so far as it goes. But when religion confuses its own inevitably limited picture of the transcendent Reality with the Reality itself, it is making a mistake.

It is a very dangerous one.

Why? Because the next step is to assume that your image of God is the only true one, and all others are therefore false. This was a mistake made by the faith of ancient Israel, and it was transmitted like a heritable disease to its offspring, Christianity and Islam. It has been the source of most religious hatred and persecution. We are not yet free from it.

The Divine Consort

By this point we have learned a little more about Yahweh. We could say other things about him. He was a storm god, and the Bible often links him with storm imagery. In Job 38:1, for example, Yahweh "answered Job out of the whirlwind." He is also a god of battles, leading his people to war. Exodus 15:3, in one of the oldest passages in the Bible, says Yahweh "is a man of war."

I have used masculine pronouns to speak of Yahweh, and the Bible does the same. He is a male god. Of that there is no question.

Over the last few decades, feminist thinkers have objected to this picture. If God is infinite and transcendent, why should we think of him in masculine terms alone?

There's no good reason to do so. In fact people have shown a universal instinct to view God in feminine terms, for example, as a divine mother. The oldest religious artifacts in existence are those strange figurines, dating back sometimes tens of thousands of years, that depict a naked, obese woman with enormous breasts—the Great Goddess, as many have supposed. In America today, where so many people are anxious about being fat, these figurines are not particularly alluring. But in an age when people often did not have enough food to survive a winter, the figures probably represented fertility and abundance. They may have looked very attractive, even sexy, to the people of the time.

Was the faith of Yahweh immune to this pull toward a feminine God? Not as much as we might think. Thus the archaeologist William G. Dever could publish a book entitled *Did God Have a Wife?*

In Canaanite myth, El had a wife, a female consort, whose name was Asherah. Her name is probably derived from a phrase from the Ugaritic language spoken in Syria in biblical times: *atirat-yammi*, "she who treads upon Sea," "Sea" being a personified chaos monster.

So exactly how closely connected was she with Yahweh in this period (from c.940 to 586 BC)? Raphael Patai, whose book *The Hebrew Goddess* is one of the most important works on this subject, sums up the picture *from the Bible's point of view*: "It appears that, of the 370 years during which the Solomonic Temple stood in Jerusalem, for no less than 236 years (or almost two-thirds of the time) the statue of Asherah was present in the Temple, and her worship was a part of the legitimate religion approved and led by the king, the court, and the priesthood and opposed by only a few prophetic voices crying out against it at relatively long intervals." Saul M. Olyan, a professor at Brown University, has written that Asherah "was an acceptable and legitimate part of Yahweh's cult in non-deuteronomistic circles. The association of the asherah and the cult of Yahweh suggests that Asherah was the consort of Yahweh in circles both in the north and the south."

Olyan uses *asherah* as both a proper name and a common noun. That's because the Hebrew language in this period did the same thing. *Asherah* can serve both as a proper name for the goddess and as a common noun for a cult object representing her, possibly a wooden image. One ancient Jewish tradition says that the *asherah* was either a tree or a tree with a cult object beneath it. Hence translators have rendered *asherah* variously as "tree" and "grove."

Certain inscriptions from the monarchical period illustrate this point. One, dating from the eighth or ninth century BC, reads, "I [b]lessed you by (or 'to') Yahweh of Samaria and by his Asherah." Another inscription reads, "To [Y]ahweh of Teiman . . . and to his Ashera[h]." We've already encountered Teiman, or Teman, in northwestern Arabia: it was Yahweh's original home. Asherah might have been with him from the beginning. In these cases, the "Asherah" was more likely a cult object than the goddess per se (the distinction is not always clear). The Bible says these "trees" or "groves" are abominations. In the Deuteronomic account, the priests in the Temple discover a lost scroll of the Law of Moses and read it to the young King Josiah (2 Kings 22:8–11). This would have taken place in or around 620 BC. Shocked by his nation's infidelity, Josiah orders a purge of the Temple. He "commanded Hilkiah the high priest, and the priests of the second order, and the keepers of the door, to bring forth out of the temple of the Lord all the vessels that were made for Baal, and for the grove, and for all the host of heaven: and he burned them without Jerusalem in the fields of Kidron" (2 Kings 23:4).

The "grove" here was undoubtedly an image of Asherah. Certainly she was connected with a tree motif. This was partly because the tree is a symbol of life, especially in an arid climate. Some images portray Asherah with a tree growing out of her pubic triangle. Hence she symbolizes life in this sense too.

Asherah's foes were the prophets and those who wrote the Deuteronomic history. Where did this history come from? As we've just seen, Josiah purged the Temple after hearing a rediscovered scroll of the Law read by the priests. The standard view today is that this scroll was an early version of the book of Deuteronomy, and that it was not rediscovered but had been written specifically for the occasion. The priests forged it to prove to Josiah that their views of Yahweh's religion went back to Moses.

And Deuteronomy condemns Asherah worship. This is how it tells the children of Israel to deal with the Canaanites: "Ye shall destroy their altars, and break down their images, *and cut down their groves*, and burn their graven images with fire" (Deuteronomy 7:5; emphasis added). The "groves," again, are *asherim*, images of Asherah. But as we've seen, even the Deuteronomist has to admit that Asherah was welcome in the Temple throughout most of the period from its construction c.940 to 586 BC.

Here we wind up with two theories that are at odds with each other.

Version one: Moses had a revelation at Sinai in which he was given the Law and was charged to worship Yahweh alone. The people of Israel agreed to this covenant. But when they entered the land of Canaan, they slid back and started worshipping all sorts of foreign gods, including Asherah. The priests in Josiah's time purged the faith of these evil influences and restored the worship of Yahweh to its pure and original form. This is the story you read in the Bible.

Version two: Originally the Israelites worshipped Yahweh as their main god, but not their only one. They thought of Asherah as his consort and worshipped her too. But at some point—we cannot say exactly when—a new "Yahweh alone" movement arose among some prophets and priests, especially in Judah, as well as a few kings "who did what was right in the eyes of Yahweh." At first this movement was in a minority, but when Josiah came to the throne, this party gained his favor. Josiah carried out their will. He destroyed cult images—or, if you prefer, idols—that had been in the Temple most of the time since it was built.

This is the story that a number of reputable scholars have come to accept (with variations among individual scholars). Margaret Barker even argues that in the time of the First Temple (as the period from c.940 to 586 BC is called), the standard worship was devoted to a trinity of gods: El, Yahweh, and Asherah.

Which version is the true one? I find it hard to say. There is too much evidence lost, too many texts changed. As we've seen in so many cases, the Bible claims one thing, but the actual evidence from the period often shows just the opposite. Whether Asherah was part of the picture at the beginning, during the days of Moses, is hard to decide, at least until some new evidence comes to light.

In any event, Josiah died in 609 BC, and the Temple was sacked by the Babylonians only a couple of decades later, in 586.

The book of Jeremiah has an interesting passage about this matter. After the Temple's destruction, people who "had burned incense to other gods" tell Jeremiah: "We will certainly do whatsoever thing goeth forth out of our own mouth, to burn incense to the queen of heaven* and to

---

*In Canaanite myth, the queen of heaven was called Astarte. She is often identified with Asherah.

pour out drink offerings unto her, as we have done, we, and our fathers, our kings, and our princes, in the cities of Judah, and in the streets of Jerusalem: for then had we plenty of victuals, and were well, and saw no evil. But since we left off to burn incense to the queen of heaven, and to pour out drink offerings unto her, we have wanted all things, and have been consumed by the sword and by the famine" (Jeremiah 44:17–18).

In short, many in Judah believed that the Temple was destroyed not because the people had profaned it with the worship of the goddess (as Jeremiah and the Deuteronomist claimed) but because they had *abandoned* her worship.

In the long run, the "Yahweh alone" movement, including the Deuteronomic circle and the biblical prophets, won the day. They created the forerunner of the Judaism of Christ's time as well as of the Judaism of today.

So the history was written by the "Yahweh alone" movement. When the Jews returned from exile in Babylonia and rebuilt the Temple (after 539 BC), the priests and the prophets were now all of that party. It was they who wrote the Deuteronomic history. It was also they who compiled and edited the Pentateuch as well as the writings of the prophets. This is the core of the Hebrew Bible as we now know it. It explains why we see biblical history the way we do.

But the goddess did not vanish completely from the Jewish faith. Later parts of the Bible, such as the book of Proverbs, mention a personified figure of "Wisdom," who has a female form: "Doth not wisdom cry, and understanding put forth her voice? She standeth in the top of high places, by the way in the places of the paths" (Proverbs 8:1–2). The Hebrew word for *wisdom*, *ḥokhmah*, is grammatically feminine. Still later, the mystics of Judaism speak of the Shekhinah, the "presence" of God. In the Bible, this word does not seem to mean much more than its face value, but in later Judaism, the Shekhinah herself is personified as a feminine aspect of God, and she is spoken of almost as a separate being. The medieval Kabbalists claimed that in the present, fallen world, the Shekhinah has been estranged from the God above. Indeed they said that all religious acts should be performed "for the sake of the reunion of God and His Shekhinah."

Maybe it is happening. Today many people are drawn to fresh visions of the divine feminine. There is a widespread sense that these ancient archetypes are reappearing to claim their rightful place in our spiritual consciousness. That may be so, but it's more likely that they have never really gone away.

6.

Fall and Return: The Exile and Its Aftermath

AFTER THE NORTHERN kingdom was destroyed in 722 BC, the Assyrians, under the king Sennacherib, tried to conquer Judah too. In 700 BC they besieged Jerusalem. The Bible says that the city was saved by a miracle. "The angel of the Lord went out, and smote in the camp of the Assyrians an hundred fourscore and five thousand: and when they arose early in the morning, behold, they were all dead corpses. So Sennacherib king of Assyria departed, and went and returned, and dwelt at Nineveh," his capital (2 Kings 19:36–37).

If there is any truth to this account, it probably points to a plague that swept the Assyrian army. Plagues came regularly and frequently in those days. Whether it was a miracle or not, to those besieged inside Jerusalem it must have felt like one.

Assyria never conquered Judah, partly because Assyria itself went into serious decline in the seventh century BC. Nineveh was sacked by the Babylonians in 612 BC. The biblical prophet Nahum exults over this destruction of Judah's old enemy.

The people of Judah did not cheer for long. The Babylonians under King Nebuchadnezzar II soon set upon them.

The Dilemmas of Prophecy

The prophets themselves did not agree about what should be done about this new threat. One, known as Hananiah, assured the people that the Babylonian threat would soon vanish and that they should resist it, as they had done with Assyria. Another, Jeremiah, said the opposite, telling Hananiah, "The Lord hath not sent thee; but thou makest the people to trust in a lie" (Jeremiah 28:15). Jeremiah advised giving in to the Babylonians.

The last king of the Davidic line, Zedekiah, chose to believe the prophets who preached resistance. "Zedekiah rebelled against the king of Babylon" (2 Kings 24:20).

Zedekiah's decision proved unwise. Nebuchadnezzar came back, conquered Judah, captured the king and his family, and put out his eyes after forcing him to watch his sons being killed (2 Kings 25:7). "And he [Nebuchadnezzar] burnt the house of the Lord, and the king's house, and all the houses of Jerusalem, and every great man's house burnt he with fire" (2 Kings 25:9).

Thus the Temple of Solomon was destroyed. This took place in 586 BC, on the ninth day of the month Av in the Jewish calendar. To this day the Jews commemorate it (along with the sack of the Second Temple in AD 70) on Tisha B'Av ("the ninth of Av"), which falls in July or August. They consider it the saddest and most ill-omened day in the year.

To explain what happened in a geopolitical sense, if you look at a map, you will see that present-day Israel lies between Egypt and Mesopotamia. These two areas were the strongholds of the great powers of that era. (Mesopotamia was controlled first by the Assyrians, then by the

Babylonians.) As these powers sought to expand, they were bound to clash. Palestine was often the battlefield.

At the beginning of this period, around 1100 BC, Egyptian power was undergoing a long decline. But the power of Assyria had not yet reached its peak. For a period of a few hundred years, say from 1100 to 800 BC, the smaller countries in between, including Israel and Judah, had some space in which they could operate more or less freely. But as first Assyria and then Babylon increased their domains, Israel and Judah were natural targets. They were too small to stand up against these great empires.

The clash between the prophets such as Hananiah, who preached resistance to the Babylonians, and those such as Jeremiah, who preached capitulation, tells us something about the problem of prophecy. After events had unfolded, it would have been easy to tell the true prophets from the false. Jeremiah predicted correctly; thus he was a true prophet. If he had been wrong, the Bible might have featured a book of Hananiah.

But at the time how was the ordinary Israelite—or for that matter the king—supposed to tell which prophet was right? It could hardly have been as clear as the Bible makes it seem. In fact Jeremiah's record for prophecy was rather unimpressive. In the 620s, the entire region was being menaced by a people "from the north country" (Jeremiah 6:22). They were the Scythians, a seminomadic tribe based in what is today southern Ukraine. They swept down through the territory of the Medes (in present-day Azerbaijan) to Egypt.

Jeremiah foresaw terrible destruction from these people of the north: "They shall eat up thy vines and thy fig trees: they shall impoverish thy fenced cities, wherein thou trustedst, with the sword" (Jeremiah 5:17).

But in fact these disasters did not materialize. The Scythians left Judah and Jerusalem more or less unscathed, and their incursions were more of a raid than an attempt at permanent conquest. The failure of Jeremiah's prophecy put him back into obscurity, and his self-confidence was shaken enough to keep him from prophesying for fourteen years.

Jeremiah had had other failures as well. About Jehoiakim, one of Josiah's successors as king of Judah, who "filled Jerusalem with innocent blood," Jeremiah had declaimed, "Therefore thus said the Lord concerning Jehoiakim the son of Josiah king of Judah; . . . He shall be buried with the burial of an ass, drawn and cast forth beyond the gates of Jerusalem" (Jeremiah 22:18).

What actually happened? The Deuteronomist simply says that "Jehoiakim slept with his fathers"—indicating that his death and burial were perfectly normal according to the customs of the time (2 Kings 24:4–5).

As these things suggest, prophecy does not stand up too well to scrutiny. Here is another little-known (or little-admitted) fact: *many of the prophecies in the Bible never came true.* What I have given above are only two examples. We will see more.

The Roots of Evil

You may have noticed that I've avoided speaking of *Judaism* when I've been talking about the religion of the monarchical period (also known as the era of the First Temple, or for the time after Solomon, of the divided monarchy). This is for a reason. The religion of that time was so different from present-day Judaism that it is hard to call them by the same name.

After the sack of the Temple, everything changed. The people of Judah (or at least their most prominent citizens) were deported to Babylon. There they absorbed many influences that had never touched them before. These influences were the seeds of Judaism as we know it today.

To take one simple example, the Jews changed their alphabet. In the monarchical period, Hebrew was written in a script that was completely unlike what we think of as Hebrew today. It was the old Phoenician alphabet, the first ever devised, which the Israelites shared with their neighbors such as the Moabites (with the usual regional differences). After the

Babylonian Exile (586–539 BC), the Jews adopted a new alphabet from the Aramaic language. It was sometimes called "the Assyrian letters." As one old *midrash* (commentary) on the book of Esther says, "Hebrew is a spoken tongue but has no script of its own. The Hebrews chose for themselves the Assyrian script and the Hebrew tongue."

These Assyrian letters were somewhat more squarish versions of what is the Hebrew alphabet today. But they are similar. Anyone who knows the modern version can read texts from the period after the Exile (though of course with some difficulty).

The Exile forced another, much greater change upon the Jews. They had to rethink their notions of divine justice—the issue that theologians call *theodicy*.

Before the Exile, divine justice was rooted in Israel's covenant with Yahweh. If they followed it, they would prosper. If they strayed from it, they would be punished.

For the final catastrophe of the sack of the Temple, the Deuteronomist blames the wicked king Menasseh, who ruled for fifty-five years until his death in 642 BC. "Menasseh seduced [the people of Judah] to do more evil than the nations whom the Lord destroyed before the children of Israel." As a result, the Lord proclaims, "I will wipe Jerusalem as a man wipeth a dish, wiping it, and turning it upside down" (2 Kings 22:9, 13).

The Deuteronomist's explanation seems a bit forced. After all, he has to face the fact that Menasseh was followed by Josiah, who reigned for thirty-one years (from 640 to 609) and who instigated sweeping reforms. Josiah purified the nation's worship of its "groves" and its idols and restored the pure faith of Yahweh alone. Didn't this work to Judah's credit? In the end, no. "The Lord turned not from the fierceness of his great wrath, . . . because of all the provocations that Menasseh had provoked him withal" (2 Kings 23:26).

Such was the decree of the Lord. It may have seemed harsh, even in those grim times. The prophet known as Second Isaiah* hints as much when he proclaims at the end of the Exile, "For [Jerusalem] hath received of the Lord's hand *double for all her sins*" (Isaiah 40:2; my emphasis). So Judah's punishment, however righteous, may have seemed out of all proportion to what the nation deserved.

The Exile ended in 539 BC. The Babylonian (or Neo-Babylonian, as it is usually called) empire had fallen to the Medes and the Persians under Cyrus the Great. Cyrus reversed the Babylonian practice and allowed the Jewish exiles to return to their homeland and rebuild the Temple.

Second Isaiah gives Cyrus the highest praise possible, calling him the Lord's "anointed" (Isaiah 45:1). In Hebrew this word is *m'shichu* (from *mashiach*). Previously it had been used only to refer to the kings and high priests of Israel. No other foreign king was so honored in the Bible. Only later did the word come to mean "Messiah."

The Jews did rebuild their Temple, slowly and fitfully, thus beginning what is called the period of the Second Temple (539 BC–AD 70). Nonetheless, the problem of evil continued to nag at the Jewish sages—as it does with us today. We as humans have a fundamental sense of fairness, of justice. This sense is, to all appearances, universal. Thus we expect the universe—and God himself—to live by a code of justice as well. Especially since, as the Bible keeps reminding us, it is God himself who has established what is just.

But often the world does not seem just. The righteous suffer, the wicked flourish. It's true, of course, that most people most of the time end up getting exactly what they deserve. But the equation never works

---

*Scholars today divide the biblical book of Isaiah into three parts. The first thirty-nine chapters (with some interpolations) is attributed to Isaiah himself, who lived during the reign of Hezekiah in the late eighth century. Second Isaiah, comprising chapters 40–55, was written around the end of the Exile, c.539 BC. Third Isaiah, comprising chapters 56–66, dates from after the Exile. As usual, the issue is far more complex than I have just indicated, but this summary will do for my purposes here.

out completely. There is always some remainder left after the good deeds are reckoned against the bad.

Second Isaiah gives a stark answer to this problem in one of the greatest and most profound verses in the Bible: "I form the light and create darkness: I make peace and create evil: I the Lord do all these things" (Isaiah 45:7).

That *is* the answer. Like it or not, there is no other possible. There is only the One, the Source. Everything arises from it, light and darkness, peace and evil. All other answers are only equivocations. As the twentieth-century theologian Paul Tillich puts it, "The holy originally lies below the alternative of the good and the evil; . . . it is both divine and demonic."

In its way the book of Job, usually dated to the time of the Exile (or later), says the same. Job is a cryptic book, using archaic spellings as well as many words that don't appear anywhere else in the Bible.

The story is too well known to be retold here. The righteous Job is forced to suffer because of a kind of bet between Yahweh and the Adversary (the literal Hebrew meaning of the word *satan*). The dramatic tension of the book lies in this simple fact: Job suffers for no fault of his own. The book of Job is a response to the theodicy of the Deuteronomist and his kin, under which all suffering is purely and completely a matter of merit. Job keeps protesting his innocence.

Finally Yahweh himself appears out of the whirlwind. In one of the Bible's most awe-inspiring passages, he confronts Job and says, "Where was thou when I laid the foundations of the earth? declare, if thou has understanding" (Job 38:4). Yahweh goes on to show his majesty and power: "Canst thou bind the sweet influences of Pleiades, or loose the bands of Orion?" (Job 38:31).

Yahweh speaks of a great sea monster called Leviathan. Scholars connect this beast with the primordial sea monster of Canaanite myth, whom the gods must subdue so that an ordered creation may begin. But to Yahweh, Leviathan is not a primordial adversary. Instead Yahweh says, "whatsoever is under the whole heaven is mine" (Job 41:11). To Yahweh, Leviathan, terrible as he is, is a mere goldfish in a bowl.

Job is cowed by this vision. He says to Yahweh, "I know that thou canst do everything, and that no thought can be withholden from thee" (Job 42:2). Job repents "in dust and ashes," and all that he has lost is restored to him.

The book of Job is one of the great works of world literature, and its depths and subtleties are not easy to fathom. Some, such as the great psychiatrist C. G. Jung, have seen Yahweh's response to Job as a mere show of force—a view that Jung sets out in his *Answer to Job*, published in 1952. But I cannot agree.

Yahweh's answer is not merely a display of power: it is a revelation. It reveals that the ways of God, and the workings of the universe, are far greater than humans understand and *can* understand. These workings include even what we call evil. We like to praise ourselves as superior to the other animals, with our capacities for language and technology and abstract thought. But we may differ from the animals in another way as well: we at least have a glimpse of how little we know. The answer to Job reminds us of this fact.

Satan's Arrival

The answer to the problem of evil given by Job and Second Isaiah—that it arises from the primordial Source just as good does—is overwhelmingly powerful. But it is also extremely stark. Not everyone can face it, and there is a strong urge to find some more satisfying account of divine justice. Consequently after the Exile, something new enters into Judaism. Compare these two passages. One, by the Deuteronomist, dates to around 600 BC:

And again the anger of [Yahweh] was kindled against Israel, and he moved David against them to say, Go, number Israel and Judah.

(2 Samuel 24:1)

The other, from Chronicles, dates to no earlier than 450 BC and could well be later:

And Satan stood up against Israel, and provoked David to number Israel.

(1 Chronicles 21:1)

It's clear that for various reasons David was not supposed to take a census of the people. In the first passage, it is Yahweh who tempts David to take the census; in the second, it is Satan—the Adversary.

The first passage above points up some of the faults for which Yahweh is blamed today. He is capricious and at times evil-minded. His wrath is kindled against Israel for vague and unspecified reasons. He has David number the people and then punishes them for it: seventy thousand people die of a plague (2 Samuel 24:15).

The second passage is apparently more sophisticated. Instead of blaming Yahweh for tempting David, it blames Satan, the Adversary. Yahweh is no longer the villain.

Satan appears in Job, and he appears here in Chronicles. The only other book in the Hebrew Bible to mention him is Zechariah, written in the fifth century BC.

Thus *all references to Satan in the Hebrew Bible date from after the Exile.* The two passages above highlight this fact.

There are, in fact, very few evil spirits of any kind in the Bible. When they appear, they generally have one thing in common: they are sent by the Lord, for example: "But the Spirit of the Lord departed from Saul, and an evil spirit from the Lord troubled him" (1 Samuel 16:14).

Why should this be? Second Isaiah has already given the answer: everything comes from the Lord, both good and evil.

After the Exile, the Jews began to see things differently. They were exposed to the Zoroastrian religion of the Persians. Zoroastrianism, founded by a prophet known as Zoroaster or Zarathustra, is among the oldest of the great world religions. Thus its origins are very faint and far removed. Scholars disagree about the dates of Zoroaster's life, although most say he lived sometime around 1000 BC. In any event Zoroastrianism started in present-day Iran, and it was the official faith of the Persian empire of biblical times. It survives to this day among the Parsees, most of whom live in or near Mumbai, India.

The faith of Zoroaster teaches that the world is made up of two conflicting forces: Ahura Mazda, the good and the light, versus Ahriman, the dark and the evil. Historians of religion usually say that Judaism got its concept of the Devil from Zoroastrianism.

If you bracket out all evil and ascribe it to a malign force opposed to God, you've made it much easier to say that God is all good. But in a way it defers the question rather than answering it. How did evil arise at all? Did it arise against God's will? Did he create it as a means of testing us? If so, why didn't he choose a less painful way? The questions go on and on, and if one of them is resolved, it usually just creates five new ones.

That's why I have said the answer of Second Isaiah is the only one that makes much sense. Admittedly it is hard for us to swallow. The Jews of the Second Temple found it hard to swallow as well. Nor was it completely satisfying to blame the Devil for all evil. (Why, after all, does God permit him to do it?) They were forced to come up with another, better answer, and this one too came from Zoroastrianism. Scholars call it *apocalyptic*.

The Dawn of Apocalypse

Today the word *apocalypse* usually refers to some imagined disaster that will cause the world to end. It didn't have this meaning at first. *Apokálupsis,* in the original Greek, simply means "revelation." In fact it is found in the first verse of the biblical book of Revelation, which says it is "the Revelation of Jesus Christ."

The book of Revelation (in the singular, by the way; it is not "Revelations") is one of the most influential books of Western civilization. It has had such an impact that its name came to be applied to all works of its type. In ordinary language, *apocalyptic* is an adjective only. But in theology, it is used as a noun to refer to a whole genre of writings, known as *apocalypses*. They can be broken down into two overlapping categories: (1) those that speak of otherworldly visions and journeys; and (2) those that predict the End Times. They form the literary genre called *apocalyptic*.

The book of Revelation itself (like many other texts in the genre) fits into both categories. But of the two meanings of *apocalyptic*, the second is by far the more important, and it is the one I will deal with here.

I will say more about Revelation when I discuss the period in which it was written—the late first century AD. But its roots go much further back—to something called the Day of Yahweh.

You will remember that Yahweh is a god of battles and leads his people into battle. In monarchic times, Yahweh's devotees started to speak of a "Day of Yahweh"—a kind of final battle in which his enemies would be defeated once and for all.

Amos, writing around 760 BC, refers to this idea for the first time in the surviving literature. But he makes it clear that he has not invented this concept. Nor, he insists, will it be a day of victory, as the people think: "Woe unto you that desire the day of [Yahweh]! to what end is it for you? the day of [Yahweh] is darkness, and not light" (Amos 5:18).

Amos turns the idea of the Day of Yahweh on its end. Instead of vindicating Israel, it will be a day of judgment for those who have violated Yahweh's Law—particularly by oppressing the poor.

Some of the prophets before the Exile elaborated further on Amos's theme—Zephaniah, for instance, who preached during the reign of King

Josiah (640–609 BC). Zephaniah leaves no doubt that the Day of Yahweh "is a day of wrath, a day of trouble and distress, a day of wasteness and desolation," and so on (Zephaniah 1:15). But because of the Exile and the problems of evil and suffering that it brought up, the prophecies of the Day of Yahweh began to flourish especially in the postexilic period.

The sack of the First Temple ended, more or less permanently, the life of a free and independent Judah. From then on, with only brief interruptions, the fate of the nation that was now called Judea lay with great and distant powers: Persia; the Hellenistic empire of Alexander the Great and his successors; Rome. The hope of the earliest days—that the nation would live honorably and peacefully under Yahweh's shield—grew faint.

Thus the helplessness of the Jews in the hands of their imperial masters seemed more and more evident. To counterbalance it, the postexilic prophets made the Day of Yahweh look increasingly grand and momentous.

Take the book of Zechariah. The prophecies in Zechariah 9–14 talk about the Greeks, so they must date to the time during or after the conquests of Alexander (who died in 323 BC). Zechariah 14 gives an awe-inspiring picture of the Day of Yahweh, on which the Mount of Olives outside Jerusalem shall be split in two from east to west, and "living waters shall flow out from Jerusalem, half of them toward the eastern sea and half of them to the western sea.... And [Yahweh] will become king over all the earth." In those days even "every cooking pot in Jerusalem and Judah shall be sacred to [Yahweh] of hosts" (Zechariah 14:8–9, 21; New Revised Standard Version).

This passage presents an apocalyptic vision of sorts, in which Jerusalem shall be secure forever and all nations will go up to the Temple to sacrifice at the Jewish feast of Booths or Sukkot. But we are still basically in a recognizable world, with rain and sun and harvests.

The crowning apocalyptic text of the Second Temple period goes much further than that. It is the book of Daniel. Set in the sixth century BC, during the Babylonian Exile, it portrays Daniel as a wise man in the court of Nebuchadnezzar and, later, "Darius the Mede." Actually there was no King Darius the Mede—the Darius it is probably talking about, who ruled from 522 to 486 BC, was a Persian. But this is only one of many historical facts in this text that have been blurred over. That's because the book of Daniel was written about four hundred years after the time it was set in.

To use a technical term, Daniel is a *vaticinium ex eventu*—a "prophecy" written only after the events it supposedly foresees. This prophecy appears in Daniel 10–12, which tells of the coming of "the abomination that maketh desolate" (Daniel 11:31). This refers to events of 167 BC, when the Hellenistic king Antiochus IV Epiphanes, who then ruled Judea, tried to set up an altar, and possibly an image, of Zeus in the Jerusalem Temple. This was an abomination to the monotheistic Jews. Antiochus did not stop there, "for the temple was filled with debauchery and reveling by the Gentiles, who dallied with prostitutes and had intercourse with women in the sacred precincts." To make matters worse, "people could neither keep the sabbath, nor observe the festivals of their ancestors, nor so much as confess themselves to be Jews" (2 Maccabees 6:4, 6; NRSV).

The outcome, Daniel predicts, will go far beyond the mere defeat of Antiochus. It will usher in "the time of the end." More astonishingly still, he says, "many of them that sleep in the dust of the earth shall awake, some to everlasting life, some to everlasting contempt" (Daniel 12:2, 4).

What Daniel predicted did not take place. Instead the Jews, led by the priestly family of the Maccabees, rose up, drove out Antiochus, and established an independent Jewish kingdom that lasted around a century. Because Daniel connects Antiochus's "abomination that maketh desolate" with "the time of the end," he obviously doesn't know about this less spectacular outcome. As a result, scholars argue that the book of Daniel must have been written no later than 164 BC, when the Jews were victorious.

The Day of Yahweh here is the Lord's final judgment upon everyone and everything—both the living and the dead. The apocalyptic genre here takes its full-blown form.

This idea of the resurrection of the dead was a late development in Judaism. This passage in Daniel (along with another one in Isaiah 26:16, which probably dates to the same period) is the only place where resurrection is mentioned in the Hebrew Bible.

The Laurasian Novel

But the idea of the end of the world goes much further back. You may remember that in chapter 3 I mentioned a Harvard professor named E. J. Michael Witzel, who has explored common themes among the world's mythologies. He concludes that many of the world's mythic themes can be traced back well beyond the bounds of written history. The Flood story, as we've seen, is among the most ancient and universal.

Witzel also says there is a more or less consistent narrative (he calls it a "novel") that can be found in the myths and scriptures of the peoples of Eurasia, North and South America, and even Polynesia. From their common features, he argues that this narrative very likely dates as far back as 40,000–20,000 BC. Using a name taken from geology for one of the protocontinents, Witzel calls this the "Laurasian mythos." It encompasses the history of the world from the generation of the gods to the end of time. As such, it recapitulates the human life cycle from birth to death: "Laurasian 'ideology' seems to be based on a fairly simple idea, the correspondence of the 'life' of humans and the universe." Of course, this "life" would have to include death. Witzel writes:

Laurasian mythology also tells of the destruction of our world. It may take place as a final worldwide conflagration—the Götterdämmerung or Ragnarök in the Edda, Siva's destructive dance and fire in India; by molten metal in Zoroastrian myth or by devouring the world; or by fire and water in Maya and other Mesoamerican myths; or as in the Old Egyptian tale of Atum's destruction of the earth.

Witzel includes the biblical apocalypse in this picture. Like most scholars, he sees Zoroastrianism as the immediate source of this idea. Along with the idea of the Devil, it percolated into Judaism around the sixth century BC, during or after the Exile. From there it went into Christianity. "The end of the world, judgment of humans, and emerging paradise in Zoroastrian myth," he says, are the source "from which the Christian belief in the 'end,' the final judgment, and paradise are derived."

As Witzel shows, Zoroaster did not invent the idea of the end of the world. But he may have been the first to connect it with theodicy—the concept of divine justice.

Witzel's theory suggests how limited our view of reality is. We know of existence in terms of a human life span—birth, growth, aging, death. So we see the universe—even the gods—in the same way. Are we right to do this? Do we have any reason to believe that the cosmos resembles us so exactly? The Greek philosopher Protagoras said that man is the measure of all things. Really? Or is it rather that, as humans, we are bound to see things this way?

Wisdom, some have said, is the ability to hold contradictory ideas in your mind at the same time. That may be our best recourse here. It's probably true that, as humans, we will inevitably see the universe as a human being writ large. But we also have to be faithful to our own experience and to our own condition. Yes, we are limited to seeing the world in anthropocentric—human-centered—ways, but that too is part of our thrownness. We have to acknowledge that thrownness and accept that while ours is a limited view, it's still *our* view. We will never see the universe as an angel sees it or as a cockroach sees it, and we may as well accept that fact. We will always see the universe in a human context.

Someone today may smile at the naïveté of ancient and primitive peoples, who were so foolish as to believe that the universe is born like a baby and grows and dies. But how far have we progressed? Scientific cosmology tells us today that the universe began with a Big Bang and will probably compress back into itself and end with a Big Crunch. How different is this, really, from the Laurasian mythos, with its genesis of gods and final worldwide conflagrations?

There *is* at least one difference. Unlike modern science, the Zoroastrians and the Jews after them said that the cosmos would be subject to a *moral* reckoning—a judgment of the quick and the dead, as the Christian creed puts it. Thus the universe has an ultimate meaning in moral terms. There is a justice in it that will play itself out in the end.

Of course the world, even and especially the human world, does not seem to hold up to the standards of justice as we understand them. At this point, believing that ultimately justice will be done is a matter of faith. There is no getting around that.

That is our predicament today. We are gripped in tension between the worldview that we were born with (and which we cling to more than we might think), which tells us that the universal *is* moral, and the brave new scientific worldview, whereby the universe has no ultimate justice or moral meaning.

How are we supposed to choose?

In the end, there may be no way. In any case, we did not create the universe and it is not accountable to us. But we still have to live our lives in a meaningful way.

We have seen that we imagine the life of the universe as reflecting the span of a human life. This may or may not hold true in the end. But the final judgment as foreseen by Zoroaster and the Jews after the time of Daniel is telling us that in the end our *own* lives have a moral meaning and accountability.

The apparent injustices that occur every day suggest that this account may not be settled up in the course of our lives from birth to death. It will only be settled afterward—whether immediately, upon our deaths, or ultimately, in a general resurrection in which those "that sleep in the dust of the earth shall awake, some to everlasting life, some to everlasting contempt."

Maybe, you will say, we need to believe this. We thirst for justice in human life, and we thirst for justice in the universe as well, so we find it if we can and imagine it if we can't. So it may be. But maybe our very desire is telling us that it is actually there. After all, would you ever feel thirsty if there were no such thing as water?

Part Three

Palestine in the Time of Christ

Jesus in His Context

IT'S NOT EASY for an American in the early twenty-first century to understand what it must have been like to be a Jew two thousand years ago. The United States is, at this writing, the richest and most power- ful country in the world. Although we as a nation seem to make end- less mistakes, they are *our* mistakes and no one else's. We do not have foreign armies marching into our land, taking our money, or ordering us around.

The Jews in Judea (by this time there were many who lived in other countries as well) had no such privileges. They were at the mercy of other, much larger powers who by no means had their best interests at heart. If the Jews had any breathing room, they owed it to the fact that one power was in decline and another one had not yet arisen to take its place.

Such was the situation in Judea around 150 BC, after Antiochus had been driven out. Antiochus belonged to the Seleucid dynasty, which ruled Syria and Asia Minor as a remnant of Alexander's conquests. At this time the Seleucid empire was facing a much bigger challenge than a revolt in Judea: the burgeoning Roman republic.

Again the Jews had some breathing room. Around 140 BC, the Maccabees established a kingdom ruled by their family, which became known as the Hasmonean dynasty. But the Jews did not have their freedom for long. In 63 BC (curiously, the same year as the final collapse of the Seleucids), they were conquered by the Roman general Pompey. The historian Tacitus writes: "Gnaeus Pompey was the first of the Romans to conquer Judea, and by right of victory he entered the Temple. Thus it became known that the holy seat was empty, with no images of gods in it, and that its inner sanctum had nothing to reveal."

Was this true? Was the Temple's Holy of Holies really empty, or was it rather that the priests had hidden the sacred objects before Pompey could see them?

In any case, after 63 BC Judea was under Roman domination and, with very short breaks, would remain so for centuries. The period between 49 and 31 BC marked a series of civil wars in Rome, first between Pompey and Julius Caesar and, after their deaths, between Mark Antony and Caesar's adopted son Octavian. In 31 BC, Octavian defeated Antony in a sea battle at Actium, off the coast of western Greece, and became supreme master. In 27 BC Octavian was named *princeps*—"first citizen"—and took the name *Augustus*, meaning, as in English, "august." He deftly described his move as the restoration of the republic. Historians don't see it that way. They see it as the beginning of the Roman Empire.

In this conflict, the Hasmoneans did not choose their friends wisely. They tried to take the opportunity of civil war to break free from Rome, but failed. The Romans removed them from power in 37 BC, to be replaced by Herod, who ruled over the whole of Palestine until his death in 4 BC. Herod was a client king—that is, he ruled his own domain semi-independently, but owed fealty (and tribute) as a vassal to the Senate and people of Rome.

A Mountain Covered in White

Herod was the most ambitious ruler that Judea had had in centuries. He knew his limits—he did not try to revolt or break his ties with Rome— but he did embark on several enormous architectural projects. The best-known was his restoration of the Temple in Jerusalem, which Herod exalted to an unprecedented magnificence. The historian Josephus gives a breathless description:

> The outside of the building lacked nothing to astonish mind or eye. It was covered on all sides with massive plates of gold. When the sun came up, it radiated so fiery a flash that people had to avert their eyes as if they were looking directly at the sun. To strangers approaching from a distance it looked like a mountain covered in white. On the roof there were sharpened gold spikes to stop birds perching and fouling it.

Josephus also discusses the Temple's supposedly empty Holy of Holies. Since Josephus came from a priestly family, he would have some reason to know what it held. He is rather equivocal about the matter. In some parts of his works he insists that it contained nothing at all, but in others he says that what was in it "we are not at liberty to reveal to other nations."

You may remember that the biblical descriptions of the Holy of Holies of Solomon's Temple say that it contained golden cherubim (*-im* is the masculine plural in Hebrew). In the ancient Near East, cherubim were not fat little babies, as we imagine them today. They were fully grown winged human figures, often with the body of a lion.

The cherubim in the actual Temple may have been, like the God described in Genesis, both male and female. And while the biblical account describes these cherubim as chastely touching their wings, some rabbinical traditions say they were locked in embrace. One Talmudic sage, Rabbi Qetina, who lived in the late third and early fourth centuries AD, said, "When Israel used to make the pilgrimage, they [i.e., the priests] would roll up for them the *Parokhet* [the Veil separating the Holy from the Holy of Holies], and show them the Cherubim which were intertwined with one another, and say to them: 'Behold! your love before God is like the love of male and female!'"

The "love of male and female" harks back to the old motif of Yahweh and Asherah. Did Asherah remain Yahweh's consort even up to the time of Christ, hidden from the eyes of Pompey, and maybe even from ordinary Jews, by veils and ruses?

In any case, the project of restoring the Temple outlasted Herod's own life: begun in 23 BC, it was not finished until AD 64. Ironically, its completion led to its destruction. Eighteen thousand people were put out of work, leading to social unrest that in turn caused Judea to revolt from Rome in AD 66. The Jews were defeated, and the newly completed Temple was sacked by the Romans under Titus, a general and later emperor, in 70. It has never been rebuilt.

The Temple forms the backdrop to the life of Christ. It is the Temple whose destruction he predicts; it is the Temple's moneychangers that he drives away; and it is the Temple's priests that connive to destroy him.

The Quest of the Historical Jesus

As I've said in chapter 1, the historical problems of the New Testament are in many ways as great as those of the Old, but they are different problems. The Gospels are firmly set in the context of their time. Unlike the age of David and Solomon, it is a time about which a great deal is known. We know about the history of Judea in that period; we know of its leading personalities. Archaeology confirms its details.

But Jesus himself was not a major figure in the politics and events of his time. There is scant mention of him in the ancient sources. There are two brief passages in Josephus's *Antiquities of the Jews,* written at the end of the first century AD, that mention him. Here is the first one:

> Around this time there was a man named Jesus, a wise man, if indeed it is proper to call him a man. For he was a miracle worker and a teacher of those who accept the truth with pleasure. He attracted many Jews as well as many from the Greek world. He was the Messiah. And when Pilate, at the instigation of our leading men, condemned him to the cross, those who cared for him from the outset did not stop. For he appeared to them alive on the third day, just as the divine prophets had said about him, along with innumerable other wondrous things. And the group known after his name as Christians still remains among us.

This passage doesn't appear in all the manuscripts of this text, and some scholars hold that it was put in later by a Christian scribe. But most scholars believe that the core of this passage was in fact written by Josephus (who lived from AD 37 to c.100), even if it was later touched up by Christian hands. It is not easy to tell which parts were original and which added later.

Here is the second passage:

> [Ananas] assembled the sanhedrin of judges, and brought before them the brother of Jesus called the Christ, whose name was James, and some others. He accused them of breaking the law and handed them over to be stoned.

To fill in the context, Ananas was a priest—wicked as usual. James was stoned in AD 62.

Congratulations. You have now just read all of the surviving non-Christian texts written about Jesus in the first century AD.

The first and longer passage has been called the *Testamonium Flavianum*, the "testimony" of Flavius Josephus to the life of Christ. Some have argued that the passage is completely spurious and was put in only later by a Christian scribe. But most scholars agree that at least some part of it is genuine.

Why? Well, let's assume the contrary. Let's grant the point that the *Testamonium Flavianum was* spurious—that it was not written by Josephus but by a Christian long after. Therefore it has to be taken out of Josephus's text. Very well. But if you argue this, you have just dug yourself into a deeper ditch. Because there is the *second* passage in Josephus, about the stoning of James the brother of Jesus "who was called the Christ." What do you do about that? No one doubts that this part is genuine. But if this is the *only* reference to Jesus, it means that Josephus does not introduce Jesus elsewhere. In that case, Jesus would have been so well known that he needed no introduction.

In the end, it's more reasonable to assume that both passages are genuine (although the first no doubt includes later insertions). The second passage implies that Jesus is familiar to the reader because Josephus has already mentioned him.

References to Jesus by pagan Roman authors, including Tacitus, Pliny the Younger, and maybe Suetonius, come from the second century. They are extremely brief and tell us almost nothing about Jesus the man.

As for the Gospels, as we've seen, the four Gospels in the New Testament are the oldest surviving ones, possibly with the *Gospel of Thomas* added. How much of them can really be called "Gospel truth"?

The crucial point in this investigation came in 1834–35, when a German Protestant scholar named David Friedrich Strauss published a book called *The Life of Jesus Critically Examined*. In it he put forward the startling thesis that parts of the Gospels were made up of legends that had become attached to Jesus after his time.

The book roused a furor. Strauss published a second edition in which he backtracked somewhat from his original thesis, but the damage was done. His career as a clergyman was ruined. At the same time scholars could not ignore his disturbing though all-too-plausible theory.

Here is the upshot: *the Gospels in the New Testament contain much material about Jesus that is not factually true.* If you were to call up any New Testament scholar at any nonfundamentalist seminary or divinity school and ask if he agreed with this statement, in all probability he would say he did.

This fact is not exactly a secret, but it is not often stated clearly or explicitly. Nevertheless, if you don't know this, you don't even have a starting point for thinking about the historical Jesus.

There is nothing out of the ordinary in Strauss's idea. Legends attach themselves readily to charismatic figures. One of the most familiar examples in American history is the story of George Washington chopping down the cherry tree. This event probably never took place. It comes from an early but very popular biography of Washington written by one Mason Weems. But when I was a child I certainly was told that it was a true story.

To say that the Gospels contain mythic or legendary material is, of course, not the end of the problem but the beginning. How do you decide what is true and what is legendary? There are no surviving copies of *The Jerusalem Daily Bugle* from AD 33 to check the facts against. The only texts that are even remotely contemporary are the two passages from Josephus that I have just given, and they tell us only the smallest amount.

In fact, you may respond, how do we *know* that some of the things in the Gospels aren't true? Maybe they *are* all true. After all, many people believe they are.

There are two main reasons. The first has to do with contradictions in the Gospel accounts. In Samuel Beckett's *Waiting for Godot*, the character Vladimir says, "How is it that of the four Evangelists only one speaks of a thief being saved. The four of them were there—or thereabouts—and only one speaks of a thief being saved.... Why believe him rather than the others?"

His friend Estragon replies, "People are bloody ignorant apes."

Vladimir is right. Of the four Gospels, only Luke mentions a repentant thief. Mark and John simply say that there were thieves crucified with Jesus (Mark 15:27; John 18:18). Matthew says that both thieves mocked him (Matthew 27:44).

There are any number of such discrepancies in the Gospel accounts. Many of them, like the one I've just mentioned, are not all that hard to reconcile. You could, for example, assume that Mark and John just neglected to mention this little detail, and that at first both of the thieves reviled him (as Matthew says) and then one of the thieves later repented (as Luke says).

For many centuries these problems were dealt with more or less this way. Churchmen compiled various "harmonies of the Gospels" that settled the issue for most people. It was only after skepticism came into its own during the Enlightenment in the eighteenth century that scholars began to demand—and failed to find—more consistency in the Gospel accounts.

Consistency is the smaller of the two problems. The other is much greater. What do you do with all the supernatural things in the Gospels—the healings, the changing of water to wine, the feeding of the five thousand, the resurrection itself?

Before the Enlightenment, there was no discussion of the matter. You had to believe in these things as a matter of faith. It was dangerous to do otherwise. But as the churches began to lose their hold on intellectuals in particular, again more demands were made of the Gospel texts.

Strauss's answer solved this problem. These things didn't happen; they were just stories that were attached to Jesus after his lifetime.

Unfortunately this answer again created at least as many difficulties as it solved. If you grant that the Gospels were not all literally true, how do you decide which parts are true and which are false?

Certainly the miracles were, from the point of view of modern rationalism, easy enough to discard. But what else has to go? There is almost no external evidence to judge them against.

Certainly there are ways of handling the evidence that are better than others. One criterion that scholars use is multiple sourcing. Take the fact that Pontius Pilate, governor of Judea from AD 26 to 36, condemned Jesus to death. Nobody doubts this; it is in all the Gospels, even possibly in Josephus (as we have seen above). It is the only thing about Jesus that Tacitus tells us. Scholars have no difficulty accepting this fact as historical truth. It is multiply attested; it involves no miracle or supernatural occurrence; and it fits in with what is known of the time.

But take another little detail that is just as well attested: the fact that it was the priests and scribes of the Jerusalem Temple who conspired to have Jesus destroyed. This too is multiply attested; it is in all four Gospels. It involves no supernatural occurrence, and it also fits in with what we know of the time: Judea at the time of Christ was a theocracy ruled by the priests in subjection to Rome. This fits exactly what the Gospels say.

But scholars don't like to think that it was the priests rather than the Romans who had Jesus killed. This possibility creates certain difficulties that scholars would rather avoid. So they often tell us that it was the Romans' idea to put Jesus to death—even though this contradicts the evidence.

There are some important reasons for this reluctance in this particular case, but I will go into them later. In any case, scholars over the last two hundred years have gone into a complete about-face. They used to believe—*had* to believe—that all the Gospels were literally true, no matter what kind of shoehorning this belief required. Today scholars can believe that practically nothing in the Gospels is literally true.

Four Colors

In recent mainstream scholarship, probably the most extreme position has been taken by the Jesus Seminar. This is a group of liberal scholars who have gone through the Gospels and tried to decide—by consensus—which parts were really true and which were things tacked on to Jesus by later hands. The Seminar was mostly active in the 1980s and '90s, and over two hundred scholars have taken part in it at one point or another. Although it never formally disbanded, it became far less active after the death of its founder, Robert W. Funk, in 2005. The Seminar published its conclusions in several books, the best-known of which is *The Five Gospels* (*Thomas* is the fifth), which appeared in 1993.

The Five Gospels is a colorful artifact. The sayings of Jesus from all of these Gospels are printed in four different colors. Red means that Jesus almost certainly did say it; pink, that he probably did say it; gray, that he might have said something vaguely like it; and black, the final color, means that in the view of these scholars, Jesus almost certainly did *not* say it.

As I page through this volume, I have trouble finding anything printed in red. There are a few items: "Pay the emperor what belongs to the emperor, and God, what belongs to God" (the scholars' rendition of the familiar "Render unto Caesar" verse of Mark 12:17); "Love your enemies" (Matthew 5:44); and the parable of the Good Samaritan. The Lord's Prayer gets cut with a heavy hand: only the words "Our father" (Matthew 6:9) are printed in red. While there is some pink and gray, most of what Jesus said is in black. In fact, the scholars conclude, "eighty-two percent of the words ascribed to Jesus in the gospels were not actually spoken by him."

How have the scholars come to this conclusion? Their methods say a great deal about the quest of the historical Jesus from Strauss's time in the mid-nineteenth century to the present, because most of this scholarship works on similar assumptions. Besides the criteria I mentioned earlier, such as multiple sourcing, there are others. In the first place, there is "methodological skepticism"—"when in sufficient doubt, leave it out."

Like all tools, this approach has its uses, but like all tools, it is not the right thing to use in any and all circumstances. Historians principally rely on one thing: primary sources, which are, for example, either eyewitness accounts or as close to them as we can get. In this case, these are the five Gospels. A historian, it would seem, has to have a certain amount of respect for these sources. They are all he has, and his theories not only have to explain them, but they have to explain as many of them as possible while presenting a consistent picture. Maybe one can dismiss the miracles and supernatural occurrences, but *The Five Gospels* is just talking about the *words* of Jesus. A method that eliminates 82 percent of these words seems to have a problem at its core.

Why has it been so easy for scholars to ax so much of what the Gospels say?

One answer has to do with the old question "Cui bono?" Who benefits? If a story or saying of Jesus is, by the scholars' estimation, viewed as holding up some kind of later claim made by the church, it is highly suspect. An obvious example is this verse: "Thou art Peter, and upon this rock I will build my church; and the gates of hell shall not prevail against it" (Matthew 16:18). Peter had a high standing in the early Christian community. Thus it's easy to believe that these words could have been put in Jesus's mouth later on to bolster Peter's standing.

It would be foolish to pretend that nothing of this kind ever happened. Clearly it did. The verse about Peter may be an example (after all, it appears only in Matthew).

But there is another consideration: By all accounts very soon after Jesus's death (if not before), his disciples saw him as a divine being. They followed him with great loyalty. If the tradition is correct, most of them died martyrs' deaths. The same is true of many of the other earliest believers.

If this is so, these followers would want to preserve the Master's sayings and deeds as accurately as possible. This is not to say that they always did. It *is* to say that they had strong reason to try. They must have succeeded at least to some degree. This consideration should be balanced against the claim that nearly everything about Jesus was made up later to further the interests of one faith community or another.

In any case, what do you decide to eliminate? On the basis of who Jesus was. Who was Jesus? That depends on whom you ask. The scholars of the Jesus Seminar have a very clear concept: Jesus was an itinerant Near Eastern sage. He didn't say much: "like the cowboy hero of the American West . . . , the sage of the ancient Near East was laconic, slow to speak, a person of few words." Other features: "The prophet or holy man does not initiate cures or exorcisms. . . . Those who seek help either petition in person or have someone petition for them. . . . Jesus does not initiate debates or controversies."

There is some truth to this picture, of course. But this type of scholarship is like the art of sculpture. A sculptor has a block of stone; he has a picture in his mind of the statue he wants to carve; and he carves away whatever part of the stone doesn't fit that picture. That is sculpture. But it is not scholarship—certainly not historical scholarship. Not if it means you have to throw practically all of your evidence away.

Writing history, it seems to me, is a process much more like this: A man has a pile of papers on his desk. They include all sorts of things— official government reports, interview transcripts, letters, even scraps of rumor. He has to take these and turn them into a coherent story that says as accurately as possible what happened in the past. He can, of course, eliminate some of these sources and decide which are reliable and which aren't. The government report is more to be trusted than the rumor (or is it the other way around?). But if he reaches a point where his story requires him to throw most of his own evidence out, he has taken a wrong turn somewhere.

Other scholars, equally or better qualified, start with completely different pictures of Jesus. They carve away different parts of the sources, and they end up with conclusions that bear little or no resemblance to one another.

Scholars—the best and most reputable scholars—do not agree about who Jesus was. Some, like many in the Jesus Seminar, see him as a wisdom teacher. They don't believe that he was an apocalyptic prophet preaching the end of the world, as some of his sayings seem to imply, so they throw out these passages. Other scholars say the opposite: that he *was* an apocalyptic prophet, so they would leave these parts in and throw practically everything else out. Still others, such as Geza Vermes and Morton Smith, see him as a wonder-working charismatic leader of a kind that has appeared in Judaism periodically over the centuries. They might be less inclined than their colleagues to discard the miracle stories.

All these scholars are working from exactly the same evidence—the Gospels first and foremost. But they reach opposite conclusions because they start with opposite preconceptions. The main evidence you have is the Gospels, and because you can throw out more or less anything you like in the Gospels, the picture you come out with is the picture you came in with.

Did Jesus Exist?

The Jesus Seminar is among the most radical approaches to the historical Jesus. But there are those who go further. They say that Jesus never lived at all.

The Jesus Mysteries: Was the "Original Jesus" a Pagan God? by Timothy Freke and Peter Gandy is one of the best-known books in this field. They write: "The Jesus story was not a biography at all but a consciously crafted vehicle for encoded spiritual teachings created by Jewish Gnostics." (The Gnostics were a movement in the early centuries AD prizing gnosis— direct knowledge of the divine—rather than faith or sacrifice as the key to salvation. I talk about this movement in my book *Forbidden Faith: A Secret History of Gnosticism*.) These Gnostics supposedly lived in the late first century AD and wanted to recast the pagan mystery religions—especially their themes of death and resurrection—into a new form, so they cooked up the myth of Jesus. Freke and Gandy stress the similarities between the story of Jesus and those of pagan gods such as Osiris and Dionysus.

Another popular item in this category is the 2007 film *Zeitgeist*. It argued that Jesus was nothing more than a revamped version of the Egyptian god Horus, along with some other Near Eastern deities.

There are any number of problems with these claims. For one thing, their proponents often give incorrect and sometimes absurd facts to support their positions. The correlations that *Zeitgeist* describes between Jesus and Horus are more or less nonexistent. Contrary to what the film says, there is no evidence in Egyptian myth that Horus was born of a virgin (actually he was the son of the goddess Isis and her brother Osiris), or that he had twelve disciples, or was baptized at the age of thirty.

As for the similarities between Jesus and Osiris as described by *The Jesus Mysteries*, Bart D. Ehrman, an American New Testament scholar, writes:

> What, for example, is the proof that Osiris was born on December 25 before three shepherds? Or that he was crucified? And that his death brought atonement from sin? Or that he returned to life on earth by being raised from the dead? In fact, no ancient source says any such things about Osiris (or about the other gods).

As Ehrman points out, Osiris is not a dying and resurrected god as such. He is killed and dismembered by his wicked brother Seth and put back together by his wife and sister, Isis. But Osiris isn't really resurrected to life on earth. Instead he gets a new job as lord of the dead. Ehrman concludes:

> What we know about Jesus—the historical Jesus—does not come from Egypt toward the end of the first century, in circles heavily influenced by pagan mystery religions, but from Palestine, among Jews committed to their decidedly antipagan religion, from the 30s [AD].

New Testament scholars argue, often vehemently, about nearly every detail of Jesus's life. But practically all of them would agree with Ehrman's remarks above.

I've taken these quotes from Ehrman's book *Did Jesus Exist? The Historical Argument for Jesus of Nazareth*, which debunks the idea that Jesus was a fictional creation cooked up by certain unknown sources. Ehrman's arguments are thorough and persuasive, and I won't try to repeat them here. But there are a couple of things worth noting.

There is no evidence anywhere for a group of Jewish Gnostics in the first century who would have reason to recast the pagan myths into a new story about a fictitious Jesus. So at the very least, you have to invent this group out of thin air—as opposed to Jesus, for whom there *is* direct evidence. Furthermore, even if such a group of Jewish Gnostics did exist, it would have made no sense for them to concoct a Jesus who was alive *at that time*, or even very recently. People would have found it easy to take apart this claim. If these Gnostics had created such a myth, it would have been like most myths—about the long-gone past.

Another matter: The four Gospels do differ. But their very differences show that they came from independent sources. They were not all written by the same people, or by the same group. If they had been, they would have been much more consistent. The Gospels, fragmentary and contradictory and baffling as they are, attest to what most scholars believe: that there was a real, historical Jesus who was remembered in different ways by different people, although he is recognizably the same man in all accounts.

At any rate, this is the kind of argument that scholars use in sorting through the evidence for and against the historical Jesus. Although they by no means agree even on some essential points, they do agree that he really lived, and that he lived in Palestine in the first third of the first century AD.

What else do they tell us? At this point it would be best to look at Jesus in the chronological order of his life.

8.

The Life of Jesus: Origins

My wife and I disagree about Santa Claus.

She remembers the enjoyment of believing in Santa Claus when she was a child. So she wants our sons, ages six and seven, to have the same experience. And they certainly do believe in Santa Claus. Last year my older son, who wanted an Xbox for Christmas, said that one way we could get it without having to pay for it would be to have Santa bring it for us. (In the end I caved in and bought them a PlayStation 4.)

My memories are a bit different. I too remember the excitement of believing in Santa Claus, putting out milk and cookies for him, and finding the presents on Christmas morning. But then when I was around seven, Kevin Moran, the fresh little kid across the street, told me that there was no such thing as Santa.

Upset and confused, I told him he was wrong. But I did ask my mother about it, and she admitted the truth. I found this experience painful. Not only was I disappointed to learn that Santa Claus didn't personally drop by the house every Christmas Eve, but I was displeased by the fact that nervy little Kevin Moran had told me the truth and my nice, loving mommy had not.

As a result, there is a compromise in our household. My wife talks to the boys about Santa Claus, but since I don't want to take part in what is effectively a lie, I keep my mouth shut. If the boys ask me about Santa, I simply say, "Ask your mother."

After reading a bit more, you may think of me as your own personal Kevin Moran. Not about Santa Claus, but about the birth of Jesus.

Two Nativities

Everyone knows the Christmas story: the journey to Bethlehem; no room at the inn; the little baby born shivering in the manger; the three wise men coming from the East; the angel announcing Christ's birth to the shepherds; the jealousy of wicked King Herod; the slaughter of the innocents.

How much of all this really happened?

Another little-known fact: *scholars believe that none of the Nativity story is true*. None—zero.

To take one example, I look at a copy of *The Historical Jesus: The Life of a Mediterranean Jewish Peasant* by John Dominic Crossan. Crossan is a highly respected scholar. *The Historical Jesus* is a large and detailed work, comprising nearly five hundred pages of densely packed text covering just about everything Jesus said and did—or was believed to.

About the Nativity, however, Crossan says very little. Speaking of the accounts of virgin birth and Jesus's alleged descent from the line of David, he simply says that neither of these claims "gives us any biographical information about the historical Jesus."

Most other scholars would agree. To begin with, of the four canonical Gospels, Mark and John say nothing about a virgin birth, a Nativity, or anything of the kind. For them the story of Jesus begins with his public career. That leaves us with Matthew and Luke. Both of these Gospels have elaborate and touching Nativity stories, which have formed the basis for our beliefs and imaginings about the birth of Christ. But there is—just to start with—one big problem.

These two stories have very little in common. Matthew has the wise men, their visit to wicked King Herod, the slaughter of the innocents, the flight into Egypt. Luke has the annunciation, the birth in a manger, the adoration of the shepherds. Our picture of the Nativity is a mixture of the two.

Comparing them, Crossan observes, "The only common features, apart from the names of Jesus, Mary, and Joseph, are the virginal conception and the birth at Bethlehem."

Even the dates don't match. Matthew has Jesus born during the reign of Herod the Great, who died in 4 BC. If you want to add a year or so to that for Joseph and Mary to take Jesus to Egypt and to wait for Herod's death before returning home, you come up with a date of 5 or 6 BC. Some scholars prefer a date between 8 and 6 BC. (This would coincide with a conjunction of Jupiter, Saturn, and Mars in 7 BC. It was regarded as a great portent at the time and may be connected to the "star in the east" in Matthew's nativity: Matthew 2:2.)

Luke's date is very different. Joseph and Mary go to Bethlehem because of a census ordered "when Cyrenius was governor of Syria" (Luke 2:2). Cyrenius—or Publius Sulpicius Quirinius, to give him his full Roman name—was a historical figure. He was governor of Syria in AD 6.

So Matthew and Luke give dates for the birth of Jesus that are more than a decade apart.

By the way, there *is* evidence for the census under Quirinius. In fact, because (as we've seen) the Jews regarded censuses as impious, it roused an enormous revolt in Judea. Luke himself mentions it in Acts 5:37. On the other hand, there is no evidence that Herod ever slaughtered all the babies in Bethlehem—although it would not have been out of character for him to do it.

Son of David?

There is another fact about the Nativity story that scholars question: the idea that Jesus was born to the royal line of David. Both Matthew and Luke give detailed genealogies (Matthew 1:1–17; Luke 3:23–38). Unfortunately, again they don't agree. Both Matthew and Luke trace Jesus's ancestry back to David, but through completely different lines. Matthew has Jesus's descent passing through the royal line itself, starting with David's son Solomon. So Jesus's ancestors are the kings of Judah that we read about in the Old Testament. But Luke traces Jesus's line of descent back to David's son Nathan, about whom we know nothing apart from his name.

This discrepancy has troubled Christian authorities since antiquity. One way out has been to say that Matthew is tracing Joseph's line of descent, while Luke is tracing Mary's. So when Luke says that Joseph was the son of Heli (Luke 3:23), he's really saying that Joseph is the son-*in-law* of Heli.

Like many such arguments, it is convincing to the exact extent that you wanted to believe it in the first place.

There is, of course, the further point that because Jesus was supposed to have been born through a virgin birth, Joseph was not really his father at all.

Does that mean that Jesus wasn't really descended from King David? Most scholars would say so. Here, in a nutshell, is what they say: After his death, Jesus's followers started to think of him as the Messiah. Since the Messiah was supposed to come from the line of David, the disciples made up a story that Jesus came from this line.

As I say, this is the common scholarly consensus. But I can't bring myself to agree with it completely. After all, Jesus's descent from David appears in many different sources—not only in all four Gospels, but in

Romans 1:3, written sometime between AD 56 and 58, which says that Jesus "was made of the seed of David according to the flesh."

Paul is writing only about twenty-five years after Jesus's death. He knows Jesus's disciples personally. He is writing to people in Rome whom he has never met, and he is not trying to persuade them that Jesus was the son of David but taking it as something that they will immediately recognize and agree to. That Jesus was descended from David seems to have been an early and widespread, if not universal, belief among the early Christians.

Why, then, are scholars so reluctant to believe it? In the first place, because the two different genealogies don't match. In the second place, because they say it is unlikely that Jesus's family would have possessed such a genealogy to begin with. (Eusebius, a fourth-century historian, says that Herod burned all the genealogical records to mask his own humble background.) Furthermore, scholars say, Jesus clearly did not come from the highest social class.

Actually not much is known about Jesus's social class. It all hangs on one thin verse: "Is not this the carpenter, the son of Mary, the brother of James, and Joses, and of Juda, and Simon? and are not his sisters here with us? And they were offended at him" (Mark 6:3; in Matthew 13:55, Jesus is "the carpenter's son"). The context is of Jesus teaching in his hometown synagogue—obviously a role in which people were not used to seeing him.

This is the sum total of the evidence about Jesus's social background (assuming that the detail is correct). To be a carpenter is to be a member of the artisan class, which was not particularly exalted. Whether the family had any money or not is anyone's guess. A carpenter could be anything from a poor wretch hammering rude benches together to an esteemed master craftsman.

Is this any kind of occupation for someone of the magnificent line of

David? Well, it doesn't rule out a Davidic descent. The world is full of aristocratic families who have fallen on hard times.

Jesus seems to have been widely known as a descendant of David. A passage in Mark suggests as much. When Jesus and his disciples are leaving the town of Jericho, blind Bartimaeus "sat by the highwayside begging. And when he heard it was Jesus of Nazareth, he began to cry out, and say, Jesus thou son of David, have mercy on me" (Mark 10:46–47). Even the blind beggar Bartimaeus seems to know that (1) Jesus was from Nazareth and (2) Jesus was a descendant of David.

In short, I am saying exactly the opposite of what most scholars would say. I am saying that Jesus was *not* given a Davidic ancestry after his followers had decided that he was the Messiah. Instead he was believed to be descended from David. That fact, among other things, gave his disciples to believe he was the Messiah.

Whether Jesus really was biologically descended from David is, of course, impossible to say.

The Lost Years

As you've already noticed, the historical Jesus has become a Rorschach blot. You can see almost anything you want in him. For no part of his life is this fact more clear than when you approach the "lost years"—his entire life up to the beginning of his public career.

How long were these lost years? Luke is the only Gospel writer who tries to date Jesus's career by known historical events. As we've seen, he says Jesus was born in AD 6. He also says that John the Baptist began preaching in the fifteenth year of the reign of the emperor Tiberius: AD 29 (Luke 3:1). Jesus, Luke says, was "about thirty years of age" when he was baptized by John (Luke 3:23).

These dates don't fit together. On the one hand, if Jesus had been born in AD 6 and started preaching (soon after his baptism) at age thirty, this brings us to AD 36—too late, if only because Pilate was removed from office that year. On the other hand, if Jesus started preaching in AD 29, he would have been twenty-three when he was baptized. Although he was not an old man by any means, he would seem to have been somewhat older than this.

For these reasons and others, scholars don't take Luke's dates seriously. Most scholars hold that Jesus was born during the reign of Herod the Great (that is, sometime before 4 BC) and that his public career took place around AD 30. The length of this career is not entirely clear, though its traditional length is three years.

As for what Jesus did before he stepped onto the public stage, all sorts of theories abound: that he went to Egypt, that he went to India or some other exotic location. None of these views has any evidence behind it. Another, somewhat more plausible idea is that Jesus was an Essene. While there is no evidence for this either, it's at least true that Jesus and the Essenes lived in the same time period.

The origins of the Essenes are obscure, although they can be traced as far back as the second century BC. Their name is equally mysterious. The best guess is that it comes from the Aramaic word *'asey*, meaning "healer," since, as Josephus puts it, "in their anxiety to cure disease they learn all about medicinal roots and the properties of stones." They were a strict and austere Jewish sect, mostly celibate, who dwelled semimonastically in small communities. They were given to certain occult practices. Josephus says, "Some of them claim to foretell the future, after a lifelong study of sacred literature, purifications of different kinds, and the aphorisms of prophets; rarely if ever do their predictions prove wrong."

In at least one case, an Essene gave a correct prediction. When Herod was a schoolboy, an Essene named Menaemus or Menachem told him that he would someday be king. Herod was delighted. When he gained the throne, he rewarded the Essenes handsomely, bestowing them with many privileges as well as (probably) giving them some land on the northwestern coast of the Dead Sea.

There, at Qumran, the Essenes established a community, and one of its purposes seems to have been to bury old scrolls. The Jews did not burn their copies of sacred texts when they were worn out. They did not even burn heretical works, because these too contained sacred names. Instead such texts were buried. The Essenes took their task very seriously and preserved the scrolls in ceramic jars—maybe with posterity in mind. They were unearthed starting in the late 1940s. Today they are known as the Dead Sea Scrolls. The relation of the scrolls to the Essenes and their teachings is a long, intricate, and much-disputed topic, and it wouldn't suit our purposes to go into it here.

To return to the original question: was Jesus an Essene? There are some intriguing parallels. One is their attitude toward oaths. Josephus writes, "Every word [the Essenes] speak is more binding than an oath; swearing they reject as something worse than perjury, for they say a man is already condemned if he cannot be believed without God being named." Compare this to Jesus's words in the Sermon on the Mount: "Swear not at all; ... But let your communication be Yea, yea; Nay, nay; for whatsoever is more than these cometh of evil" (Matthew 5:34, 37).

There is another intriguing similarity. As the book of Daniel shows, some, maybe most, Jews at this time believed in the resurrection and judgment of the dead. But they were not entirely sure about what happened to the soul between the individual's death and the final judgment. Many thought that the soul simply slept. This view was implied in the Hebrew Bible. Ecclesiastes states it bleakly: "For the living know that they shall die: but the dead know not any thing, neither have they any more a reward; for the memory of them is forgotten" (Ecclesiastes 9:5).

The Essenes thought differently. Josephus observes, "Teaching the same doctrine as the sons of Greece, they declare that for the good souls there waits a home beyond the ocean, a place troubled by neither rain nor snow nor heat, but refreshed by the zephyr that blows ever gentle from the ocean. Bad souls they consign to a darksome, stormy abyss, full of punishments that know no end."

This passage is extremely revealing. It suggests that the idea of heaven and hell came out of Greece—probably from the mystery religions known as Orphism and Pythagoreanism. The Essenes combined this doctrine with that of reincarnation, an idea that made its way into the Kabbalah but never caught on in Christianity.

In short, by Jesus's time Jewish thinking about eschatology (the study of the Last Things, including death and the final judgment) had shifted from its previous ground. More and more the Jews were tending to believe that right after death the soul went to a pleasant existence if it was good, to a gloomy one if it was bad.

Jesus in the Gospels teaches a doctrine very much like this one. See, for example, Mark 9:45: "And if thy foot offend thee, cut it off: it is better for thee to enter halt into life, than having two feet to be cast into hell, into the fire that never shall be quenched." Or the parable of the rich man and Lazarus in Luke 16:19–31, which says of the rich man, "In hell he lift up his eyes, being in torments, and seeth Abraham afar off, and Lazarus in his bosom."

It's possible, then, that Jesus did teach the doctrine of heaven and hell so beloved of Christians today. He may have learned it from the Essenes. Or they could have introduced it into Judaism as a whole.

All the same, Jesus was almost certainly not an Essene. The Essenes were hyperobservant of the Jewish Law—so much so that they were not allowed to relieve themselves on the Sabbath. (I suppose you could train yourself to do this if you had to.) Jesus's casual attitude toward the Law— gleaning ears of wheat to munch on during the holy day and so on— would not have squared with them. Jesus may have heard the Essenes teach, he may even have studied with them at some point and taken some ideas from them, but if he had ever been an Essene, he had broken with them by the time he started preaching.

The Essenes do not appear in the New Testament, at any rate not under that name. Nevertheless, there may be some indirect references to them. The Gospels mention a mysterious group called the Herodians, for example in Mark 3:6: "And the Pharisees went forth, and straightway took counsel with the Herodians against him, how they might destroy him."

Who were these Herodians? There was no sect of that name. But it is possible that they were the Essenes, who received great favors from Herod. No Essene would have called himself a Herodian, but it may have been a derogatory name given to them by outsiders, just as Catholics a hundred years ago were derogatorily called "papists" and "Romanists." If this identification is correct, then the Essenes were enemies of Jesus.

Jesus's Sources

Until fairly recently, it did not occur to anyone to ask about possible sources for Jesus's teachings. After all, if you are the omniscient Second Person of the Trinity, talking about your background and education seems beside the point.

But as Jesus comes more and more to take on human dimensions in the eyes of scholarship, it does start to make sense to talk about sources and influences for his thought.

The most obvious is the Jewish tradition. Jesus in the Gospels quotes from the Old Testament and uses it in his disputations with his various foes. Take for example the passage in Matthew 12:1–7, in which the Pharisees reproach him and his disciples for plucking ears of grain on the Sabbath. Jesus replies: "But he said unto them, Have ye not read what David did, when he was an hungred, and they that were with him; How he entered into the house of God, and did eat the shewbread, which was not lawful for him to eat, neither for them which were with him, but only for the priests? . . . But if ye had known what this meaneth, I will have mercy, and not sacrifice, ye would not have condemned the guiltless."

Jesus is alluding to the passage in 1 Samuel 21:6, where David eats the "shewbread," the sacred bread that only the priests are allowed to eat. Jesus then alludes to Hosea 6:6, which says, "For I [the Lord] desired mercy, and not sacrifice."

Some authors have tried to take out all of Jesus's disputes with the Pharisees, saying they are not historical, on the (usually unstated) assumption that Jesus was such a nice guy that he never would have argued in this way.

Others argue from a different angle. Here is Reza Aslan, author of the highly unreliable bestseller *Zealot: The Life and Times of Jesus of Nazareth*: "The vast majority of biblical scholars would agree that the illiteracy rates in Jesus's world were somewhere around 98 percent. 98 percent of Jesus's fellow Jews could neither read nor write. The notion that a tekton, as Jesus is referred to in the Bible, a woodworker, which would make him the second-lowest rung on the social ladder in his time just above the slave and the indigent and the beggar, would have had any sort of formal education, let alone the kind of education necessary to debate theological points with the scribes and the Pharisees, is difficult to reconcile with what we know of the history of the time."

This kind of reasoning doesn't really work. The monumental figures of history are not statistics, they are not faces in the crowd. They are unique and powerful individuals. Their stories are often unusual, even weird.

Look at it this way. Say that two or three thousand years from now, very little historical material has survived from the twentieth century. Scholars come across a story about an unemployed bum who could not even get into art school, but who rose to become dictator of Germany and started the biggest war in the history of the world.

How could you believe this? Unemployed bums are lazy. So, often, are art students. They are almost never possessed of burning ambition and usually have no leadership skills. So why should anyone believe such a ridiculous story?

And yet the career of Adolf Hitler is among the best-documented things in history.

This consideration should give us pause when we look at statistical likelihoods and suchlike when dealing with historical figures.

In the end, it is very difficult to cut out all the denunciations of the scribes and Pharisees from the historical account of Jesus—if only because it then becomes impossible to see why Jesus would have had enemies that wanted to kill him.

Overall it makes more sense to assume that Jesus did have a detailed knowledge of the Old Testament. His disputations also suggest that he had some knowledge of the traditional art of Jewish learned debate, in which the parties throw scriptural quotes at each other in attempt to get the better of the argument.

Beyond that, it is impossible to say where Jesus gained his knowledge, and to what extent it was through training and education and to what extent it was natural ability. At this point it will probably not surprise you to learn that scholars don't put much credence in Luke's story in which the twelve-year-old Jesus disputes with the doctors of the Law in the Temple (Luke 2:41–50).

So, then, Jesus's life and thought fit within the context of the Judaism of his day. But there is another element that is harder to explain. A great deal of Jesus's teaching is about interpersonal ethics and behavior, for example: "Give to him that asketh thee, and from him that would borrow of thee turn not thou away" (Matthew 5:42), or in his call to forgive: "Take heed to yourselves: If thy brother trespass against thee, rebuke him; and if he repent, forgive him" (Luke 17:3).

These ethical utterances are among the most admired and influential words of Jesus, but they don't fit all that well into the context of Judaism at that time, which focused heavily upon the fulfillment of the Law and upon the collective responsibility of the people. In the Hebrew Bible, forgiveness is not a matter of personal ethics: all the calls for forgiveness are from the Lord on behalf of certain individuals or the nation as a whole.

Where, then, did Jesus get his emphasis on the more personal side of moral behavior? Up to a point William Blake was right when he wrote, "There is not one Moral Virtue that Jesus Inculcated but Plato & Cicero did Inculcate before him what then did Christ inculcate [sic]. Forgiveness of Sins."

Although Blake is unaware of it, Cicero, the great Roman statesman and philosopher, actually does praise forgiveness—*clementia*—in a number of passages. Cicero died in 43 BC, nearly forty years before Jesus was born. Even so it is not likely that Jesus knew anything about him or his writings. They were in Latin, and Latin was not widely studied in the eastern Mediterranean world of Jesus's time: Greek was the lingua franca. Jesus might have known Greek, but he almost certainly did not know Latin.

So I am not arguing that Jesus read Cicero. Instead I am arguing that both Jesus and Cicero may have been drawing on a philosophical discourse that was widespread in classical antiquity. This discourse started with Socrates in the fifth century BC. Unlike the philosophers who went before him, Socrates was not interested in abstract speculations about the origins of the universe. He was concerned with what made human life conscious and meaningful. Largely through his pupil Plato and Plato's pupil Aristotle, Socrates's ideas spread throughout the world of philosophy and helped show how individuals could live in an ethical and responsible way. These ideas further spread into the world of thought through such schools as the Cynics, Stoics, and Epicureans.

Cicero, an educated Roman, certainly studied the works of the great Greek philosophers; in fact he wrote about them. But where and how would Jesus have gotten his knowledge? There is no evidence that he was directly familiar with the Greek philosophers or their works. He does not quote them, and his ideas are different enough that there are no traces of direct influence.

But there is the city of Sepphoris. Sepphoris was a bustling Hellenistic city in Galilee, less than four miles from Jesus's hometown of Nazareth. In fact Sepphoris was traditionally said to be the birthplace of Jesus's mother, Mary. In Jesus's time the city was the site of an enormous civic restoration project on which, some have suggested, Jesus himself may have worked as a craftsman.

Unlike Jerusalem, the center of Jewish resistance to Roman and Hellenistic influence, Sepphoris represented an accommodation with the larger world of the empire. It is possible, no doubt likely, that Greek philosophers of some sort had a presence there. They may have influenced Jesus, not only through an emphasis on personal ethics and morality but in their style of discourse. Again in imitation of Socrates, many philosophers used informal conversations—as opposed to lectures—to communicate their ideas. This practice resembles Jesus's own interactions with his disciples and his rivals.

John Dominic Crossan speaks of Jesus as a "wandering Cynic philosopher," which would connect him much more closely with one of these Greek philosophical schools. The Cynics were not what we think of as cynics today. The name comes from the Greek *kúon*, "dog." They were sometimes mocked for their uncouth, doglike behavior—which they then embraced as a virtue, extolling the natural simplicity of dogs against human artificiality. The Cynics, aggressively unconventional, often had no fixed abode and flaunted morality and etiquette. Diogenes, the most famous of them, lived in the fourth century BC. Once reproached for masturbating in public, he replied, "If only one could achieve the same effect by rubbing an empty stomach!"

Was Jesus a Cynic in this sense? Probably not. After all, there is quite a distance between plucking a few ears of grain on the Sabbath and public masturbation. But Jesus may have picked up on some of the thought and behavior of the many wandering teachers who belonged to any and all of the Hellenistic philosophical schools.

Beyond that it is impossible to say more. It would be pointless, for example, to argue that Jesus got 30 percent of his ideas from the Cynics, 40 percent from the Stoics, or anything of the kind. The influences are not that close or that direct. Nonetheless, he may have encountered Greek philosophers, in Sepphoris or even farther afield, and been inspired by them in both teaching and practice.

9.

What Jesus Taught

So much for the background of Jesus. What did he teach?

If you go through the canonical Gospels, you will find that Jesus's teachings break down roughly as follows:

1. Ethical teachings about the proper relationship with one's neighbor and with God. The Sermon on the Mount in Matthew 5–7 is the most famous example. These teachings are perhaps Jesus's greatest contribution to the world's religious life and thought. They are well known and for the most part clear. I've discussed some of their implications in my other books, especially *Conscious Love* and *The Deal*, so I won't say much about them here.

2. Tirades against the religious hypocrisy of his day. In his early ministry in Galilee, he assails the Pharisees, the Sadducees, and possibly the Essenes. When he goes to Jerusalem, he takes on the priests of the Temple.

3. Enigmatic pronouncements on the kingdom of God or the kingdom of heaven. Many of the parables fall under this category. This

is among the most mysterious parts of Jesus's teaching, and it comes as no surprise that theologians disagree about what he meant by it.

4. Statements, also enigmatic, about Jesus's own nature and mission and his relation to Jewish concepts of the Messiah and the Son of Man.

5. Apocalyptic utterances about the destruction of the Temple and the end of the world.

You could go on breaking down these categories almost indefinitely, but these rough divisions will suit our purposes here.

As we look at them, two things become clear.

In the first place, they do not fit well together. They produce a complex and contradictory Jesus, one who is at once declaring the imminent end of all things and giving lessons about how to lead a decent day-to-day life.

In the second place, as we shall see, if you attempt to take out any of them, the whole picture of Jesus collapses upon itself.

Jesus and Revolution

Let's start with the second of the categories that I have given—Jesus's tirades against the religious hypocrisy of his day. Here is what the Jesus Seminar says about his rants against the Pharisees: "The Pharisees are routinely condemned in the gospels. The polemic more accurately reflects conflicts between the synagogue and the Christian communities that produced the gospels in the last quarter of the first century than it does the situation of the historical Jesus."

The argument goes like this: Jesus really did not have that much conflict with the religious leaders of his day. His denunciations of the scribes and Pharisees were put into his mouth later on, in the last quarter of the first century, when Christianity was breaking decisively with Judaism.

Why should the Pharisees have been singled out? Because, the theory goes, the Pharisees were the ancestors of the rabbinical Judaism that arose out of the ashes of the Second Temple and forms the basis of today's Judaism. The Gospels, particularly Matthew, have Jesus denouncing the Pharisees as a way of putting distance between Christians and Jews.

There are at least two problems with this argument. To begin with, even Mark, by most accounts the oldest and most historically accurate of the Gospels, nonetheless still has Jesus at odds with the Pharisees as well as with the "Herodians." We've already encountered this verse: "And the Pharisees went forth, and straightway took counsel with the Herodians against him, how they might destroy him" (Mark 3:6).

But let's grant the point that all of Jesus's arguments with the sects of his days were stuck in later. So let's take them out.

Now there is a big hole in the narrative.

Suddenly there is no clear reason that anybody would want to have Jesus killed. And obviously *someone* wanted to have Jesus killed. Otherwise you have to take out the crucifixion as well, and the story of Jesus caves in completely without that.

How do the scholars get around this problem?

One common step is to make Jesus a political revolutionary, as was done by Reza Aslan in *Zealot: The Life and Times of Jesus of Nazareth*. Aslan writes: "The notion that the leader of a popular messianic movement calling for the imposition of the 'Kingdom of God'—a term that would have been understood by Jew and gentile alike as implying revolt against Rome—could have remained uninvolved in the revolutionary fervor that had gripped nearly every Jew in Judea is ridiculous."

There are a number of problems with these claims. To begin with, it is very far from obvious—and in my view incorrect—that the term "kingdom of God" as used by Jesus had any political import. Certainly few, if any, of the parables about the kingdom of God make any sense interpreted in this way. Nor is it clear that the pre-Christian uses of that phrase have any such meaning.

But the problem is much bigger than that. To assume that Jesus was a political revolutionary requires some monkeying with the evidence. There is almost nothing in Jesus's statements anywhere that has a political tone—certainly not against Rome. "Render unto Caesar," the closest he gets to a political statement as such, is an evasive answer. But then the coin in question *does* have Caesar's image and superscription, so the coin is in fact Caesar's. Therefore Jesus is saying that there is no reason not to pay taxes to Caesar. Hardly a revolutionary act.

This is not to say that Jesus loved Rome. But let's assume that, minimally, he was a wise man. A wise man does not take actions that he knows to be futile. And sedition against Rome would certainly have been futile, as the Jews so grimly learned forty years later.

In any event, if you want to argue that Jesus really was a political revolutionary and was killed by the Romans for that reason, you have to assume that he made any number of political pronouncements that have simply been lost to all sources.

Furthermore, you have to throw out practically all the evidence in the Gospels, which unanimously state that it was the priests and the Pharisees who wanted to have Jesus destroyed.

Not to mention the verses that extol peace and love and turning the other cheek.

So to make Jesus a political insurgent you have to discard a great deal of evidence that we have, and make up a great deal of evidence that we do *not* have. This argument comes about as close to begging the question— the most elementary of all logical errors—as you can get.

If it's such a flimsy theory, why does it keep surfacing? In the first place, it is very difficult for the American intelligentsia today to take seriously anything that has to do with spirituality. To make an issue a social or political or economic one is the only way they can make it comprehensible to themselves or acceptable to mainstream intellectual opinion. Thus they understand Jesus most easily as a political agitator.

There is another reason, however, and it is worth going into.

Over the last couple of generations scholars have been more and more inclined to say that it was the Romans and not the priests who wanted to have Jesus killed—even in the face of the evidence. Why?

Because of an awkward little matter known as "blood guilt." We see its origins in Matthew 27:24–25, during the trial of Jesus: "When Pilate saw that he could prevail nothing, but that rather a tumult was made, he took water, and washed his hands before the multitude, saying, I am innocent of the blood of this just person: see ye to it. Then answered all the people, and said, His blood be on us, and on our children."

In the centuries of recrimination between Christians and Jews, this verse has been used as evidence of the Jews' collective responsibility for killing Christ—for deicide (a word that I have always found irresistibly comic despite its tragic consequences). The idea of blood guilt has helped inspire anti-Semitism, which took especially monstrous forms in the twentieth century.

Thus in the last seventy years Christian scholars have done everything they can to backpedal from this charge of blood guilt. Understandably.

Nonetheless, saying that it was the Romans who wanted to have Jesus killed still goes against the existing evidence—which says that it was the Jerusalem hierarchy that instigated the death of Christ. Pilate, the cruel Roman governor, was apparently indifferent to the fate of this man who was supposedly so seditious.

From a moral point of view, the solution is clear. You can believe that the priests wanted to have Jesus killed without blaming the whole Jewish people for it. Probably most of the Jews of Christ's own time had barely even heard of him. The Jerusalem mob that was crying for his blood—

if this really happened—no doubt amounted to a few dozen people bribed by the priests.

In any case, it's absurd to blame an entire people for something that a tiny number of their ancestors may have done two thousand years ago. Speaking personally, like many Americans I am of European ancestry. What kind of connection do I have with my forebears from two thousand years ago? At that point they were probably still painting themselves blue and guzzling mead from the skulls of their enemies.

Nor is it anti-Semitic to say that the Jerusalem priests of AD 30 were wicked and corrupt. Josephus says much the same thing—and he was not only a Jew, but a Jew of the priestly class.

As a result the most sensible conclusion is what the Gospels claim: that Jesus incensed the religious authorities of his time by criticizing their greed, hypocrisy, and corruption, and they conspired to have him killed for it.

So we can be faithful to the sources—and I am speaking here in a historical rather than a religious sense—without slipping down a slope of anti-Semitism.

The Kingdom Within

Let's turn now to the third major subject that Jesus addresses: the kingdom of God or the kingdom of heaven. (The difference between these two terms is subtle and obscure, and for our purposes it's best to take them as synonymous.) This is by far the most difficult aspect of Jesus's teaching. As Wikipedia says, "No overall agreement on the theological interpretation of 'Kingdom of God' has emerged among scholars."

And in fact it's not too easy to learn what this kingdom of God is from the theologians.

Let's start with Catholicism. It's hard to find anything even remotely resembling a definition of the kingdom of heaven in the *Catechism of the*

Catholic Church, the church's definitive statement of doctrine. Here is something that comes close: "'To carry out the will of the Father Christ inaugurated the kingdom of heaven on earth.' Now the Father's will is 'to raise up men to share in his own divine life.' He does this by gathering men around his Son Jesus Christ. This gathering is the Church, 'on earth the seed and beginning of that kingdoms [*sic*].'"

As far as I can tell from this passage, the kingdom of heaven is the collective body of redeemed believers that will come into its own after the Last Judgment. The Catholic church as a corporate body is a precursor of this kingdom. Pope Benedict XVI calls this the "ecclesiastical" interpretation, adding that it "has come gradually to dominate the field, especially in modern Catholic theology."

But how does this description relate to anything Jesus himself says about the kingdom? What about the parables? How is the church like "leaven, which a woman took, and hid in three measures of meal, till the whole was leavened" (Matthew 13:33)? Or "treasure hid in a field" (Matthew 13:44)? Or seed cast in the ground (Mark 4:26)?

Let's see if the Protestants can do any better. Reinhold Niebuhr, one of the most distinguished theologians of the twentieth century, describes the kingdom of God as "God's sovereignty over history." But to say that the kingdom of God is "God's sovereignty" is pretty circular. As for history, it has not radically changed over the last two thousand years. It is still largely a story of lies, selfishness, and cruelty. One would do well to stay away from any God who was sovereign over that.

Of course Niebuhr does not mean this. He means that God's sovereignty over history will be disclosed at the end of time, in which the quick and the dead shall be judged and the moral accounts of humanity will receive their final reckoning. As mainstream Christianity has always taught.

It was possible for Christ's first disciples, who were so close to his own time, to believe in the imminent end of the world. In fact Paul's first letter to the Thessalonians, the first of the New Testament texts to be written, is partly intended to soothe the fears of Christians who were afraid for their loved ones who died before Christ's return.

It is harder to believe in such things today. The universe is not, we know, six thousand years old but in all likelihood closer to fourteen billion years old. On this scale God's sovereignty over history is so remote that it doesn't offer much comfort.

Pope Benedict mentions another way of viewing the kingdom of heaven—what he calls the "mystical" interpretation. This approach has been far more prominent in Eastern Orthodoxy than in either Catholicism or Protestantism. In the passage below, for example, Nikiphoros the Monk, who lived in the late thirteenth century, gives some directions for prayer:

> Seat yourself, then, concentrate your consciousness, and lead it into the respiratory passage through which your breath passes through your heart. . . . Train your consciousness not to leave your heart quickly, for at first it is strongly disinclined to remain constrained and circumscribed in this way. But once it becomes accustomed to remaining there, it can no longer bear to be outside the heart. *For the kingdom of heaven is within us* (cf. Luke 17:21), and when your consciousness concentrates its attention in the heart and *through pure prayer searches there for the kingdom of heaven*, all external things become abominable and hateful to it. (Emphasis added.)

Thus in the Orthodox mystical tradition, which goes back—continuously, I believe—to the earliest days of Christianity, *the kingdom of God is an internal state*. (This particular practice is called the "prayer of the heart." The passage above contains partial instructions only, by the way.)

If we accept this premise, much of the riddle evaporates. It also becomes clear how this idea of the kingdom of heaven came to be buried. In fact the hidden or lost nature of this kingdom—its being, for example, like a treasure in a field—is the point of some of the parables. Because if the kingdom is an internal state and you have no experience of that state, you will not understand it, nor will you believe that it even exists.

Actually this too is a major part of Christ's message, and it explains his tirades against the scribes and Pharisees. The scribes do not know these truths, because they are not merely a matter of book learning, and to believe they are is to be completely deluded. "Woe unto you, scribes and Pharisees, hypocrites! for ye shut up the kingdom of heaven against men: for ye neither go in yourselves, neither suffer ye them that are entering to go in" (Matthew 23:13).

Jesus's denunciations apply, of course, to the spiritual pettifoggers of our own time too.

Very well then. If the kingdom of God is an internal state, what kind of state is it? Let's begin with something very basic and obvious and yet usually overlooked. There is something in you that *is conscious*, that *is aware*. It is not your body, nor is it even your thoughts and feelings, because you can step back inwardly and observe all these things as if from a distance (this is the point of many meditative practices). Here are some names for it from around the world: the Atman, the Self, Buddha nature, "I am that I am."

As these examples suggest, this truth is known to practically all religions. Of course it is—because if it is true, it must be universally true, and many people will have discovered it in their own ways.

This consciousness, this "true I," is, in most of us, embryonic. It is there and it can never go away—in fact, it is said, this is the only part of you that is truly immortal. (It may be connected to the "something eternal" mentioned by Thornton Wilder.) Nevertheless, you can be all but unaware of it. You can go through your life completely oblivious to it, caught up in the exterior thoughts and concerns that the New Testament calls by the name of "the world." You can go to your grave this way, having lived your life in sleep. Most do. This is, in fact, why many people say they don't know who they are.

Hence this "I" is like a seed. It is sown in all of us, but in most of us it falls on stony ground or is eaten by birds. It is the pearl of great price, which a merchant sells all he has to buy, because it is the only real and genuine and true thing within us. It is like leaven, because even though it is very small and usually unnoticed, it "leaveneth the whole lump"— meaning that your life and your experience would not exist without it.

What I have just said explains a great deal about the kingdom of heaven, but it doesn't explain everything. It doesn't tell us, for example, what it may mean to "enter the kingdom of heaven" (as in Matthew 7:20; 18:3; 19:23, and similar passages).

To enter the kingdom of heaven is to take this little seed of the true "I" and cultivate it until "it is the greatest among herbs, and becometh a tree, so that the birds of the air come and lodge in the branches thereof" (Matthew 13:32). Following the ethical teachings of Christ is part of this cultivation; so are certain types of spiritual practice, like the prayer of the heart.

This view of the kingdom of God is extremely ancient. It was expressed by the third-century church father Origen in his treatise *On Prayer*. Origen writes, "Those who pray for the coming of the Kingdom of God pray without any doubt for the Kingdom of God that they contain in themselves, and pray that this Kingdom might bear fruit and attain its fullness. For in every holy man it is God who reigns."

What are the results? The apostle Paul says, "For the kingdom of God is not meat and drink; but righteousness, and peace, and joy in the Holy Ghost" (Romans 14:17).

There is another, still deeper consequence. You come to realize that *this "I," this Self, is the same in all of us.* This fact too is known to all the great traditions. The Hindu Brihadaranyaka Upanishad, for example, says, "This Self is the Lord of all beings; as all spokes are knit together in the hub, all things, all gods, all men, all lives, all bodies, are knit together in that Self. . . . Your own Self lives in the hearts of all."

Christianity often speaks of the relation of the body to its parts as a way of describing this fundamental unity. This idea is especially important to Paul: "So we, being many, are one body in Christ, and every one members one of another" (Romans 12:5).

The I That Is We

You may have noticed that in all this talk about Christ's teachings, I haven't said anything so far about love. Isn't love one of the most important messages that Christ had to bring?

Yes. And this is the time to bring it into the discussion.

It's almost impossible to write about love without sounding mawkish or cynical. But we might start with one curious yet important fact.

Love is the source both of tremendous hope and of tremendous disappointment. This is most obvious, no doubt, in romantic love, as we can see in the great love poets of history—or in the latest pop hit that's blaring on the radio.

The hope lies in the promise of eternal, undying, unconditional love—the kind of love that everyone seeks. The disappointment comes from the fact that not everyone finds this kind of love.

It's possible that people are looking for the wrong thing in the wrong place.

If you sort through all the verbiage, you will, I believe, find two and only two kinds of love. One is highly conditional and transactional. If you're good to me, I'll be good to you. If you're not, I will pay you back in kind.

This kind of love has a biological basis. Political psychologist Drew

Westen observes, "Natural selection favors animals that practice *reciprocal altruism*, the tendency to help each other out."

You can call it reciprocal altruism, or you can call it conditional, transactional love. In my book *Conscious Love* (which discusses these subjects in much more detail), I have called it *the love of the world*. It is what the world knows as love. Even supposedly unconditional kinds of love are often really versions of this worldly love.

Many romantic films have a moment in which the heroine looks over at an elderly couple sitting nearby in a diner or restaurant. The two old people are radiant. We can see that they have spent their lives together, been through many ups and downs. Their love has proved itself over the decades. On the heroine's face we see the question, "Will I ever find love like this?"

How could anyone be so harsh as to call this the love of the world—conditional, transactional love?

And yet that is what it is.

Literally.

As you'll remember, marriage is a legal contract. And a contract, as a lawyer once told me, is a promise that the law will enforce. All of the care, all of the nurturing that one partner may have given to the other, no matter how selfless and noble, is really nothing more than honoring the promises made at the altar.

If the other person doesn't live up to these promises, which are (minimally) some degree of sexual fidelity and kind treatment, the other person has the right to end the contract. If a woman puts up with abuse beyond a certain point, people start to wonder what's wrong with her for *not* leaving the marriage.

I could say the same thing about most of the other types and versions of love. Friendship is highly transactional, and while family relations aren't supposed to be, in the end they are. This often plays out during the holidays at the end of the year, when family members reckon the accounts and tally up excesses and deficits—often with the usual recriminations.

All of these, then, are forms of the love of the world.

I'm not, by the way, denouncing this state of affairs. Transactionality is one of the main ways in which humans have managed their relations with one another, and if there were no such thing, any kind of organized collective life would be impossible.

Since this is so—and has been so for as long as anyone knows—why should we upset ourselves about it? Why should we find ourselves longing for something more?

Because there is another kind of love. It is not transactional or conditional. It is unconditional and endless. It is probably the only kind of love that is not likely to cause a certain amount of damage.

This is the love of which Christianity speaks. Because the English word *love* has to cover so many different meanings and nuances—a source of confusion and unhappiness in its own right—sometimes the word from the Greek New Testament is used to name this unconditional love: *agape* (pronounced ah-*gah*-pay). Taking a phrase from G. I. Gurdjieff, I have called it *conscious love*. With agape, you are conscious enough to see the other person clearly and wish for and do only what will genuinely benefit him or her.

Unconditional love is as real as the other kind. But it is much rarer. Pain often comes when people delude themselves into thinking that transactional love is unconditional love when it is nothing of the kind.

A man and a woman meet. They fall in love. They go around saying things like, "I don't have any attachment to this person. I just want what's best for her." Then, after six weeks of fighting, they break up and wish each other nothing but evil.

I don't want to belabor the point. But in the end the situation seems to be this: There is conditional, transactional love—reciprocal altruism, if you like. And there is unconditional love: agape.

It isn't wise to get too sentimental about agape. In fact agape is the opposite of sentimentality. It is pure and clean, but it is also impersonal.

It has to be. Personal love is conditional love. Why? Because it means that you love someone *because* she is that person. Unconditional love is extended to all—unconditionally.

For that reason (and this is a fact that is often overlooked), agape isn't particularly warm. Liddell and Scott's Greek lexicon, the definitive work in English, even says that the verb from which *agape* is derived can imply "regard rather than affection."

You may find this fact somewhat peculiar, but then you look at the Gospels and you realize that Jesus isn't terribly warm either. He is kind, but he is also somewhat remote and impersonal. He is often dismissive of his family, for example. When he is told that his mother and brothers are waiting to see him, he shows no interest, saying, "Whosoever shall do the will of my Father which is in heaven, the same is my brother, and sister, and mother" (Matthew 12:50).

Agape is not personal love; it is the opposite. It is *not* based on personal preference or kinship or race or class. Rather it arises out of the knowledge that this "I" is the same in all of us and that at the deepest level of being there is no difference between you and me.

Many times you hear the expression "we are all one." What could this possibly mean? In day-to-day life we are most assuredly *not* one. The advantage of one person is the disadvantage of the other. You get the girl, I don't; I get the job, you don't.

According to the world—and according to the love of the world—we are not one. I am not you. We are linked only by our mutual interests and advantages. It is only agape that is truly based on the realization that if I follow the "I" far enough into myself, I reach an "I" that is "we."

This awareness, and this kind of love, produces quite different results from the personal kind. The most famous description appears in 1 Corinthians 13, where the apostle Paul praises it at length. The King James Version here translates *agape* as "charity" to suggest that something other than conventional love is at stake. "Charity suffereth long, and is kind; charity envieth not; charity vaunteth not itself, is not puffed up" (1 Corinthians 13:4).

Thus, as you can see, agape comes about naturally as a result of entering the kingdom of heaven.

I'm not, by the way, trying to vilify transactional love while extolling agape. Each has its place. We are linked by advantages and interests as much as by anything else. And as the dictionary tells us, agape can seem a bit cold. Each kind of love has its role. Unhappiness comes only when you mistake one for the other.

The Apocalyptic Jesus

In the discussion of Jesus's teachings above, I have taken the Gospels' evidence about Jesus more or less at face value. That's because I think his teachings as described up to this point are reasonably clear. Maybe Jesus *didn't* say every last thing in the Sermon on the Mount. Maybe some of the parables about the kingdom of heaven *don't* go back to him. Maybe some of the denunciations of the scribes and Pharisees *were* tacked on later. But the basic message comes out the same.

It will come out different only if you decide—for whatever reasons of your own—to eliminate a whole category of sayings, whether it is about the kingdom of heaven or about scribes and Pharisees or whatever else you pick. And this strikes me as being very high-handed with the evidence.

From here on, however, the problem becomes harder to sort out. Here what Jesus really said—as opposed to what was put into his mouth later—*does* make a great deal of difference to what one decides about his original teachings. And there is no authoritative external criterion for figuring out how much in the Gospels is genuine and how much was added. Thus the conclusions are going to have to be much more tentative.

To show what I mean, let's turn to Jesus's apocalyptic messages. The core of these messages is found in a section of the synoptic Gospels called the Apocalyptic Discourse. It is found in Matthew 24, Mark 13, and Luke 21. Scholars generally agree that Matthew and Luke relied on Mark's account to write their own, so let's take Mark.

You may remember that scholars generally date Mark to around AD 70. What's their reasoning? Much of it relies on this chapter. If you were to read the thirteenth chapter of Mark completely fresh and without any preconceptions, you would probably come to this conclusion: Jesus was predicting a Roman invasion of Judea and the sack of the Temple, to be shortly followed by the end of the world.

Scholars do not, as a rule, believe that Jesus really made these predictions. They may have been *vaticinia ex eventu* (*vaticinium ex eventu* in the singular): supposed prophecies that were actually cooked up after the events they are supposed to predict.

Say that I want you to believe in a holy man who died in 1910. It would help my case considerably if I could get you to think he predicted the two world wars and the assassination of John F. Kennedy, along with the 9/11 debacle for good measure. So I might concoct some prophecies of this sort and put them in his mouth.

Today recordkeeping is good enough that this would be hard to accomplish. But in the first century, it would have been much easier.

Thus scholars date Mark to around AD 70 because it's the most likely context for verses such as this one, where Jesus says about the Temple, "Seest thou these great buildings? there shall not be left one stone after another, that shall not be thrown down" (Mark 13:2). The Temple was sacked in 70.

Thus, scholars say, this prophecy is a *vaticinium ex eventu*: Mark has put a prediction of the sack of the Temple into Jesus's mouth. So the Gospel would have to be written after AD 70. But not too much later, because Jesus goes on to say: "In those days, after that tribulation, the sun shall be darkened, and the moon shall not give her light. . . . And then shall they see the Son of man coming in the clouds with great power and glory."

If this passage had been written much later than 70, it would have been harder to claim that the end was at hand. But Jesus insists that the time is coming soon: "Verily I say unto you, that this generation shall not pass, till all these things be done" (Mark 13:30).

If you assume that "this generation" is the generation that Jesus was speaking to in AD 30, then forty years later the time of their passing would be coming very soon. And so would the end of the world.

Hence scholars date Mark to around 70.

Now we are left with a question: how many, if any, of these predictions did Jesus actually make?

There is another complication. The discourses of Jesus in the Gospels were probably not really discourses that he gave as wholes. They are much more likely to be assemblages of related sayings that were later put together by the authors of the Gospels.

So did Jesus really predict the sack of the Temple, to be followed by the final judgment? Did he predict one thing, and not the other? Did he predict both things separately, so that it was the Gospel writers who put them together this way?

There is no good answer. As you can see, it depends a great deal on exactly how much of this prophecy is genuine—that is, goes back to Jesus. And there is no way of knowing that independently.

The balance of the evidence favors the general scholarly opinion. It's much easier to believe that these prophecies were written after the fact than that Jesus spoke them. The only factor to the contrary is the possibility that Jesus, forty years earlier, could have foreseen the coming storm of revolt and suppression and told his followers about it. That is possible. After all, the situation in Judea was extremely tense in Jesus's own day. Any intelligent observer (even setting aside powers of prophecy) might well have concluded that it was bound to explode sooner or later.

In that case, what about the predictions of the end of the world? It's true that the crushing of the revolt and the sack of the Temple brought about an end to *a* world—the world of the Second Temple. But on the rest of the planet, everything continued much as it always had. The moon continued to give her light, and as the saying goes, cats continued to have kittens.

So there is some temptation to think that all the prophecies in the Gospels were made up later and put in Jesus's mouth by his too-eager followers. But this view has some problems too.

To begin with, it is certain that in the earliest days of the Christian movement—soon after Jesus's death—there was intense apocalyptic expectation. People were looking for the end to come very soon. We have already seen this hope in 1 Thessalonians, dated to between 50 and 52. It is the first New Testament text to have been written. "But I would not have you to be ignorant, brethren, concerning them which are asleep, that ye sorrow not, even as others which have no hope. . . . For the Lord himself shall descend from heaven with a shout, with the voice of an archangel, and with the trump of God: and the dead in Christ shall rise first" (1 Thessalonians 4:13, 16. By the way, this is the source of the Rapture doctrine beloved of fundamentalist Christians today). The Thessalonians are worried that some of their friends and family members will die before Christ comes. What will happen to them then? Paul is telling them not to worry: the dead will be resurrected and taken up first.

Paul had to deal with fears of this kind among the earliest Christians. Thus there was an intense apocalyptic expectation. The simplest way to explain this is that this expectation goes back, in some way or another, to Christ himself.

I think it would be hard to say more than that. How much goes back, and in how much detail, would be almost impossible to sort out given the current evidence.

Many scholars, including some of the most esteemed ones, say that Jesus was basically an apocalyptic prophet, preaching the imminent end of the world. The most famous proponent of this view is Albert Schweit-zer, who sets it out in his classic study *The Quest of the Historical Jesus*. Schweitzer's portrait of this historical Jesus is not very inspiring. Schweit-zer's Jesus is a madman. He decides he is the Messiah. Then he gets the insane idea that he will bring about the last judgment if he dies on the cross, so he gets himself crucified. (Of course the resurrection was made up later.) If Schweitzer's Jesus were alive today, he would be standing on a street corner with a sandwich board reading THE END IS NIGH.

To this day many scholars still follow Schweitzer's view of Jesus as apocalyptic prophet. I have difficulties with it myself. Some of them are like my objections to the idea of Jesus as political agitator. If the immedi-ate end of the world really was his major theme, why did he spend so much time talking about other things? If he really thought the end of the world was here, why should he bother with ethical teachings or with denouncing priests and scribes? If you are warning people on a sinking ship, you are not going to be lecturing them about the Golden Rule.

Again, you also have to suppose that Jesus delivered a huge number of warnings that somehow have not come down to us. You have to monkey with the evidence in ways that, at best, look highly irresponsible.

As a matter of fact, scholars who hold to this theory *do* cut out practi-cally everything Jesus is reported as saying. If this were the only prob-lem, it would be bad enough. But it also means that you have to imagine that after Jesus's death, his disciples must have formed a kind of Jesus committee that made up his ethical teachings, the teachings about the kingdom of heaven, and the rest.

Some scholars try to do something like this. Here's an example. The German theologian Walter Schmithals says that Jesus's ethical state-ments "must belong to a different strand of tradition, which was closely related to the corresponding Jewish piety, as shown by numerous rabbin-ical parallels."

Schmithals is saying that Jesus did not say the things in, for example, the Sermon on the Mount. They were commonplace pieces of rabbinic wisdom that were somehow attracted to him, like bits of paper to an electrically charged comb. Or someone cut out all these statements from somewhere else, pasted them in, and attributed them to Jesus.

These claims don't stand up well. The ethical statements in the Gospels show a clear, powerful, unique moral voice. A third of the world's population tries to live by them to this day. You don't create such a voice by pasting together proverbs out of rabbinical fortune cookies.

In any case, if this was what happened, whoever glued these teachings together would be of more interest than Jesus himself.

In the end, Jesus's teachings can't be written off as a committee composition or a bunch of proverbs that were strung on to his name afterward. This may hold true for some of them, but certainly not all and probably not most. They are too great and too original. Besides, if Jesus were a fictional creation, the picture of him would be much clearer and more consistent than it is. Instead we have what scholars say we have: a fuzzy picture of a man who lived a generation or so before the Gospels were written and about whom there were many memories and, no doubt, still more speculations.

And if you make Jesus into an apocalyptic prophet, as Schweitzer did, you fall into the same problem that he fell into. For Schweitzer, the historical Jesus and the Christ of faith have practically nothing to do with each other. But then how do you get from one to the other? Where and how did the Christ of faith arise? Schweitzer doesn't tell us. At the end of his book he simply shrugs his shoulders and walks away.

One popular answer is to say that Paul conjured it all up. But that is not the picture presented by Paul himself or by any source. Paul keeps insisting that what he is teaching is what he has been taught. He does argue with the apostles, especially James the brother of Jesus, about whether Gentile believers have to keep the Jewish Law. The debate some-times becomes quite heated. But there is no debate about who Jesus is or about what he taught. These are all taken as given.

This leaves us with one major part of Jesus's teachings to be dealt with: who he was and who he said he was. To explore this issue, let's look at his public career.

10.

The Life of Jesus:
The Public Career

Jesus's public career began with his baptism by John. It ended with his crucifixion. He did a number of things in between.

That is about as precise a sequence of Jesus's career as we have.

Why? Remember that Mark is the earliest of the Gospels in the New Testament. Matthew and Luke used it to write their accounts. John arguably used it as well.

One of the earliest surviving testimonies about Mark comes from the church father Papias in the early second century. Papias writes:

> Mark, who had been Peter's interpreter, wrote down carefully, but not in order, all that he remembered of the Lord's sayings and doings. For he had not heard the Lord or been one of His followers, but later, as I said, one of Peter's. Peter used to adapt his teachings to the occasion, without making a systematic arrangement of the Lord's sayings, so that Mark was quite justified in writing down some things just as he remembered them. For he had one purpose only—to leave out nothing that he had heard, and to make no misstatement about it.

Scholars today do not necessarily believe Papias's testimony on every point. The Gospel may or may not have been written by Mark, who may or may not have been Peter's disciple. But scholars generally agree that the chronology in Mark only vaguely resembles the sequence of events as they actually happened.

If this is the case, and if the other evangelists based their accounts on Mark, we can't trust the Gospel narratives to give an accurate account of exactly when in his career Jesus said or did anything.

But all sources agree that Jesus's entry into public life started with his baptism by John.

The Precursor

At this point it can hardly surprise you to hear that much of what the Gospels say about John the Baptist is doubted by scholars. They don't for the most part put much credence in the beginning of Luke's Gospel, in which John is Jesus's cousin and John's own birth is foretold to his father by an angel. Nor do they believe, for example, that John said of Jesus, "He must increase, but I must decrease" (John 3:30).

What, then, do we know of John? He practiced baptism—a type of immersion that somehow purified the candidate. Our sources don't exactly agree about what this baptism was supposed to accomplish. Mark says, "John did baptize in the wilderness, and preach the baptism of repentance for the forgiveness of sins" (Mark 1:4).

The main source about John apart from the New Testament is Josephus. Josephus doesn't quite say the same thing. This is what he says: "John called to baptism the Jews who listened to him and practiced virtue, exercising justice toward one another and reverence toward God. For the baptism would only be acceptable to him if they employed it, not for the remission of sins, but for the sanctification of the body, just as the soul had been purified by justice."

Josephus says the baptism was performed *after* the soul was purified "by righteousness." Mark makes it sound as if the baptism itself was part of the purification. In either case, John's practice seems to circumvent the purification process set out in the Jewish Law, which involved not only ritual bathing but costly sacrifices at the Temple. If John was practicing his baptism as an alternative to these, he would have been very much at odds with the Jewish establishment of his day. He would have been imply-ing (if not actually stating) that their rites were corrupt and could not purify anybody.

As a matter of fact, none of the sources talk about any conflict between John and the Jerusalem priesthood—maybe because John never (to our knowledge) went to Judea but stayed to the north, in Galilee. Instead he was put to death by the command of "Herod the tetrarch"—Herod Anti-pas, son of Herod the Great. Josephus says Herod was alarmed by John's popularity, which he feared would lead to revolt. The Gospels say that John condemned Herod for marrying his queen Herodias, his brother's ex-wife. Of course both of these possibilities could be true.

The Gospels connect John with "Elias," or the prophet Elijah, one of the most mysterious and haunting figures in the Jewish tradition. ("Elias" is the Greek form of the name, generally used in many New Testament translations; translations of the Old Testament generally use the Hebrew form, "Elijah.") Elijah, "an hairy man, and girt with a girdle of leather about his loins" (2 Kings 2:1), stood up against wicked King Ahab and Queen Jezebel and foretold their doom. The performer and recipient of many miracles, Elijah in the end was taken up to heaven in a fiery chariot.

John in the Gospels is associated with Elijah. John too is a man of the wilderness, "clothed with camel's hair, and with a girdle of a skin about his loins; and he did eat locusts and wild honey" (Mark 1:6).

Why is the link to Elijah so important? Because of a prophecy in the Old Testament: "Behold, I will send you Elijah the prophet before the coming of the great and dreadful day of the Lord" (Malachi 4:5).

The Gospels identify Elijah—and this prophecy—with John the Baptist. Jesus tells his disciples, "Elias is indeed come, and they have done unto him whatsoever they listed" (Mark 9:13), referring to his execution by Herod Antipas.

In recent years, some have tried to use this identification between Elijah and John as proof that the Bible teaches reincarnation: John was the reincarnation of Elijah. This is going too far with the evidence, because there is almost no indication that the Jews of the first century believed in reincarnation. More likely Elijah was seen as a type, a prefiguration of John, at least by Christians.

In all four Gospels, John baptizes Jesus. But the Gospels differ in certain details. This is a good opportunity to illustrate one of the basic points of New Testament criticism.

The principle is this: A story starts out simple. It is then elaborated on, with all sorts of details added that say more about the author's prejudices than about what actually happened.

So let's take the four Gospels in the order in which scholars say they were written.

In Mark, John preaches repentance for the forgiveness of sins. He foretells the coming of one "mightier than I" (Mark 1:7), who is of course Jesus. Jesus comes to be baptized and sees the heavens open and "the Spirit like a dove descending upon him," and a voice saying "Thou art my beloved Son, in whom I am well pleased."

Matthew preserves this basic structure. But he inserts some more details. John condemns the Pharisees and Sadducees as a "generation of vipers." He also warns of a coming retribution, in which "he that cometh after me . . . will burn up the chaff with unquenchable fire" (Matthew 3:11–12). In Matthew, John also balks at first at baptizing Jesus: "I have need to be baptized by thee, and comest thou to me?" (Matthew 3:14). So Matthew's Gospel inserts some condemnation of the scribes and Pharisees, and shows John honoring Jesus as a being higher than himself.

Luke's version is more elaborate still. John quotes the prophet Isaiah, speaking of himself as "the voice of one crying in the wilderness" (Luke 3:4). Like Matthew, Luke depicts John as denouncing a "generation of vipers" (Luke 3:7), except that these are no longer the Pharisees and Sadducees, but the Jews as a whole. John also baptizes soldiers and tax collectors—the very personification of the Roman occupation. Thus Luke, slightly later than Matthew by five or ten years, suggests that the Christian community has distanced itself more from the Jews than Matthew does. The "vipers" are no longer a couple of sects, but the Jews as a whole.

The Gospel of John, the last of the four, does not actually say that John the Baptist baptized Jesus. Instead it says he "bare record, saying, I saw the Spirit descending from heaven like a dove, and it abode upon him" (John 1:32). C. H. Dodd, perhaps the foremost commentator on the Gospel of John in the twentieth century, points out that this Gospel almost never mentions either baptism or the Eucharist directly. Dodd believes that the evangelist saw these as secret initiations, not to be revealed to outsiders.

Clearly there are different overlays in each version. In Mark, John simply baptizes Jesus, and it is Jesus who sees the Spirit descend. Similarly in Matthew and Luke. But by the time we get to the fourth Gospel, it is John himself who is bearing witness, and baptism itself is not even mentioned.

These details give some clues to the development of the Gospel tradition. Scholars tend to assume that Mark, being the oldest and simplest, is frequently the closest to historical truth, while John, the fourth Gospel, has little if any connection with the historical Jesus. Thus as time goes along, the story becomes more elaborate, the status of Jesus is continually raised, and the actual facts are pushed farther into the background. (I doubt that it's quite so simple, but this is a rich mine for disputes and there is no space to go into them here.)

To go back for a moment, there is a curious detail in Josephus's description of John's baptism. If it is for "the purification of the body," it would have to be done more than once—often, in fact. Nobody takes a shower thinking it will last for the rest of his life.

And this is exactly the practice of the sole surviving community that traces its teachings back to John the Baptist: the Mandaeans, who use ritual immersions in water as a central part of their religion. The Mandaeans used to be concentrated in the marshy areas of southern Iraq, where the Tigris and Euphrates flow together and water is plentiful. Over the past decades, however, they have been displaced. They have suffered greatly from persecution by Saddam Hussein and from the American invasion. Numbering around seven thousand in 2014, they are an endangered minority.

At any rate, if Mandaean practice is any guide to what John taught, his baptism may have involved many periodic immersions in water. The Gospels contrast John's baptism with the baptism of Christ. Mark has John say, "I indeed have baptized you with water: but he shall baptize you with the Holy Ghost" (Mark 1:9). This may suggest that John baptized once, with water, meaning that the baptism had to be repeated. The Christian practice, which baptized both "with water and the spirit," had to be done only once. Hence it was higher and purer, at least in the eyes of the Christians.

There is another detail. John 4:2 says, "Jesus himself baptized not, but his disciples." If there is any truth to this statement, it may mean that Jesus himself did not put much stock in baptism but allowed his disciples to do it because they found it useful.

Miracles

The Gospels records the acts and the sayings of Jesus. In the previous chapter, I tried to outline the teachings that lie behind his sayings. As for his acts, most of them involve miracles of one sort or another.

So now we have to ask what we're supposed to make of miracles. Since the eighteenth century, the mind-set of the West has tended to deny that miracles ever happen; there is always a rational explanation. Often there is. But sometimes these rational explanations require more credulity than the miracles themselves.

In fact it was partly the search for rational explanations of the miracles that launched the quest for the historical Jesus in the eighteenth century. Up to that point the miracles were—had to be—taken at face value. The Gospels were infallible Scripture, and Jesus the incarnate Second Person of the Trinity. No further explanation was needed. But as the Enlightenment began to scatter its beams of reason, it cast doubt on supernatural explanations of all kinds.

As it turned out, the rational explanations left something to be desired too. They reach their fullest expression in a life of Jesus written by one Heinrich Eberhard Gottlob Paulus. Its nearly twelve hundred pages were published in 1828. Paulus can explain all the miracles simply and naturalistically. The resurrections that Jesus performs are simply "deliverances from premature burial." The Jews buried their dead within three hours, Paulus claimed. Thus they would have inevitably buried any number of people who were in comas or trances. The Jewish love of miracles "caused everything to be ascribed immediately to Deity, and secondary causes to be overlooked; consequently no thought was unfortunately given to the question of how to prevent these horrible cases of premature burial from taking place!" Jesus, through his unusual insight, simply rescued and revived a few of these unfortunate individuals.

Jesus's own resurrection happened the same way. He died unusually quickly for someone who was crucified (in a mere three hours). But in fact he had merely gone into a cataleptic trance. The cool tomb and the aromatic unguents revived him. He stripped off his shroud and found some gardener's clothes that he put on, which explains why Mary Magdalene thought he was the gardener (John 20:15).

You get the idea. Paulus's explanations may even be right in some instances, but taken as a whole they seem forced.

At the beginning of this book I mentioned the work of David Friedrich Strauss, who took the inquiry into the historical Jesus to the next stage. In his magnum opus, published in 1834–35, Strauss argued that many of these stories were simply myths that became attached to Jesus's memory after he died. Practically everyone who has followed after Strauss has built upon this insight in one way or another. No one can dismiss this claim completely.

To begin with, charismatic figures tend to inspire stories of miraculous events and occurrences. You don't need to go far afield to confirm this idea. Just read some of the amazing stories of encounters with the shade of Elvis Presley—his appearances, his healings, his words of inspiration. Which shows that in the United States today, people's minds work much as they did in first-century Palestine. Why should we expect otherwise?

Furthermore, some of the miracle stories in the Gospels are clearly written with symbolic meanings in mind. This is particularly true in the Gospel of John. The story of the wedding in Cana, for example, employs a profound symbolism of several layers of the inner life, represented by the stone cisterns, the water, and finally the wine into which it is changed. (I will say more about this in chapter 15.) If there is a factual kernel to this story, it's probably tiny.

Thus we seem to be justified in merely tossing away all the miracle stories as superstitious fictions. And yet, I think, this is taking a step too far. For more than one reason.

Recently I was watching one of the countless TV documentaries on Jesus. A scholar—I forget which one—said, "In those days, miracle workers were a dime a dozen." And here is C. H. Dodd on the miracles in John's Gospel: "A serious enquirer in the Hellenistic world, though he might be impressed by such miraculous cures, would not be ready to find in them evidence such as are here advanced. After all, such cures were frequently reported." I could find similar statements in many other scholarly works.

What could possibly have been going on? So far from being fictions, *miracles in Jesus's time were commonplace.*

I don't think this fact can be explained away with the usual rationalizations (people were uneducated, superstitious, and so on). There is too much evidence to the contrary, even from educated and enlightened ancient sources. Up to a point the miracle workers could have been performing sleight-of-hand magic, but sleight-of-hand magic can't explain actual occurrences of healing.

Something else must have been going on.

I believe it was. But it raises an extremely difficult subject—so difficult that, to my knowledge, no one yet has gone into it with any depth.

You may have heard the expression *consensus reality*. Psychologist Charles Tart uses a stronger one in his book *Waking Up: Overcoming the Obstacles to Human Potential*. He calls it *consensus trance*.

It is the state of waking sleep in which practically all of us go through our lives.

There are many dimensions to this idea, but let's start here: Tart is an expert in hypnosis. He points out that you can hypnotize people to perceive things that are not there, and *not* to perceive things that *are* there. A woman is hypnotized and told that a mosquito is around. She starts swatting and itching. But there is no mosquito.

Another man is hypnotized and given a different suggestion. A bottle of ammonia is passed in front of his nose, and he can't smell it.

Formal hypnosis is a limited procedure. The session lasts for maybe an hour, and the subject, usually a grown adult, goes home and lives his life the way he always has. The suggestion is not very powerful and wears off.

Consensus trance is something very different. It is imposed on us when we are extremely helpless and innocent, and it is reinforced in all sorts of ways that are frankly coercive. As Tart points out, these methods are involuntary. The subject did not ask to be hypnotized. They use physical force, and also use love and validation as rewards. Guilt is also used.

This trance is induced in us from infancy, by our parents and by everyone around us. From then on, it continues relentlessly. Tart writes, "Consensus trance induction starts in conditions that give far more power and influence to the cultural hypnotists than is ever given in ordinary hypnosis induction." It takes a village—or rather a society—to hypnotize a child.

Part of this hypnosis involves beliefs about what is real and what is not real. Cultures implant very different messages into their members about this matter. For my sons in middle-class America, zombies are funny cartoon characters. In Haiti, zombies are *not* funny cartoon characters. They are taken very seriously.

A zombie is a dead person who is buried and resurrected, but who remains in a catatonic state, subject to the control of someone else. There are the usual theories about this: social conditioning, drugs, and the like. No doubt they are valid to some degree. Nonetheless, in Haiti zombies are real. Cases are reported, and there is even a law on the books that forbids turning someone into a zombie. Even in our increasingly benighted time, a legislator who proposed such a law in this country would be a laughingstock.

Similarly, when I read accounts of life in Africa, I have the impression of people who dwell in a megalopolis of spirits—good, bad, ancestors, enemies.

You could say that they have been hypnotized to believe in, even see, these things. Or have we, in our culture, been hypnotized into *not* seeing them?

In first-century Palestine, the miraculous was far more vivid and present than it is in technology-infested America. Does that mean that they imagined all sorts of miracles in their superstitious blindness? Or does it mean that, because there was a collective belief that they *could* happen, they actually *did* happen?

Thinking about these issues in any depth is like taking a psychedelic drug.

In any event, I believe that, at the very least, it's best to avoid smug and obvious answers. They merely reinforce our particular form of collective trance.

Besides, even in our materialistic flatland, miracles do happen. Even medicine admits that healings take place for reasons that medicine cannot explain. It has grudgingly given them the name of "spontaneous remissions," invoking a mysterious occult force known as the "placebo effect."

To sum up: I don't believe that the miracles of Jesus happened exactly and literally as the Gospels describe. Strauss was right: myth and legend do intrude. Furthermore, there is an element of symbolism (particularly in the Gospel of John) that needs to be taken into account. But I do think we need to avoid the credulity both of blind belief and of blind skepticism.

The Messiah's Passion and Death

We now come to a long-deferred issue: who was Jesus, and who did he think he was?

Ultimately we can't answer these questions. We have no access to Jesus's thought processes. Moreover, his statements about himself are very cryptic. And we have no final criterion to tell us which of them are authentic and which were added later by a church that was groping with these issues itself.

Take this verse, beloved by fundamentalists: "I am the way, the truth, and the life: no man cometh unto the Father, but by me" (John 4:6). This verse might mean that Jesus is the only source of salvation, and so it is taken by many people. But most scholars do not believe this statement is genuine. They don't believe that Jesus said this, or anything like this. As I've pointed out, they don't think *any* of these statements in the Gospel of John are authentic.

So if we take all these out, what does it do to our understanding of who Jesus was?

As I've said, I think there is good reason to believe that Jesus was believed to be descended from David. It is possible that he claimed to be the Messiah, and on the whole, I tend to think he did. But it is impossible to say definitively. Why? Because, as I've said, a great deal depends on the authenticity of verses whose authenticity is very much in dispute.

For example, according to Mark, during Jesus's trial, the high priest asks him, "Art thou the Christ [i.e., the Messiah], the son of the Blessed? And Jesus said, I am: and ye shall see the Son of man sitting on the right hand of power, and coming in the clouds of heaven" (Mark 14:61–62. I will put off the question of who the Son of Man was until chapter 14).

If this passage is authentic, or is based on an authentic anecdote, Jesus claimed he was the Messiah. But many scholars don't think it is. The Jesus Seminar scholars point out that Jesus's answers in parallel passages in Matthew (27:11) and Luke (22:70) are more ambiguous and evasive, and probably closer to the truth.

It's also possible that Jesus allowed others to *believe* he was the Messiah. In Mark 8:27–30, he asks his disciples who they think he is. Peter says, "Thou art the Christ." Jesus neither affirms nor denies this. Instead, again rather ambiguously, he charges them "that they should tell no man of him."

If this passage is authentic (and the previous one is *not*), Jesus may have allowed his disciples to believe that he was the Messiah without coming out and saying so. But again, the Jesus Seminar concludes simply that "this is a stylized scene shaped by Christian motifs"—meaning that it's a story about Jesus made up by the Christian community after his death.

I mention the opinion of the Jesus Seminar here not because I agree with them, but to show how much depends on the authenticity of verses like these. And that is a matter about which there is very little agreement.

Originally the Messiah simply meant the "anointed"—the kings and priests of Israel. After the Babylonian Exile, it came to mean a figure who would fulfill Israel's hopes of deliverance. The prophets focused these hopes on a restored house of David: "And I will pour upon the house of David, and upon the inhabitants of Jerusalem, the spirit of grace and of supplications" (Zechariah 12:10).

As a matter of fact, scholars aren't completely clear about how the Jews conceived of the Messiah in Jesus's time. That's because the texts from that period don't mention him very often. James H. Charlesworth, a professor at Princeton Theological Seminary, says, "it is impossible to derive a systematic description of the functions of the Messiah from the extant references to him" in the literature of Jesus's time.

In the final estimate, if you remove Jesus's messianic claims entirely, it becomes much harder to explain how the priests were able to put him to death. Their *motive* is quite clear: they were angered by his sharp condemnations. But this was not grounds for capital punishment. It could well have been Jesus's messianic claims that enabled them to have him convicted of a capital crime.

If Jesus made such claims, it is almost impossible to believe that he did so in order to provoke insurrection. In his way Jesus was less political than John the Baptist, since John provoked Herod, tetrarch of Galilee, by criticizing his unlawful marriage. There is no indication that Jesus did anything like this.

Jesus's messianic claims were evidently spiritual, as the Gospels say. He may not have actually said, "My kingdom is not of this world," as John writes (John 18:36). But it must have been what he believed. As we shall discover, it also jibes perfectly with who the Son of Man was supposed to be.

In any case, Mark says that the priests and scribes assembled for a nighttime trial in which they convicted Jesus of blasphemy. Scholars have questioned whether this trial really took place. From what is known of Jewish trial procedure of that period, the Sanhedrin (the supreme Jewish council) did not meet this way—at night, for example.

In that case Jesus's trial can only be explained by saying that it was conducted irregularly and illegally. If you want to deny this possibility, you would have to argue that the priests and scribes of Christ's time were above such base practices. But all the evidence—from Josephus as well as the New Testament—suggests that in fact they were more than capable of such things. And certainly a history of legal irregularities over the centuries would fill many volumes.

Mark, like the other Gospels, suggests that Pontius Pilate, the supreme secular authority in Judea, did not want to crucify Jesus and tried to prevent it. This claim too has been questioned on the grounds that Pilate, by all accounts, was unusually cruel and harsh. He would be removed from office in AD 36 for suppressing a revolt in Samaria with unusual brutality. Because the Romans were ordinarily brutal enough, we can only guess what this must have meant.

Admittedly there is not much evidence for Pilate's clemency in any other situations. But this doesn't mean that he always acted in an unfailingly brutal way. No one behaves in ways that are completely consistent, and that is as true for cruel people as it is for most of us.

Furthermore, if Pilate knew that Jesus was not a threat to Roman rule (which he could easily have known from his own spies and informers), he would have no reason to execute him and at least two good reasons *not* to execute him. In the first place, Roman law may have been harsh, but in its way and for its time, it was fair. And it was against the law to execute an innocent man. In the second place, Pilate would not have liked the idea of jumping when the priests snapped their fingers. He might have resisted for this reason alone.

My account above does not, it is true, agree with many scholarly theories today. But they tend to fall apart on their own. Some say Jesus was crucified as a political agitator. In that case, where are all his political remarks? They must have been lost, or suppressed! But by this reasoning I could argue anything. I could argue that Jesus worshipped a monkey god but that all his statements to this effect have been lost.

Others claim that Jesus was a simple teacher of wisdom who never had a nasty word for anybody. But if this is true, how did he fall afoul of the authorities?

To restate the picture I have sketched above: Jesus infuriated the religious authorities by condemning their greed and hypocrisy. They hated him and wanted to have him destroyed. They had him convicted on the grounds that he claimed to be the Messiah (which quite possibly he did) and therefore an insurrectionary (which he almost certainly was not). Pilate did not believe the priests, but in the end he let them have their way.

This theory has two advantages over many of the others that are now circulating. In the first place, it is coherent and understandable in the context. In the second place, instead of ruling out huge pieces of evidence—large portions of the Gospels—it tries to preserve and account for as much of them as possible.

I'm not taking this approach out of reverence for sacred scripture. I'm doing it because, to my mind, it is the most intellectually honest and thorough way of dealing with historical evidence.

But it would be hard to account for *all* the evidence. As Samuel Beckett noticed, only one of the four Gospels speaks of a thief on the cross being saved. Although I think the core narrative stands up to investigation, any number of differences and discrepancies still remain. Many, even most, of them must have been due to simple misremembering and to the mutations that stories undergo in an oral tradition.

The Empty Tomb

By all accounts, Jesus suffered and died under Pontius Pilate. Of course the story does not end there. There is still the climactic moment of Jesus's life: the resurrection.

To rise from the dead in bodily form goes about as far against commonsense wisdom as you can get. Once Strauss set out his theory of myth, it became natural to say that the resurrection was nothing more than that: a myth that became attached to Jesus's memory after his life. Some scholars still make this kind of argument. They might claim, for example, that originally the followers of Jesus recognized his symbolic presence in the Eucharistic meal, and this later mutated into a tale of a literal resurrection.

Views of this kind have serious problems. The most serious is that they can't account for the evidence: a number of Jesus's followers claimed to have seen him after his death. Paul mentions this fact in a passage that I quoted earlier in this book. I will quote it again:

> For I delivered unto you first of all that which I received, how that Christ died for our sins according to the scriptures;
> And that he was buried, and that he rose again the third day according to the scriptures:
> And that he was seen of Cephas, then of the twelve:
> After that, he was seen of above five hundred brethren at once; of whom the greater part remain unto this present, but some are fallen asleep.
> After that, he was seen of James; then of all the apostles.
> And last of all he was seen of me also, as of one born out of due time.
> *(1 Corinthians 15:3–7)*

Paul is writing sometime in the decade of the 50s, well within the lifetime of Christ's disciples. He has heard of their visions of the risen Jesus firsthand, and connects his own vision with them.

In short, by the earliest known account, Jesus's disciples claimed to have seen him alive after he died.

There is another reason for paying some heed to the testimony for the resurrection. Otherwise it becomes impossible to understand how the Christian movement caught on so electrically and spread so fast. If the crucifixion really had been the end of the story, Christianity would have fizzled out. Jesus's life would have been a failure. The disciples would have gone home to Galilee broken and defeated—just as the Gospels describe them before Christ's appearance.

If you deny that the disciples saw the risen Jesus, you have to make up some alternative story about why Jesus became seen as divine or semi-divine more or less immediately after his death. And those alternative stories are universally weak and implausible.

It's true that the stories in the Gospels have difficulties of their own. We have already seen how Mark, the oldest and most historically accurate of the Gospels, simply ends with an empty tomb. The women who have come to anoint Jesus find he is not there. A "young man" (another angel) tells him that he is risen. They flee in terror. That is the end of Mark's story.

The other Gospels tell of Jesus's encounters with disciples. These stories are perplexing. For one thing, they don't resemble one another.

In Matthew, Jesus appears to the disciples as a whole and charges them to spread his teachings to "all nations."

In Luke, Jesus appears to two disciples on the road to Emmaus. They don't even know who he is at first. But after he shows his wounds and proves that he has a physical body by eating some fish and honey, they recognize him. In the end Jesus is "parted from them, and carried up to heaven" (Luke 24:51).

In John, Mary Magdalene sees Jesus near the tomb, but she too fails to recognize him. He has to identify himself to her. He later appears to the rest of the disciples, helps Peter with his fishing, and tells the "beloved disciple"—usually identified as John—that he, John, will "tarry till I come."

These stories do share some features. They say the risen Jesus has a physical body: after all, the body is missing from the tomb. But this body has some unique properties. Jesus seems to be able to change his shape enough to disguise his identity. He can also materialize and vanish at will. Apart from these details, the stories are all different, and there is almost no overlap between them.

Scholars generally don't put much credence in these episodes. At the same time they have to admit that the rise of Christianity is impossible without the belief in the resurrection. Paul puts it at the center of Christian teaching: "If Christ be not risen, then is our preaching vain, and your faith is also vain" (1 Corinthians 15:4).

One of the best discussions of this problem that I know of appears in the recent book *How Jesus Became God* by the New Testament scholar Bart D. Ehrman. He argues that even from a purely historical point of view, we have to accept that the disciples had some kind of experience of seeing the risen Jesus. But that, according to Ehrman, is as far as the historian can go. The historian can say that by all accounts the disciples had some experience like this, but he cannot say whether or not that experience was real. At that point he would start to trespass into matters of faith.

I'm willing to go a little further than Ehrman does. People have encounters with dead friends and relatives all the time. In the 1990s, I was editor of *Gnosis*, a now-defunct magazine on mysticism. We often got articles from people about their encounters of this kind—appearances from parents, friends, children. *Gnosis* didn't publish articles like these, so I almost always sent them back, but they kept coming anyway. I imagine their writers didn't know what else to do with them.

I have also known people who have had such experiences. One friend of mine says his father appeared to him after his death to tell him to wear a suit to the funeral.

You can believe that people have these experiences without committing yourself to a belief in an afterlife. Skeptics, in fact, love to write them off as hallucinations laced with wishful thinking.

Personally, I am not so sure. But this issue takes us into the realm of parapsychology, which is outside the scope of this book.

At the very least it makes sense to assume that the disciples did have some visions of the risen Jesus, whatever those visions may have been. These experiences were enough like one another to be mutually recognizable. The disciples were even able to accept Paul's vision as genuine, although Paul had not known Jesus and had persecuted his followers.

A mainstream scholar can accept the resurrection as subjective experience, but not as objective event. Hence scholars tend to reject another central part of the resurrection story: the empty tomb.

However you want to interpret it, people see ghosts all the time. These ghosts are disembodied. They are ethereal and sometimes transparent. Ghosts do not have bodies as living humans do.

The Gospels, on the other hand, say that the risen Jesus did have a body of some kind—and that his physical body was missing, suggesting that it was transformed in some kind of way.

Why should anyone doubt the empty tomb story? It appears in all four Gospels, including Mark, the earliest. Thus from a documentary point of view, it's both early and multiply attested—meaning that, all else being equal, you have to take it seriously as a part of an authentic tradition.

This fact takes the discussion into a whole new arena. Scholars may admit that people might have had a vision of a recently deceased man (which is fairly common). But they balk at the story of the empty tomb, because that would mean he *did* physically rise.

Ehrman puts the empty tomb among one of the many question marks that hang over the resurrection. Of course he is right—at least until some startling new evidence comes to the surface. Which isn't terribly likely.

If Jesus didn't rise physically, what happened to his body? Some scholars doubt not only that there was an empty tomb, but that there was a tomb at all. John Dominic Crossan says Jesus's body was eaten by dogs. Bart Ehrman is more cautious: "My view now is that we do not know, and cannot know, what actually happened to Jesus's body. But it is absolutely true that as far as we can tell from all the surviving evidence, what normally happened to a criminal's body is that it was left to decompose and serve as food for scavenging animals."

Nevertheless, this is not what the sources say about Jesus. They say that his body was taken down and buried in a tomb belonging to one Joseph of Arimathea. They also say that the tomb was empty three days later, and that a risen Jesus, who seemed to possess some sort of body, appeared to his disciples afterward.

What does a conventional scholar do with this kind of story? It's one thing to believe that people have visions of recently deceased friends and relatives. That's fairly common. But people don't see dead relatives who have risen from their graves.

To speak personally again, there is an old maxim that I take very seriously: Neither accept nor reject.

You don't have to believe that such things actually happened. After all, you weren't there, and we don't even have any accounts surviving that were written by anyone who was. I certainly don't think you have to believe these things to gain your soul's eternal salvation.

On the other hand, you're not forced to the opposite conclusion either. Anyone with any sense knows that the world is full of things that are not explained and cannot be explained by conventional means. To deny this fact is to become a true believer of another stripe.

There is another thing to consider: Jesus remains a living presence. Over the centuries he has appeared to many people. Many accounts witness to this fact. Some of them are clumsy and incoherent, and not a few sound frankly insane. But not all of them. Here is one, by author Dan Wakefield:

One night when I am nine years old I go to bed, say the Lord's Prayer, and before going to sleep (I am clearly and vividly awake during this whole experience), I feel or sense—I experience—my whole body filling with light. The light is white and so bright that it seems almost silver. It is not accompanied by any voice or sound, but I know quite clearly the light is Christ, the presence of Jesus Christ. I am not transported anywhere, I am all the time in my room at the top of the stairs in our house at 6129 Winthrop, Indianapolis, Indiana, a place as familiar as my own hand. Everything is the same as always, my bed and the desk across from it, the pictures on the wall of my favorite football heroes, like Tommy Harmon of Michigan. Everything is normal and solid and real, the only thing different is the Light, and after it has infused me, maybe I too am different, or in some way changed—not better or brighter or nicer but simply changed, the way a person is changed by deep experience, altered in how the world is perceived, more open to the unexplainable, the great mysteries, the gift of grace. The light is not frightening to me as a child, but reassuring, like a blessing. It is so real that in fact it seems today like the very bedrock of my existence.

Was this an encounter with the risen Jesus? I don't know. It's Wakefield who connects this light with Jesus. For my part, I would simply say that these encounters with the risen Christ, past and present, are part of the evidence and must be taken seriously, just as all religious experience must be taken seriously.

The Birth of the Church

JESUS REMAINS A mysterious figure. There is much we do not know and will not know about him. Some of this enigma is, as it were, journalistic: many facts are missing. Some of it, though, has to do with Jesus himself, who was a figure of such depth that in the end it's impossible to explain him through the usual attempts at psychohistory. All great religious figures have some of this mystery.

As little as we know about Jesus, we know even less about his disciples. In fact we know almost nothing about them. In the Gospels, they almost always serve as a foil for Jesus's teaching. Often he insists they are misunderstanding him. They are listed as twelve, but the names on the various lists of these twelve don't completely match. We hear very little about them after Jesus's death.

There is, of course, the book of Acts, the second half of a literary pair written by Luke. For me, Acts has always been the least satisfying of biblical books. In the first place, despite Luke's best efforts, none of the disciples has anything like the power and charisma of Jesus, so after the

Gospels their stories seem lackluster, even with their healings and miraculous escapes from prison.

In the second place, Acts doesn't tell us much about the apostles (as the disciples are called after Jesus charges them to preach the Gospel). Peter and John appear, as does Philip, who baptizes an Ethiopian eunuch. About James, the brother of John, we learn only that Herod killed him "with the sword" (Acts 12:2). In Acts 13 and for the rest of the book, the focus shifts almost exclusively to Paul.

In fact, if you were to read the New Testament cover to cover, you would conclude that it was about two men: Jesus and Paul. Apart from them, there is very little. Only some general epistles (attributed to the apostles James, John, Peter, and Jude, although they almost certainly did not write them) and the bizarre but magnificent book of Revelation.

Eusebius's *Ecclesiastical History*, written around AD 320, is one of the most important sources for the early centuries of Christianity. Much of it covers the first century, which occupies four out of ten books. It's as fascinating as it is valuable.

Eusebius sets out a marvelous array of lore and tradition. There is the story of Abgar, king of Edessa, who sends an invitation to Jesus to come and cure him of a disease. Eusebius includes both Abgar's letter and Jesus's response, which says, "When I have been taken up I will send you one of my disciples to cure you." Eventually the disciple Thaddaeus goes to Abgar and heals him.

Eusebius also tells how the emperor Tiberius received the news of the crucifixion, which took place during his reign. Evidently Pilate had sent him a report of the crucifixion and resurrection. Tiberius wanted to have Jesus declared a god, but the Roman Senate voted against it.

We also learn that John the beloved disciple and evangelist settled in Ephesus, in Asia Minor, and lived there until the reign of Trajan (AD 98–117).

These bits of history, and others like them, have their own magic. I read them and I can't help thinking there is some truth behind at least a few of them, but what that truth is would be extremely hard to determine.

But here is what scholars think: The letters between Jesus and Abgar are later forgeries. Tiberius never heard a word about the crucifixion, which would have been an extremely minor and unimportant event in his realm. John may have settled in Ephesus and lived to a long age, but then again he may not.

The apostles thus immediately fade into the background—so far, in fact, that *there are few if any firsthand descriptions of the apostles themselves.* Everything that comes through is at second or third hand.

Here's one example. It's one of very few stories of the apostles in which anyone claims to have seen or talked to one of them face to face. It comes from Irenaeus of Lyons, writing around 180. He tells the story of a bishop named Polycarp, who allegedly knew the apostle John. It involves an encounter between John and a heretic named Cerinthus, who supposedly taught that the coming kingdom of God would be a time of sexual freedom: "John the apostle went into the bath-house to take a bath, but when he found that Cerinthus was inside he leapt from the spot and ran for the door, as he could not endure to be under the same roof. He urged his companions to do the same, calling out: 'Let us get out of here, for fear the place falls in, now that Cerinthus, the enemy of the truth, is inside.'"

This claims to be an eyewitness account of one of the apostles—John, according to tradition the one who lived the longest. But it comes through Irenaeus, writing about Polycarp, who evidently lived into the mid-second century. (There is a short but vivid account of his martyrdom, again not an eyewitness account, called *The Martyrdom of Polycarp.*) The story about Cerinthus is thirdhand. We have practically no firsthand anecdotes of the apostles themselves.

Even including these, Eusebius has remarkably little to say about any of the apostles. Yet in his day there was an intense interest in them, and Eusebius had access to a wide variety of sources, at least for his time. Thus very little material about them must have come down to Eusebius in the fourth century.

As a matter of fact there is a great deal more about the apostles. I pick up Wilhelm Schneemelcher's *New Testament Apocrypha* (a standard work) and look at its table of contents. There are all sorts of Acts of the various apostles, modeled on or inspired by Acts in the New Testament. If you like you can read the Acts of Andrew, John, Paul, Peter, and Thomas—and of the twelve apostles as a whole. There is *The Passions of Bartholomew,* a *Martyrdom of Peter,* and a *Martyrdom of Matthew.* Some of these have survived. Others are known only as names.

To my knowledge, practically no scholar sees any of these texts as having any value whatsoever in telling us what the apostles said or did. None of these works is earlier than the second century—a hundred years at least after the apostles' lifetimes. Many are centuries later. Some seem to be variations on the romantic adventure novel (a genre that existed in classical antiquity).

Maybe I misspoke when I said earlier that not much is known about the apostles. Actually a great deal is known. But almost none of what is known is believed.

The Age of the New Testament

There is, by the way, a big gap between the death of Jesus around AD 30 and the surviving texts about him. To see the size of this gap, look at the sidebar on pages 170–71. It gives the dates of the New Testament books in the rough order of their composition. For the dates, I'm using Raymond E. Brown's *Introduction to the New Testament.* Brown, a Catholic priest, was among the most respected New Testament scholars of his generation.

DATES OF NEW TESTAMENT TEXTS

GOSPELS

Mark: 60–75, "most likely between 68 and 73"
Matthew: 80–90, "give or take a decade"
Luke-Acts: 85, "give or take five to ten years"
John: 80–110

EPISTLES OF PAUL

1 Thessalonians: 50–51, though possibly 41–43
Galatians: 54–57
Philemon: 55–63
Philippians: 56–63
1 Corinthians: 56–57
2 Corinthians: 55–57
Romans: 55–58

EPISTLES ATTRIBUTED TO PAUL

2 Thessalonians: after 100 (if not genuine); 51–52 (if genuine)
Colossians: after 80 (if not genuine); 54–63 (if genuine)
Ephesians: after 90 (if not genuine); 60s (if genuine)
Titus: c.100
1 Timothy: before 100
2 Timothy: around 100
Hebrews: 60s or more likely 80s

PASTORAL EPISTLES

1 Peter: 70–90

James: 70–110, "most likely in the 80s or 90s"

Jude: Unknown; probably 90–100

2 Peter: c.130

Revelation: 92–96

Source: Raymond E. Brown, *An Introduction to the New Testament* (New York: Doubleday, 1996).

This list doesn't represent the views of all scholars, because they don't all agree. Much depends on whether a given text was really written by the man it's attributed to. An enormous number of things come into play in deciding this question. They include writing style, subject matter, audience addressed, and many other considerations.

The seven letters of Paul (as given here) are the ones more or less unanimously accepted as genuine. Scholars believe that the others attributed to him were written by someone else. There is some dispute about 2 Thessalonians. Opinion is somewhat divided, although the majority probably don't think the letter is actually by Paul. Opinion about the other letters is far more consistent. The vast majority of scholars don't think Ephesians or Colossians were really written by Paul. Almost no scholars believe that 1 and 2 Timothy or Titus were written by him.

You'll find different dates for these texts in many scholarly works. The more theologically conservative the scholar, the *earlier* the date is likely to be. That's because conservative (evangelical Protestant) scholars want to see as close a connection between Jesus and the New Testament texts (especially the Gospels) as they can. Furthermore, they want to believe that the New Testament texts are to be taken at face value—including their claims of composition. So they're more likely to believe that the disputed epistles of Paul were written by him.

The more theologically liberal the scholar, the *later* the date is likely to be. Liberal scholars want to see as large a gap as they can between Jesus and the writings about him. That's because liberal scholarship tends to assume that much or practically all of what is in the New Testament reflects later theological agendas rather than historical fact. Liberal and mainstream scholars also tend to discount any possibility of supernatural things such as miracles and prophecies.

Let's take the Gospel of Mark. The date I have given—"most likely between 68 and 73," according to Brown—represents a rough mainstream consensus. We've already seen why. Mark mentions the sack of the Temple, and the sack of the Temple took place in 70: "Seest thou these great buildings? there shall not be left one stone after another, that shall not be thrown down" (Mark 13:2). For the mainstream scholar, this is a *vaticinium ex eventu*, a prophecy after the event, because the mainstream scholar either does not believe in prophecy or at any rate cannot permit himself to presuppose it for the purposes of dating.

But then I visit an evangelical Christian website, Theopedia. It says, "Though it is impossible to be sure about the composition date" for Mark, "evidence points to the latter part of the seventh decade, likely after Peter's martyrdom in AD 64, but probably before the destruction of Jerusalem in AD 70." This conservative website has less difficulty with the belief that Jesus, God incarnate, may have prophesied the Temple's destruction. Also against mainstream opinion, Theopedia even suggests that Matthew might be dated as early as 50, "when the church was largely Jewish and the gospel was preached to the Jews only." This would put Matthew that much further ahead of the events that it seems to be discussing.

As you can see, the arguments become quite intricate. In any case, I have never read anything by any scholar that was not, to some degree, conditioned by his or her own ideology.

At any rate, the list here represents a moderate mainstream view. One thing is obvious right away. Contrary to what many people assume, *the Gospels were not written first. The epistles of Paul were written first.* Paul shows no knowledge whatsoever of any of the Gospels. They hadn't been written yet.

The latest New Testament text is 2 Peter, written probably seventy years after the death of the real Peter. Why? For one thing, 2 Peter addresses an issue that didn't come up in the time of Peter himself: why the Second Coming was delayed. Assume that Peter died in Nero's persecution of 64, as traditionally believed. At that point expectation of the coming end was still intense. This is obvious in Paul's thought. It relies heavily on this expectation, and according to tradition, Paul died in the same persecution. So even up to the time the apostles died, whether by martyrdom or from old age, people still believed that Jesus was coming back very soon.

But when 2 Peter was written, people were starting to wonder. The writer says, "There shall come in the last days scoffers, . . . saying, Where is the promise of his coming? for since the fathers fell asleep, all things continue as they were from the beginning of the creation" (2 Peter 3:3–4).

Who were the "fathers"? The apostles. At the time of this letter, they were all long gone. Of course that would include Peter himself. This is one (but only one) reason that this letter could not have been written by Peter.

James, the First Pope

There is one apostolic figure who does surface, although dimly—James the brother of Jesus. He is in many ways the most enigmatic figure of all. He is not one of the twelve and is never listed among them. He is mentioned in Mark as Jesus's brother (Mark 6:3), but does not otherwise appear in any of the Gospels.

Admittedly the picture is confusing. There are three Jameses at least: James the son of Zebedee, James the son of Alphaeus (both of whom are among the twelve), as well as James the brother of Jesus. "James" is an Anglicized version of the Hebrew *Ya'akov* or "Jacob," rendered as *Iákōbos* in the Greek of the New Testament. Obviously it was a very common name.

When Jesus is alive, his brother James is completely in the background. We read, "Neither did his brethren believe in him" (John 7:5). James is not listed as an exception.

After Jesus's death, the picture changes completely. In Acts, without any explanation, James the brother of Jesus is head of the Jerusalem church. In Acts 15, it is he who gives the final ruling on whether Gentile converts need to observe the Jewish Law (they don't). Thus *James was the first head of the Christian church. Not Peter.* Jerome, in the fifth century, confirms this by writing that "James, who is called the brother of the Lord, . . . after our Lord's passion [was] at once ordained by the apostles bishop of Jerusalem."

We don't hear much else about James. In the passage from 1 Corinthians that I cited in the previous chapter, Paul says that Jesus appeared to James, but James was by no means the first to see him.

That's all the New Testament has to say about James. But there is one intriguing verse from the *Gospel of Thomas*: "The disciples said to Jesus: We know that you will depart from us. Who is to be our leader? Jesus said to them: Wherever you are, go to James the righteous, for whose sake heaven and earth came into being."

Josephus also calls him James the Righteous. In fact he suggests that the disasters of the war with the Romans were visited upon the Jews "in requital for James the Righteous, who was a brother of Jesus known as Christ, for though he was the most righteous of men, the Jews put him to death."

Jerome, in the fifth century, tells us a little more. He quotes a second-century historian named Hegesippus: "After the apostles, James the brother of the Lord surnamed the Just was made head of the Church at Jerusalem. Many indeed are called James. This one was holy from his mother's womb.

He drank neither wine nor strong drink, ate no flesh, never shaved or anointed himself with ointment or bathed. He alone had the privilege of entering the Holy of Holies, since indeed he did not use woolen vestments but linen and went alone into the temple and prayed in behalf of the people, insomuch that his knees were reputed to have acquired the hardness of camels' knees."

Jerome also quotes from the lost *Gospel to the Hebrews*, probably from the first century:

> The Lord, after he had given his grave clothes to the servant of the priest, appeared to James, for James had sworn that he would not eat bread from that hour in which he had drunk the cup of the Lord until he should see him rising again from those who sleep. And again, a little later, it says, "Bring a table and bread," said the Lord. And immediately it is added, "He took bread and blessed and broke and gave to James the Just and said to him, 'My brother, eat your bread, for the son of man is risen from among those that sleep.'" And so he ruled the church of Jerusalem thirty years, that is, until the seventh year of Nero [61 or 62].

Josephus also says that James was stoned to death at the instigation of the priest Ananas in AD 62 (see the passage on page 97) on the grounds that he had violated the Jewish Law. One story says that James got up on the wall of the Temple, preached Jesus as the Son of Man, and was stoned to death for it. It adds portentously that the Roman invasion took place immediately afterward. (Actually the invasion did not take place until AD 68.) This story appears in Eusebius's *Ecclesiastical History*, written in the fourth century.

Apart from speculation—some of it wild—this is the sum of what we know about James the brother of Jesus.

One other passage might shed light on James and his status. It is also from Eusebius. He is quoting from one Africanus, who had written a letter trying to harmonize the genealogies of Matthew and Luke. It is a fascinating passage:

Herod [the Great], who had no drop of Israelitish blood in his veins and was stung by the consciousness of his base origin, burnt the registers of their [i.e., the Hebrew] families, thinking that he would appear nobly born if no one was able by reference to public documents to trace his line back to the patriarchs or proselytes.... A few careful people had private records of their own, having either remembered the names or recovered them from copies, and took pride in preserving the memory of their aristocratic origin. These included the people ... known as the Desposyni [those "belonging to the Lord"] because of their relationship to the Saviour's family. From the Jewish villages of Nazareth and Cochaba they passed through the rest of the country, expounding the genealogy discussed above.

This passage, by the way, is one reason I take the story of Jesus's descent from David—or of the *belief* in Jesus's descent—more seriously than many scholars do.

The text also suggests that in the earliest Christian communities Jesus's family members enjoyed very high status. If so, having James as the head of the church after Jesus's death makes perfect sense.

Later, by the way, Eusebius says that Jesus's family (specifically the descendants of his brother Jude) was almost wiped out in a persecution by the emperor Domitian, who reigned from AD 81 to 96. Nevertheless, they lived into the reign of the emperor Trajan (98–117).

By this account, Jesus's family survived into the second century AD. After that they vanish from history.

The Apostolic Faith

Despite their shadowy presence, the apostles take on new importance in the early second century. Various authorities, mostly bishops, write epistles proclaiming something called the "apostolic faith" that is being threatened by all sorts of heretics who believe all sorts of things. The church's only possible hope is to cling to the original, primitive faith of the apostles.

If you want an early version of what this was—or was thought to be—you can read a short text called *The Teaching of the Twelve Apostles.* In Greek the word for "teaching" is *didachē* (pronounced did-ah-*khay*), so scholars usually refer to this text as the *Didache.* It probably goes back, at least in part, to the early second century. But the *Didache* was never regarded as an inspired text. It was lost for many centuries before being rediscovered in 1873.

The *Didache* is short. It fills seven and a half pages in a paperback edition of early Christian writings that I have. The first part sets out the Two Ways: the Way of Life and the Way of Death. Among other things, it commands Christians to "practise no magic, sorcery, abortion, or infanticide." (This is, by the way, the first condemnation of abortion that I know of in the Christian tradition. No one says anything about it anywhere in the New Testament.)

The second part of the *Didache* contains directions for performing baptism and the Eucharist and for receiving prophets—who in those days were still very much a part of the Christian community. It says, "If anyone comes and instructs you on the foregoing lines, make him welcome. But should the instructor himself then turn round and introduce teaching of a different and subversive nature, pay no attention to him." But it does not say what might constitute different and subversive teaching. In fact the *Didache* says almost nothing about doctrine at all.

The *Didache* comes from an era when certain elements of the church, especially some bishops, were feeling the need to formulate and solidify the central doctrines of Christianity in the face of what came to be called heresies. "Heresy," *haíresis* in Greek, is derived from the verb *hairéō,* "to take." Originally it simply meant "choice." Later it came to mean "sect," and still later a sect at odds with the nascent Catholic church.

Here is the picture that the church has promoted and which even scholars accepted until less than a century ago: The Christian church, founded by Christ himself and led by the apostles, was a unified and harmonious body throughout the first century. But by the beginning of the second century, various heretical groups rose up. (The Gnostics are the best-known.) The bishops of the true church had to fight these heresies and preserve the apostolic tradition. They had to formulate the apostolic teachings more clearly and make the church tighter and more solid as an organization. Hence the Catholic church (as it was starting to be called in the late second century) was born.

Most scholars no longer believe this account. They have come to see that these heresies—splinter groups with their own sometimes peculiar beliefs—were around almost immediately after Jesus's own time. New Testament scholar Gregory J. Riley writes, "Even in the same geographical area and sometimes in the same cities, different Christian teachers taught quite different gospels and had quite different views of who Jesus was and what he said and did. There does not seem to have been an original and coherent set of doctrines, even though the Church later tried hard to give an impression of early unity."

Because *heresy* is a rather loaded word, scholars tend to refer to these different groups as "faith communities." Some of these faith communities may have been founded by one or more apostles. At first no community was dominant. Only in the second century did the Catholic church, for a number of complex reasons, start on the long road to triumph.

Thomas the Contender

One early faith community was centered around the apostle Thomas. He is a marginal figure in the New Testament, chiefly remembered for doubting the resurrection until he has seen it with his own eyes. After Jesus's death, Thomas apparently went to Syria, where he formed a community there. He may have written the Gospel attributed to him. Unlike the Gospels in the New Testament, which are anonymous but "according to" the evangelists, the *Gospel of Thomas* claims to be written *by* Didymus Judas Thomas. (*Dídumos* is Greek for "twin," and *Thomas* is its Aramaic equivalent. In a third-century apocryphal text called *The Book of Thomas the Contender*, Jesus calls Thomas "my twin and true companion," but it's unlikely that Thomas was literally Jesus's twin brother. No doubt Thomas did have a twin brother, but we don't know who he was.) In the end, whether Thomas did or didn't write this Gospel is an open question.

We've already encountered the *Gospel of Thomas*. Another very short text, it takes up only twelve pages in one standard edition. It consists entirely of sayings of Jesus, sometimes in dialogue with the disciples. There is no narrative. There is no virgin birth, no baptism by John, no crucifixion or resurrection.

Thus *Thomas* resembles the sayings collections that scholars believe were the first written texts about Jesus. It is the only one that has survived. Thus it may be older than the New Testament Gospels, although many scholars don't want to admit as much. Why? The *Gospel of Thomas* smacks of Gnosticism, and Gnosticism was a heresy that (so the theory goes) rose up only in the second century. So the Gospel cannot be that early.

Such was the old view. But the new view says that these different faith communities arose in the *first* century. If so, the apostle Thomas may have started one, and he may have taught doctrines that were later called Gnostic.

How could this be?

To my mind, the only plausible answer is this: Jesus's disciples understood his teachings very differently from the outset, even in his lifetime. He himself may have adjusted his teachings to suit the minds and characters of the disciples. This is hardly a wild speculation. Any good teacher would do the same.

In fact *The Gospel of Thomas* mentions this possibility: "And he [Jesus] took him [Thomas] and told him three things. When Thomas returned to his companions, they asked him 'What did Jesus say to you?' Thomas said to them, 'If I tell you one of the things which he told me, you will pick up stones and throw them at me; a fire will come out and burn you up.'"

This passage includes a major Gnostic theme. It points to a hidden wisdom that Jesus did not necessarily share with all the disciples. The Gnostics said this hidden wisdom was gnosis—"knowledge" of the kingdom of God within us. They also said that this gnosis was not given to most people—even to most believers. This exclusivity enraged the fathers of the proto-Catholic church. After all, they didn't have this knowledge.

If there is some truth to what I've just said, the heresies that caused such hatred and division in Christianity from its earliest days were not outside imports. They may have gone back to the apostles themselves.

The Resurrection of the Body

Probably, then, there was no apostolic teaching. There were only apostolic *teachings*. Peter may have understood Jesus one way, Thomas another, John still another. But as the Catholic church began to solidify in the second century, standard doctrine needed to be set.

To tell how this doctrine came to be as a whole would require an encyclopedic work. I doubt that one person could write it, at least in any exhaustive way. But in order to have a glimpse of this process, let's look at one teaching: the resurrection of the body.

As we've seen, the accounts of Jesus's resurrection in the Gospels are vague and puzzling. They make it sound as if Jesus still has a physical body like our own: his hands and feet have nail holes, and he eats fish and honey. But this body isn't entirely like our own. Jesus doesn't look like his old self. Even his disciples don't recognize him at first. He is able to materialize and vanish at will.

It's a confusing picture. In a way it makes these stories more credible. If they had been made up later to promote some doctrine, they would have been clearer and less ambiguous.

These accounts suggest that even those who had seen the risen Christ had no clear idea of what kind of body he had. They probably didn't have the chance to think about it. When a dead man appears to you, your first reaction is not going to be theorizing.

At the same time, Jesus was supposedly resurrected, which prefigured the resurrection of humanity as a whole. So a question naturally arose: what kind of body will we have when we're resurrected? The first known Christian to try to give an answer was Paul. He discusses it in 1 Corinthians 15:35–55. He makes it extremely clear that it is *not* the physical body that is resurrected. "Flesh and blood cannot inherit the kingdom of God; neither doth corruption inherit incorruption." What is resurrected is something he calls the "spiritual body": "It is sown a natural body; it is raised a spiritual body. There is a natural body, and there is a spiritual body."

It's impossible for me to read this passage and think that Paul believed in a physical resurrection. He states the exact opposite. But the Catholic church and its descendants *do* teach the resurrection of the physical body.

For centuries the Catholic church forbade cremation for exactly this reason. If you burned up the physical body, what was going to be left to be resurrected? In 1963, the policy was liberalized. You can now cremate a body. But you have to keep the ashes all in the same place, presumably so that Jesus can find them when he comes back. As a Web site for Catholic cemeteries admonishes, "Cremated remains of a loved one are not to be scattered, kept at home or divided into other vessels among family members, just as it is clear that these practices would desecrate a body in a casket. The Church allows for burial at sea, providing that the cremated remains of the body are buried in a heavy container and not scattered."

It is one of the weirdest facts I have ever come across in the study of religion. *Conventional Christianity teaches something that is explicitly denied in its own sacred scriptures.*

How could this have happened?

In her bestselling book *The Gnostic Gospels*, scholar Elaine Pagels describes the process. Pagels says that "the New Testament accounts could support a range of interpretations, some of them very much physical, others more mystical." Christian doctrine was disparate at the beginning. All we can really say is that for Paul the resurrection was spiritual and not physical. Almost certainly others saw it that way as well.

So how and why did it change? In the first place, you may have already noticed that this idea of a spiritual body is hard to grasp. What exactly does Paul mean by a spiritual body? (In Greek it is *sôma pneumatikón*.) How does it differ from a "natural body"? (The Greek for "natural body" is *sôma psukhikón*, literally "psychic body.") And how does this "natural body" differ from the physical body, which Paul calls *sárx* ("the flesh")?

I will go into this last question in chapter 15, but right away we can see that the questions become esoteric and difficult. The raising of a spiritual body, whatever that may be, is not an idea that a rapidly spreading church is going to find handy. But the resurrection of the physical body? That's easy to understand.

So the motive for dumbing down the original teaching is obvious.

In her account, Pagels says that the orthodox bishops insisted on the physical resurrection of Jesus because they needed to establish their own authority. By this theory, Jesus rose physically from the dead. The apostles saw this happen, which is in fact what made them apostles. They passed down their lineage to bishops whom they consecrated, and so on down the generations. This was the base of the bishops' authority. Hence it was in their interest to insist on the apostolic succession, as it's still called.

Pagels's analysis is brilliant in many ways. Like much of late twentieth-century scholarship, it focuses on power and control. These facts shaped church doctrine as much as beliefs. And Pagels is certainly right up to a point. Human beings are political animals, and power and control are always living issues in human organizations.

I would only disagree in saying that there were other reasons as well. The most important is the fact that the doctrine of a physical resurrection is easier to understand, and thus more likely to appeal to the masses. The resurrection of a spiritual body, on the other hand, is hard to conceive of. It's likely to appeal only to a sophisticated elite.

These facts go far toward explaining the struggle between the proto–Catholic church and the Gnostics in the second century. They also help explain why the Catholic church won in the end.

Paul: The Great Apostle

I COULD HARDLY discuss the founding of the Christian tradition without approaching one monumental figure. Many argue that he did more to shape Christianity than Jesus himself. He is the apostle Paul. In a way all of Christian theology is nothing more than a footnote to Paul.

It would be amusing to look into the uses made of Paul over the last century. He has been a useful foil in many polemics. Often he is the villain in Christian history. By this view, everything that is good in Christianity comes from Jesus. Everything that is bad comes from Paul.

The reason is not hard to find. Paul is not an easy thinker to sort out. His writings are letters addressed to specific churches in specific situations. Often we can only guess at the issues at stake. Some epistles, especially 2 Corinthians, may be made up of several letters pasted together by a later editor. On occasions Paul seems to be thinking aloud on paper.

In fact we've already seen how thoroughly misunderstood Paul has been about the resurrection of the body. The nineteenth-century theologian Franz Overbeck quipped, "No one has ever understood Paul, and the only one who did understand him, Marcion, misunderstood him."

Maybe Marcion isn't a bad place to start.

Marcion lived in the second century. He was yet another in the long list of heretics who challenged and offended the proto-Catholic church. Among other things, he was the first man to make a canon of the Christian Bible.

Marcion's Bible would not take long to read. It consisted of the Gospel according to Luke and Paul's epistles. Everything else had to go.

Two things are obvious right away: (1) Marcion held Paul in the highest esteem, and (2) Marcion thought the Old Testament was worthless. These facts are connected. They shed light on an important and often overlooked part of Paul's theology.

Marcion said there were two Gods. One, the true, good God, was far away, completely alien to this world. The other, who made this world, was defective and evil. The God of the Old Testament was the second God. He gave the Law to the Hebrews as a kind of bondage. But the true God sent Christ to redeem us from this Law and from this world.

Marcion may have gotten the inspiration for this idea from Paul, who wrote, "Wherefore then serveth the law? It was added because of transgressions, till the seed should come to whom the promise was made; and it was ordained *by angels* in the hands of a mediator" (Galatians 3:19; my emphasis).

For Paul, the Law was not given by God. It was given by angels. What this verse seems to be saying is this: humans had gotten so wicked that some kind of law was needed to curb them. This law was, first, the general law given to Noah after the Flood (Genesis 9:1–7), which the Jews believed applied to all people universally; and second, the Law given to Moses on Sinai, which applied only to the children of Israel.

To understand all this, you have to set aside present-day images of angels as golden-haired beauties with wings. The angels in ancient Judaism and Christianity were not necessarily friendly to humans. That didn't mean they were evil (although there were evil angels too). Even the good angels served as doorkeepers to the heavenly realms. Like bouncers in a bar today, they were supposed to keep people out who didn't belong there.

These would of course include sinful humans. Because all humans have sinned, all humans are kept out. In fact, Paul suggests, the law was set up to create sin as a way of separating us from God. As Paul puts it, "I had not known sin, but by the law" (Romans 7:7). And it was the angels who gave humanity the law.

How did Paul see these angels? He gives no clear indication. But there is one unmistakable fact: Paul *never* refers to the angels in a positive way. Here's one example: "For I am persuaded, that neither death, nor life, nor *angels*, nor principalities, nor powers, nor things present, nor things to come, Nor height, nor depth, nor any other creature, shall be able to separate us from the love of God, which is in Christ Jesus our Lord" (Romans 8:38–39). Angels here are among the obstacles blocking man from the love of God.

Or take 1 Corinthians 4:9: "For I think that God hath set forth us the apostles last, as it were appointed to death: for we are made a spectacle unto the world, and to *angels*, and to men" (my emphasis here and in the previous passage). The angels are not helpful, loving figures who save you from car wrecks. They are grouped with the mocking humans who do not believe.

In the Old Testament the angels, often called the "host of heaven," are ambiguous figures. They are not powers of evil, but respected members of the heavenly hierarchy. Nevertheless, they sometimes seem to tempt people into worshipping them, and this was strictly forbidden. "If there be found among you ... man or woman, that hath wrought wickedness in the sight of the Lord thy God ... And hath gone and served other gods, and worshipped them, either the sun, or moon, or any of the host of heaven, which I have not commanded," that person is to be stoned to death (Deuteronomy 17:2–5).

If you grasp this, it's much easier to understand the controversies in early Christianity as described in Acts and in Paul's epistles. The disciples of Christ hold that even Gentile believers should observe the Jewish Law. Paul disagrees vehemently. According to him, this Law was handed down by the angels as a purely temporary means of regulating humanity until Christ should come. And, he seems to imply, the angels are not completely willing to give up this control.

The epistle to the Ephesians was probably not written by Paul, but its thought is heavily influenced by him. Here is what it says: "For we wrestle not against flesh and blood, but against principalities, against powers, against the rulers of the darkness of this world, against spiritual wickedness in high places" (Ephesians 6:12). The "principalities," "powers," "rulers of the darkness of this world" are not the emperors of Rome, but the angels.

Marcion went further and said the Great Angel, Yahweh himself, the Demiurge, was evil. Did Marcion misunderstand Paul, as Overbeck said? Yes, because Marcion saw this Great Angel as the Demiurge—a second-rate pseudodeity who does not know that there is a true God above him. Jesus was sent to us from the true God, who was totally alien to this world. By contrast, Paul believed that the Great Angel took human form in Jesus to save us from the Law—as we shall see.

But in a way, as the scholar Marcel Simon remarks, Marcion "did little more than push to their logical conclusion the results which [Paul] barely managed to avoid."

Marcion is often classed among the Gnostics, who also held that this world was the creation of the Demiurge. It's no coincidence that many of them too harked back to Paul. He did not necessarily believe that the world was created by wicked powers, as the Gnostics did. But he believed that humanity was (before the coming of Christ) enslaved to powers that were, at best, ambivalent toward man.

Sin, Original and Otherwise

It may be time to introduce a technical term from theology—soteriology. It comes from the Greek *sōtēr*, "savior." It is the study of salvation.

Salvation? What? Why do we need it in the first place?

In most of the Hebrew Bible, salvation doesn't come up. It doesn't have to. The covenant between Yahweh and Israel is simple. If the people obey the Law, they prosper. If they disobey, they are punished. It's all straightforward.

As the history of Israel and Judah progressed, more explanation was needed. There was a point at which the people had suffered for their sins, and more. But they were still under foreign yokes. There was only one way they could reconcile themselves to this discrepancy. They began to believe that a savior would come, a Messiah who would redeem them from their cruel masters. The Messiah would set the balances of justice right.

This was the Messiah that the Jews (or some of the Jews) were waiting for in the time of Jesus. As the Gospels suggest, some of them may have looked to him as this savior. But he was not. He did not save them from the Romans, nor did he try. Thus they didn't accept him as the Messiah.

Jesus suffered and died on the cross. His disciples said that they saw him afterward, resurrected. Whatever else he gave them, he did not give them any explanations. Nevertheless, they needed to understand all this in some way, and they decided that Jesus died for their sins. He was a human sacrifice for the sins of man, much as the animal sacrifices in the Temple had wiped away the people's sins in the past.

This was what Paul was told after his conversion: "For I delivered unto you first of all that which I also received, how that Christ died for our sins according to the scriptures" (1 Corinthians 15:3).

Paul developed the theory of salvation further. He tried to answer the question of just how it was that Christ could die for our sins. He held that angels had given the Law to humans so that humans would sin and fall into bondage to the angels. Every person sinned, so everyone was in bondage. The penalty is not hell (which Paul does not mention) but death.

Jesus came down from heaven (Paul hints that Jesus too was an angel—the Great Angel in fact) to save us. Jesus allowed himself to be punished and killed by "the princes of this world"—the lower angels. But there was one little secret, which none of the princes knew, "for had they known it, they would not have crucified the Lord of glory" (1 Corinthians 2:3). The angels had punished one who was sinless. By doing this, they violated their own Law. The Law was thereby made invalid. Mankind was freed.

After Paul's time, it became awkward and confusing to talk about these "princes of the world." How could the angels in heaven, the servants of God, be evil, or even ambiguous? So the doctrine was changed slightly. Now it was said that mankind had fallen prey to Satan. Christ, by dying sinless, had paid Satan the ransom of his perfect blood, and the Evil One had to release humanity.

What I have just set out in the paragraph above is called the *ransom theory of atonement*. It was the dominant theory of soteriology in the early centuries of Christianity.

Only in the fifth century, with Augustine, and later still, in the eleventh century, with Anselm of Canterbury, was this theory changed. After all, it seemed odd to say that Satan, the prince of evil, had any justice on his side, as the ransom theory said. So Satan was taken out of the picture. It was now God himself who had to be appeased.

Exactly how this was done is, according to standard theology, something of a puzzle. Evidently God had to send down part of himself to earth to be tortured to death. Thus in some way God managed to make it up to himself.

Maybe I should put this position more respectfully. After all, it is the most popular view about soteriology in Christianity to this day. It is known as the doctrine of *penal substitution*. Mankind had to pay the penalty for the sin of Adam, because, as Anselm put it, "the Divine justice . . .

allows nothing but punishment as the recompense of sin." Because all men were sinful, they would not be acceptable sacrifices to God. So God had to incarnate as a perfect, sinless man to serve as an acceptable sacrifice. To himself.

Whether I put it contemptuously or respectfully, the outcome is the same. This explanation is ludicrous. No amount of theologizing, no appeal to "divine mystery," is going to save it.

You can see how this theory of redemption progressed from something more or less reasonable in its time to something completely incredible today. In the days of the apostles, atonement was made to the gods by animal sacrifice. It was not that hard to take the step of accepting one perfect human sacrifice that would suffice for all time.

But when the God to be appeased was the high, all-good God, incapable of evil, the question became more difficult. If God was all-good and all-forgiving, why did somebody (especially somebody sinless) have to be tortured to death to appease him? And why should this all-powerful God demand blood sacrifice anyway? Of what use could it possibly be to him?

If you read conventional theology, you will find various attempts at explanation. Virtually all of them, seen with any impartiality, stumble over themselves to the point where they amount to little more than waffling. But then, as Arthur O. Lovejoy drily remarked in his classic study *The Great Chain of Being*, "The permissibility and even necessity of contradicting oneself when one spoke of God, was a principle commonly enough recognized" in medieval times, "though the benefits of it were not usually extended to theological opponents."

Along with the doctrine of penal substitution, another curious doctrine grew up—original sin. Meaning that everyone is born to sin. Little babies right out of their mothers' wombs are contaminated with it, because they are descendants of Adam.

The origins of this doctrine are traced to Paul. Here is one passage from him that supposedly supports the idea of original sin: "As by one man sin entered into the world, and death by sin; ... so death passed upon all men, for that all have sinned" (Romans 5:12).

But Paul did not teach the doctrine of original sin. He taught the view that I've explained in the previous section. He said that we are in the grip of sin not because we inherited it like some genetic disorder, but because all of us have sinned.

The Law decrees death as the payment for sin: "The wages of sin is death" (Romans 6:23). "All have sinned." Thus all are subject to death. Presumably if someone lived without sin, he would not have to suffer death. But the only person who was sinless was Jesus, and he chose to suffer death as a way of making the angels' rule invalid.

This is quite different from believing in original sin. In the first place, by the teaching of original sin, everyone is subject not only to death but to hell. This made even the Catholic church pause. Even Catholicism could not quite swallow the idea that sinless newborns who died would go straight to eternal torment. So it invented the idea of limbo (from the Latin *limbus*, "edge")—a place that was not exactly heaven, but was at least a place without suffering, for infants and other more or less innocent beings. Dante makes it the first circle of his hell.

In any event, you can see how Paul was used to justify later doctrines that he did not teach and which he probably would have found monstrous.

As for Paul being the hellfire-breathing villain and Jesus the compassionate hero, if you go by the Bible alone, you will find that Paul never says a word about hell, but that Jesus in the Gospels talks about it frequently. Make of that what you will.

The Body of Christ

So how did Paul view salvation? His ideas make most sense if you realize that an ancient and almost universal idea is in the background.

This is the idea of the Universal Man, or the Cosmic Man. Essentially it says that all of us are cells in the body of one Great Man. This being has various names in various traditions. Ancient Greek thought called it the Anthropos, which is simply Greek for "human." In Hinduism it is called Purusha.* Zoroastrianism calls it Gayomart. Judaism probably acquired this idea from the Zoroastrians in the two centuries when the Jews were subject to the Persian empire (539–332 BC). The Jewish Kabbalah calls this cosmic man Adam Kadmon. In the eighteenth century, Emanuel Swedenborg called this figure the *maximus homo* ("greatest man" or "greatest human").

Of course this Cosmic Man is a myth. Some myths are little more than amusing stories. Others express truths that cannot be conveyed any other way. The myth of the Cosmic Man is one of the latter.

The Cosmic Man, by the way, is androgynous.

The myths say something further. They say that through some sin or mistake, this Cosmic Man fell. He was shattered into countless pieces, and we are these pieces. We are part of one larger being, but we don't feel that way. We feel like a collection of separate bodies running around on planet earth.

This fall—or *the* Fall—did not take place anywhere on the time line of history, even of the history of the material universe. The material universe is the world of the Fall. Even science, from beginning to end, is merely a study of this universe of the Fall.

The world is a mixture of good and evil. Adam and Eve (the androgynous Cosmic Man) ate from the Tree of the Knowledge of Good and Evil. That is, they wanted to know what good and evil are, so they fell into a realm where good and evil are woven into our existence. Everyone, no matter how fortunate or how wretched, experiences a mixture of good and evil in life.

This, by the way, is why science neither proves nor disproves the story of Genesis. Genesis tells of a completely different level of reality. It was

---

*Readers of my book *The Dice Game of Shiva* should realize that I use the word *purusha* in a very different sense there. The word has many meanings in Hindu philosophy.

understood as taking place on a garden on earth because that was the only way most people could imagine it. But the truth—that it involves a different realm entirely—was always preserved, in both the Kabbalah and esoteric Christianity. I will talk more about it in chapter 15.

Before we go back to Paul, I need to say one other thing. In the esoteric Christian tradition, the Cosmic Man in this fallen, separate state is called Adam. Man in his anticipated state of restoration is called Christ.

This is why Paul can write, "For as in Adam all die, even so in Christ shall all be made alive" (1 Corinthians 15:22).

In Adam we are subject to death and to the rule of angels—who by rights should not be able to rule us. In Christ we are not subject to death or to the angels. Eventually we will be exalted above them. "Know ye not that we shall judge angels?" (1 Corinthians 6:3).

By accepting Christ through baptism, the individual becomes a part of the cosmic Christ. This Christ is not subject to death, nor is the Christian.

Of course freedom from death does not mean that the *physical* body is free from death. The physical body is still subject to death; in a way it *is* death. But the believer dies to the "flesh," as Paul puts it. That's why he says that the resurrection has to do not with the flesh, but with the spiritual body. The flesh is going to die regardless, because it is of this fallen world. Only the spiritual body is immortal. It is part of the body of Christ.

Paul often speaks of the collectivity of believers as the body of Christ. "For as the body is one, and hath many members, and all the members of that one body, being many, are one body: so also is Christ. For by one Spirit are we all baptized into one body, whether we be Jews or Gentiles, whether we be bond or free; and have been all made to drink into one Spirit. For the body is not one member, but many" (1 Corinthians 12:12–14).

For this reason also Paul can speak of the faithful literally being *in* Christ: "If any man be in Christ, he is a new creature" (2 Corinthians 5:17). Conversely he also speaks of Christ being in the believer: "Know ye not your own selves, how that Jesus Christ is in you?" (2 Corinthians 13:5).

Although Paul does connect the historical Jesus with the cosmic Christ, it is the latter that mostly interests Paul. "Though we have known Christ after the flesh, yet now henceforth know we him no more" (2 Corinthians 5:16).

Jesus the man, particularly by his death and resurrection, started the process of cosmic regeneration. "But now is Christ risen from the dead, and become the firstfruits of them that slept" (1 Corinthians 15:20).

Jesus, by his resurrection, is "the firstfruits of them that slept." In Paul's time Jesus's resurrection had just taken place. Thus Paul, like much of the early Christian community, believes that the final drama will come soon. At that time all those who are in Christ, living and dead, will be raised and transfigured: "Behold, I shew you a mystery; We shall not all sleep, but we shall all be changed, in a moment, in the twinkling of an eye, at the last trump: for the trumpet shall sound, and the dead shall be raised incorruptible, and we shall be changed" (1 Corinthians 15:51–52).

The picture I have just given of Paul's theology is at variance with most versions. They tend to make him look like a stodgy and sanctimonious evangelical Christian. The Paul I have described is much more mystical. In fact, for much of my account, I have relied on Albert Schweitzer's book *The Mysticism of Paul the Apostle*. Published in 1930, it is not nearly as well known as Schweitzer's *Quest of the Historical Jesus*. But it is at least as brilliant. I have never had the sense that Schweitzer really understood Jesus. But very few theologians have been better at understanding Paul.

If you take this picture of Paul as a starting point, you will find that his writings make sense in a way that they don't according to other interpretations.

Women and Homosexuals

Today feminist thinkers denigrate Paul. They say that he thinks of women as second-class citizens in the community of Christ. Jesus, by contrast, treated women more or less the same as men—which was very unusual in his day.

It's true that Paul said this: "Let your women keep silence in the churches: for it is not permitted unto them to speak; but they are commanded to be under obedience, as also saith the law. And if they will learn any thing, let them ask their husbands at home: for it is a shame for women to speak in the church" (1 Corinthians 14:34–35).

Paul also said: "But I would have you know, that the head of every man is Christ; and the head of the woman is the man; and the head of Christ is God" (1 Corinthians 11:3).

There are any number of other things that Paul is supposed to have said. Such as:

Wives, submit yourselves unto your own husbands, as unto the Lord.

(Ephesians 5:22)

Therefore as the church is subject unto Christ, so let the wives be to their own husbands in every thing.

(Ephesians 5:24)

Wives, submit yourselves unto your own husbands, as it is fit in the Lord.

(Colossians 3:18)

I will therefore that the younger women marry, bear children, guide the house, give none occasion to the adversary to speak reproachfully.

(1 Timothy 5:14)

These four passages were *not* written by Paul. They are from letters that, according to most scholars today, were written in his name but are not authentic.

Just to recap, here are the letters that Paul is today believed to have written:

Romans
1 Corinthians
2 Corinthians
Galatians
Philippians
1 Thessalonians
Philemon

Here are the letters that, according to most authorities, were *not* written by Paul:

Ephesians
Colossians
2 Thessalonians
1 Timothy
2 Timothy
Titus

The Epistle to the Hebrews, which is anonymous, was sometimes attributed to Paul as well, but this was doubted even in antiquity. No one knows who wrote Hebrews.

When criticizing Paul, it's good to keep these facts in mind. He should not be blamed for saying things that he never did say.

It's true that this leaves the passages from 1 Corinthians quoted above. (Some scholars think that the first passage, forbidding women to speak in churches, may have been inserted later, but this is highly speculative.) It would be hard to argue that Paul did not believe something of this kind. He is blamed for a misogynistic strain in Christianity that reaches an almost pathological level in some of the later church fathers.

I think this is going too far. Like the earliest Christian texts, including the *Didache,* Paul advocates a clean, sober, virtuous life. Sexual relations are to be contained in marriage. The husband is head of the household, as he was almost universally in those days. Nonetheless, Paul does not show the extreme misogyny displayed by the church fathers of later centuries.

Paul is also blamed for condemning homosexuality, which he does: "Know ye not that the unrighteous shall not inherit the kingdom of God? Be not deceived: neither fornicators, nor idolaters, nor adulterers, nor effeminate, nor abusers of themselves with mankind . . . shall inherit the kingdom of God" (1 Corinthians 6:9–10). A similar passage appears in 1 Timothy 1:8–11, but again this is not authentically Pauline.

There is no reason to pretend that Paul did not condemn homosexuality. The word for "effeminate" in this passage is *malakoí,* which simply means "soft." There is some dispute about whether the word refers to passive partners in homosexual intercourse. But the other word, here translated as "abusers of themselves with mankind," is clear. It is *arsenokoítai,* which literally means "those who sleep with males." It is a masculine plural noun. Although this word does not appear elsewhere in Greek, it would be hard to argue that it would refer to anything other than homosexual intercourse.

In this case, the conservative Christians are right: the Bible *does* condemn homosexuality. Paul does it here, and the Law of Moses is still more extreme: "If a man also lie with mankind, as he lieth with a woman, both of them have committed an abomination: they shall surely be put to death" (Leviticus 20:13). The liberals who try to argue this fact away are mistaken.

What does all this mean for us now? With regard to both women and homosexuality, Paul was writing a long time ago, under social conditions that are almost unimaginable today. His views present no real problem for us unless you regard his writings as sacred and infallible Scripture that must be followed at all costs. The same is true of the Old Testament.

This is not a position that I myself would take. You can find Paul's ideas inspiring and profound without believing, much less living by, every last thing he said. The status of women and gay people today is a matter that society should be, and is, working out in other ways and on different terms.

13.

Revelation: The Overthrow of the Wicked Angels

YOU CAN PROBABLY find more varying and extreme views about the book of Revelation than about any other book of the Bible. C. H. Dodd, the great commentator on the Gospel of John, called Revelation "muddled fantasy-thinking." But Boris Pasternak wrote in *Doctor Zhivago*, "All great, genuine art resembles and continues the Revelation of St. John."

My own opinion comes much closer to Pasternak's than to Dodd's. Nevertheless, Revelation, the culmination and climax of the Bible, presents endless difficulties. An elaborate vision that includes letters to churches in Asia Minor, the unlocking of seven seals, seven angels with seven trumpets, a false prophet, a loathsome beast whose number is 666, and the whore of Babylon, it ends with a portrait of the "heavenly city, New Jerusalem, coming down from God out of heaven prepared as a bride adorned for her husband" (Revelation 21:1).

Revelation and Apocalypse

The Greek title for Revelation, as I mentioned earlier, is *Apokálupsis*— "revelation." In fact Catholic Bibles often give the title of this book as the

Apocalypse. And, as I also said earlier, apocalypses usually describe visions of higher realities. Many of them are prophetic visions of the end of the world. That's why *apocalypse* today usually refers to the end of the world.

There are many such apocalypses among the books that didn't make it into the Bible. (Collectively these books are called the Pseudepigrapha, meaning "works with false attribution.") Jewish apocalypses are attributed to Old Testament figures such as Baruch, secretary to the prophet Jeremiah, and Ezra, possible editor of the Torah. Christian ones are ascribed to apostles such as Peter, Paul, and Thomas.

These other apocalypses are fascinating documents. They tell us an enormous amount about Judaism and Christianity, especially from the second century BC to the second century AD. But none of them has the power and resonance of the one in the Bible.

Who wrote this mysterious text?

John.

Five books in the Bible are ascribed to John: the Gospel of John, three epistles, and Revelation. Today most scholars believe they had different authors. One man wrote the Gospel. Another man, perhaps part of a Johannine faith community, wrote the epistles. The man who wrote Revelation was someone else still. Tradition says it was "the elder John." *Elder* was a term sometimes used to refer to the generation of Christian leaders that immediately followed the apostles.

But Revelation may not have had a single author. It may be a composite work, with some parts written earlier and others added on later. Teasing out these layers of composition is an intricate task, and I won't try to do it here.

One thing we can say is that the Greek in Revelation is clumsier than in the other writings attributed to John, or indeed in the rest of the New Testament. It is full of awkward and unidiomatic usages. They resemble those of a Semitic language—probably Aramaic, the language Jesus spoke—more than Greek.

When and where was it written? The earliest testimony is that of Irenaeus around AD 180. Irenaeus says that the apostle John wrote Revelation in the reign of the emperor Domitian (81–96). Most scholars have taken this statement more or less at face value. By this view, John's statement "I John, who also am your brother, and companion in tribulation" (Revelation 1:9) refers to Domitian's persecution of Christians.

There are some doubts about this theory. In the first place, evidence of a persecution under Domitian is quite slender. Some scholars don't believe that it ever happened. In the second place, scholars also believe that the famous beast whose number is 666 (Revelation 13:19) was the emperor Nero. The numerical value of "Nero Caesar," written in Hebrew characters, adds up to 666. In Hebrew, letters double as numbers, so all letters have a numerical value. Words with the same numerical value refer to things that are connected or identical. This technique is known as *gematria* (for Hebrew) or *isopsephy* (for Greek).

If this identification is right, why should John have written such a thing in the 90s? Nero died in 68, so he was no longer a threat. Some say that John was talking about a legend of a *Nero redivivus* (resurrected) that was supposedly current in the late first century. But this is something of a stretch.

The likelihood that Nero was the beast whose number was 666, along with the ominous, feverish tone of Revelation, suggests that at least part of this text was written during the Jewish War, around the time of Nero's death in 68. It was under Nero that the Romans had invaded Judea the year before.

The awkward Greek may suggest that at least some of Revelation was originally written in Aramaic and was translated only later. If so, the date in the 90s could simply mean that the final version of the text was put together and translated into Greek at that point.

Messages Past and Present

Many fundamentalist Protestants say Revelation is about *our* time. Christ will return any minute. All the prophecies in the Bible—in Daniel and Ezekiel and the Gospels as well as in Revelation—can be unlocked with the key of current events.

Take the beast whose number is 666. Setting aside Nero, countless identities have been proposed for this infamous creature. Would-be prophets associate him with some prominent figure currently on the world stage. In previous eras, candidates included Muhammad, Napoleon, and Hitler.

Late in the last century, Ronald Wilson Reagan was a popular choice. His full name consists of three six-letter words. When he retired from office in 1989, supporters bought him a house in Los Angeles's stylish Bel Air district. Nancy Reagan took hexakosioihexekontahexaphobia (fear of the number 666) seriously enough to have its street number changed from 666 St. Cloud Road to 668.

While at this stage it seems rather beside the point to see the Gipper as the climactic figure of evil in world history, the theory persists. Surfing the Internet, I come across a thread from 2008 entitled "Proof That Ronald Reagan Was the 666 Antichrist!" It's in the unlikely location of the DateHookup.com website.

Today's suspects are easy to guess. One Internet prophet observed, "On the 10th Anniversary of the twin towers Barack Obama read Psalm 46. This particular verse is the 666th chapter from the end of the Bible. It is also on the 666th by page leaf from the very beginning in the original 1611 King James 1st edition." You can also watch a YouTube video giving you "final warning" of "%100 [*sic*] Proof Pope Francis I Antichrist 666."

To return to technicalities: this approach to Revelation is known as the *futurist* view. It assumes that John the beloved disciple, on the Mediterranean isle of Patmos in AD 95, had visions of such figures as

Reagan, Obama, and Pope Francis and chose his own cryptic way of describing them.

Practically no one outside the fundamentalist world takes such interpretations seriously. Instead scholars generally hold to the *preterist* view of Revelation, which says that the author was talking about events in his own day: the first century AD. We've already seen an example of this interpretation: associating 666 with the wicked emperor Nero.

Admittedly, the futurist view is much more fun.

But the preterist view is more plausible. Revelation was written in the first century, so it's much more likely that it's about the events of the day.

The Drama of the End

The preterist interpretation doesn't solve as many problems as you might think. There are two questions that it doesn't answer at all:

If Revelation is about the time of Nero or Domitian, why should anyone bother with it today?

And why does it occupy such a hold on the human imagination, from semiliterate Internet prophets to Boris Pasternak?

To answer these questions, it may be best to start with a broad sketch of this bizarre and cryptic text.

John begins with a vision of the Son of Man, who delivers messages to be given to seven churches in Asia Minor. These messages are rather unenthusiastic. One church is told, "I have somewhat against thee, because thou hast left thy first love" (Revelation 2:4). Another is told, "Because thou art lukewarm, and neither cold nor hot, I will spue thee out of my mouth" (Revelation 3:15).

The scene then shifts to heaven, where John sees a throne, "and he that sat was to look upon like a jasper and a sardine stone" (Revelation 4:3). A book containing seven seals is produced, and it is opened by a Lamb with seven horns and seven eyes.

The seven seals are opened one by one. Each time new disasters unfold. After the seventh, "the third part of the creatures which were in the sea, and had life, died" (Revelation 8:9). Next seven trumpets are sounded by seven angels, unleashing more disasters.

These gloomy events all culminate in a "war in heaven: Michael and his angels fought against the dragon: . . . And the great dragon was cast out, that old serpent, called the Devil, and Satan, which deceiveth the whole world: he was cast out into the earth and his angels were cast out with him" (Revelation 12:7, 9).

A beast then rises out of the sea—the beast whose number is 666. Seven vials of God's wrath are poured out upon the earth. Another beast appears, with seven heads, and on it rides the whore of Babylon, "arrayed in purple and scarlet colour" (Revelation 17:4). An angel comes down from heaven and proclaims her fall.

The climactic moment comes when one who is called "Faithful and True" appears on a white horse out of heaven. He and his hosts smash the armies of the beast. The dead are raised and judged. Satan is bound and "cast into the lake of fire and brimstone" (Revelation 20:10).

Finally the prophet sees "a new heaven and a new earth." He witnesses the descent of the heavenly Jerusalem, whose foundations are "garnered with all matter of precious stones" (Revelation 21:19). The saints are granted the vision of God, and his name is on their foreheads.

To figure out what this all means in some absolute sense is not realistic. Revelation is, if nothing else, a great work of art. Great works of art are not written in code. You can't decipher them to get a single, final message. *They mean themselves.* Whatever interpretation you give is merely one of many possible perspectives. This is true for *Oedipus Rex*, for the *Iliad*, for *Hamlet*. It is also true for Revelation.

There is something else to consider. Boris Mouravieff, an authority on the esoteric tradition of Eastern Orthodoxy, writes, "The Revelation is the most transcendent message that can be expressed in words. It is useless to try to understand the Revelation through the centres of the Personality"—meaning the ordinary level of consciousness.

Bearing this caution in mind, let us proceed.

The Whore and the Beast

Let's start with the whore of Babylon. John describes her as sitting upon "a scarlet-coloured beast.... And the woman was arrayed in purple and scarlet colour, and decked with gold and precious stones and pearls, having a golden cup in her hand full of abominations and filthiness of her fornication: And upon her forehead was a name written, MYSTERY, BAB-YLON THE GREAT, THE MOTHER OF HARLOTS AND ABOMINATIONS OF THE EARTH. And I saw the woman drunken with the blood of the saints, and with the blood of the martyrs of Jesus." An angel tells him, "The woman which thou sawest is that great city, which reigneth over the kings of the earth" (Revelation 17:3–6, 18).

The scarlet beast on which the woman is sitting has seven heads, which, the prophet is told, "are seven mountains, on which the woman sitteth" (Revelation 17:8).

The interpretation is clear. If the woman is a "great city, which reigneth over the kings of the earth," the city must be Rome. The seven mountains are the seven hills on which Rome was built. The beast would be the Roman Empire, which has "seven kings"—that is, emperors. (The Romans had had no kings per se since the sixth century BC.)

Exactly which emperors these are supposed to be is a vexed question. That's because the seventh emperor—starting from Julius Caesar—was Galba, and Galba reigned such a short time (in 68–69) that it's hard to believe John had him in mind. If you want to get technical, Julius Caesar was not really an emperor. His title at the time of his death was *dictator* (an actual position in the Roman republic). So strictly speaking, Augustus was the first emperor. But then the seventh emperor would be Otho, who reigned for three months in 69, so the same argument applies. (You probably won't be surprised to learn that that period was known as the Year of the Four Emperors.)

Most likely, the number seven is used because it is so important to Revelation as a whole. In fact, the number seven occurs and reoccurs to a degree that seems almost maniacal. Seven churches, seven spirits before the throne of God, seven seals, seven trumpets, seven angels having the seven last plagues. Whatever meaning Revelation may have, the number seven is obviously a central part of it.

Seven is the number of the planets known at the time—Mercury, Venus, Mars, Jupiter, and Saturn—plus the sun and moon, all of which, in the ancient view, form a series of concentric zones or belts around the earth. Spiritual liberation is only possible, according to many teachings of the time, by ascending through these seven zones and loosening the hold each one has on the seeker.

In fact, when you are looking into ancient mysticism and you come across the number seven, it's helpful to ask yourself right away if the text is talking about the planets or their rulers (seen as angels or gods or "the host of heaven"). Often it is.*

By contrast, the Jewish tradition avoids speaking of the planets because it does not want to encourage worship of them. So it usually talks about seven heavens without referring to the planets. Certainly this was the case in this period, around the turn of the second century AD.

Revelation is telling the story of how this cosmic system is undone. When the seven seals are opened, the system begins to unravel. During the process, "the stars of heaven fell unto the earth, even as a fig tree casteth her untimely figs" (Revelation 6:13). Of course it is the Lamb—Christ—who starts this chain of events.

---

*The system actually encompasses the five planets—Mercury, Venus, Mars, Jupiter, and Saturn—plus the sun and the moon, which of course are not planets. But for the purposes of this discussion I will simply speak of the "seven planets."

The climactic moment is the war in heaven, in which Michael and his angels cast Satan and his minions down to earth.

Let me clear up one possible source of confusion here. Christian tradition often says that the Devil and his angels fell from heaven soon after the founding of the universe. In Milton's *Paradise Lost*, for example, Satan revolts, is cast down, and then decides to tempt God's new creation, Adam and Eve.

This is *not* the view of Revelation. Revelation is *not* saying that this war in heaven took place in the primordial past. It is saying that the war has taken place in the writer's own day, in the first century AD. Christ's sacrifice began this war ("Worthy is the Lamb that was slain"; Revelation 5:19). As a result Satan and his evil angels are cast down to earth. The final struggle happens on earth. The events of John's time—the persecution of Christians and the Jewish War—show how this cosmic drama plays out.

For John, then, the terrible events of his own day are occurring because Satan has fallen down to earth.

In simple terms, Revelation seems to be saying this: The previous cosmic order was wicked, headed by Satan. Christ undid this wicked order, a process symbolized by the opening of the seven seals and the casting down of Satan from heaven. The number seven refers to "the seven Spirits which were before the throne" (Revelation 1:4), probably identified with the planets. Each of these planetary zones had been corrupted and needed to be purified; hence the "seven seals" that are opened. Once this purification in the heavens is complete and Satan is cast down to earth, a parallel process takes place on earth with the pouring out of the "seven golden vials, full of the wrath of God" (Revelation 15:7).

The end of the book moves into the days to come. The Word of God leads the heavenly forces to smash the earthly powers of "the beast, and the kings of the earth" (Revelation 19:19). This time the Devil is cast down not onto earth but into hell. The quick and the dead are judged, and the New Jerusalem arrives.

Justice Restored

In the end Revelation offers a vision that is like Paul's. There are differences, of course. Paul does not speak of Satan being in heaven (although the pseudo-Pauline epistle to the Ephesians does say something similar in talking of "the rulers of the darkness of this world, spiritual wickedness in high places"; Ephesians 6:12). In Revelation, on the other hand, Satan starts out in heaven. There are good angels and bad angels, and the good conquer the bad.

But in the end the message is the same. The old order—which was not only a social and political order but a cosmic order—has been overturned by the sacrifice of Christ. Spiritual wickedness in high places has been overcome. The faithful need only await the last act, which is due at any moment.

Apocalypse was in the air at the time. The early Christians were drunk with apocalyptic hope. Christ's resurrection—which heralded the defeat of the forces of death and decay—seemed to be a sign that this restoration was coming in the immediate future.

Even after all this explanation, we are still left wondering why this odd text, which to all appearances is forecasting that the end of the world would happen in the first century AD, continues to exercise such a hallucinatory power.

Part of the answer lies in the mystery of the symbols. John does not come out and say that the Roman Empire is about to be overturned by the heavenly hosts. He makes his statements darkly and obliquely, speaking of scarlet women and horned beasts. Not only does this make his language more vivid, but it also makes it applicable to any number of future situations. It also avoids stating any prediction flat out. This is good (or at least prudent) prophetic practice. Nostradamus in the sixteenth century was adept at the same art—one reason that his prophecies too still grip the imagination. (I discuss this matter in my book *The Essential Nostradamus*.)

Still, we have to push the question further. What is Revelation trying to say to us? With all its angels and trumpets and pestilences, its central theme is yet another version of the apocalyptic message. The present world order is wicked and unjust and corrupt. It is so now, and it was so in the year 95. The world order is out of whack with the forces of the universe, because these are based on justice and right. The political and economic powers reflect this dysfunction, but they are its result, not its cause. A higher force must come and rescue us and restore the cosmic balance.

Maybe there is some objective truth to this picture. Maybe it's just wishful thinking. But as I've said earlier, it speaks to a deep need in all of us for justice, not only in the courts of law, but in the cosmos. We know this justice is not here now, not in any complete or satisfying way. We can only look dimly to the future. And we realize that any world in which justice is perfect will be far different from this one, and perhaps, as Revelation suggests, unrecognizable.

There are other ways of reading Revelation. In *The Secret Book of Revelation*, the Dutch theologian Gilles Quispel writes, "The secret Revelation of John can also be regarded as a process of individuation," referring to Jung's process of self-discovery by grappling with the contents of the unconscious through dreams and symbols. These contents must be dealt with—sometimes fought with—and integrated into a higher psychological whole, symbolized by the New Jerusalem.

In the early twentieth century, James M. Pryse wrote *The Apocalypse Unsealed*. For Pryse, the vision of Revelation has nothing to do with empires or Neros. It is about the inner transformation of the aspirant:

Many actors, apparently, play their parts in the drama of the *Apocalypse*; yet in reality there is but one performer—the neophyte himself, the sacrificial "Lamb," who awakens all the slumbering forces of his inner nature, passes through the terrible ordeals of the purificatory discipline and the telestic [i.e., initiatic] labors, and finally emerges as the Conqueror, the self-perfected Man who has regained his standing among the deathless Gods.

Pryse connects the seven seals with the chakras, the seven subtle centers in the human body. According to certain theories, these need to be opened in order for the seeker to attain enlightenment. Hence he translates *apokálupsis* as "initiation." Later in the century, other books came out along similar lines.

Each of these readings, along with many more that I haven't discussed, casts its own special light on Revelation. But if Mouravieff was right—and I think he was—its ultimate meaning may be glimpsed only by the awakened and illumined soul.

14.

The Master and Two Marys

THE BOOK OF Revelation takes us to the end of the Bible. Now let's see how Christianity relates to this Bible, and where it got some of its teachings from.

One way of glimpsing part of an answer would be to look at the fates of Jesus and two women in his life: Mary, his mother, and Mary Magdalene. Or rather, to look at the fate of their reputations in later centuries.

Christology, High and Low

Theologians often speak of *Christology*. The meaning of this word seems obvious. It's the study of Jesus Christ, isn't it?

Not exactly.

Most often Christology is used to mean a theological *position* about Jesus Christ.

Was Jesus God, a man, or something in between? Your Christology depends on how you answer this question.

There are Christologies high and low.

High Christology means you have a very exalted conception of who Jesus was. The highest Christology that I know of is that of the eighteenth-century Swedish visionary Emanuel Swedenborg. Swedenborg said that *"the absolute God is Jesus Christ, who is the Lord Jehovah. . . .* He is the Father, the Son, and the Holy Spirit combined." Swedenborg dismissed the usual view of the Trinity as nothing more than a muddle-headed idea of three Gods (a criticism that many others have made too).

The next highest, and most familiar, form of Christology is that of the Catholic and Orthodox and most of the Protestant churches. Jesus Christ is the incarnate Son of God, the Second Person of the Trinity. He is the equal of God the Father, fully God and fully man.

By contrast, a *low Christology* would say that Jesus was just a man like the rest of us. He was not born of a virgin, and he was not a divine incarnation at all.

The lowest Christology, I suppose, would be that of the authors who argue that Jesus never even existed: he was a fictitious creation made up by persons unknown. But, as we've seen, this view is not and has never been taken seriously by reputable scholars.

You may have noticed that my earlier account of who Jesus thought he was, or claimed to be, was rather vague. It was. It had to be. Any more specific answer would have been less correct.

Why? As I've already indicated, no one knows with any finality which of Jesus's statements in the Gospels are authentic and which aren't. The accounts in the Gospels are shaped by who the early Christians thought Jesus was. He undoubtedly did make some of the messianic claims about himself. Undoubtedly he did not make others, which were put into his mouth later. Exactly which statements of his fall into which category is guesswork at best.

Therefore the most careful and sensible path is to admit that we only have, and can have, a rough idea of how Jesus saw himself. I myself think he believed himself to be (and was believed to be) descended from the house of David. This shaped his concept of himself and his mission. He could well have seen himself as the foretold Messiah. But the redemption he offered to the Jews was spiritual and not political. It's possible that he saw himself also as the Son of Man, identified with the Messiah.

In any case, there is much more evidence about how Jesus came to be seen later.

Previously I mentioned *low Christology*. Some views of this kind say that Jesus started out as a man like the rest of us, but that at a certain point he was adopted as the Son of God. (That's why these theories are often classed under the label *adoptionism*.) Some early Christians believed that this adoption this took place at Jesus's baptism by John. Bart D. Ehrman argues that this was the view of Mark, which is why Mark opens his Gospel there.

Another view held that Jesus was adopted at his resurrection. This appears to be echoed at the beginning of Romans. I give this passage in Ehrman's translation:

> Paul, a slave of Christ Jesus, called as an apostle and set apart for the gospel of God, which he announced in advance through his prophets in the holy scriptures, concerning his Son, who was descended from David according to the flesh, who was *appointed* Son of God in power according to the Spirit of holiness by his resurrection from the dead, Jesus Christ our Lord. (Romans 1:1–4; my emphasis)

There are a number of reasons for believing that Paul did not originally write this. Instead it was probably an early kind of creed that Paul is quoting. He expects the believers at Rome—whom he has not yet met—to recognize it. (Notice that this passage lays heavy emphasis upon Jesus as the descendant of David.)

There are more examples, which you can look up for yourself, such as Acts 2:36; 5:31; 13:32–33; 1 Corinthians 15:3–5.

The picture would seem to be clear. Initially Jesus's followers thought he was a man who had been exalted to the right hand of God. You might assume, then, that Christology was a neat progression. Little by little, over the generations Jesus the man advanced to becoming Jesus the God.

But the picture is not so clear. In the first place, there were any number of other faith communities that saw Jesus quite differently. There were the Ebionites, Jewish Christians who believed that he was simply a man from start to finish. The Docetists were a Gnostic sect who believed that the flesh is so completely defiled that Jesus would never have put it on. Instead he was kind of a phantom who only appeared to suffer on the cross. And of course there were any number of other positions in between, both in the earliest times and in later centuries.

Even in the Christian communities represented in the New Testament, the situation wasn't that simple. Jesus's adoption was not the adoption of a man like the rest of us. Take a look at these verses from Paul's epistle to the Philippians:

> Let this mind be in you, which was also in Christ Jesus: Who, being *in the form of God*, thought it not robbery to be equal with God: But made himself of no reputation, and took on him the form of a servant, and was made in the likeness of men: And being found in fashion like a man, he humbled himself, and became obedient unto death, even the death of the cross. Wherefore God hath highly exalted him, and given him a name which is above every other name: That at the name of Jesus every knee should bow. (Philippians 2:5–10; my emphasis)

To begin with, two likely facts about this passage: (1) Philippians is dated to between 56 and 63; (2) Paul did not write it, but is quoting it. It is a preexistent hymn that his readers would have been familiar with (just like the opening of Romans). Thus Paul is not breaking any news to the Philippians. He is appealing to something they already believe.

Thus this passage was well known even when Philippians was written.

Its view of Jesus may go back to no more than ten years or so after his death. It says he was a preexistent divine being "in the form of God," who chose to be born "in the likeness of men." By his redemptive death on the cross, God exalted him higher than he had previously been, to the point where his name "is above every other name."

At this point I need to stress that *there was no doctrine of the Trinity in the earliest days of Christianity. The early Christians did not believe Jesus was God.* Theologies that made these claims started to arise only in the second century.

In the passage above, Paul seems to be arguing for what later came to be called a *subordinationist* view of Christology: Jesus was a step, but still a step, below God.

This is quite an extraordinary status to have gained so soon after his death.

The Philippians passage represents an early version of a high Christology. Although Jesus is not God, he is only one step below him and he is above everybody else, both humans and angels. Furthermore, he did not start out as a man like everyone else. He was a preexistent divine being.

Here is Bart D. Ehrman's summation: "Jesus was thought of as an angel, or an angel-like being, or even the Angel of the Lord—in any event, a superhuman divine being who existed before his birth and became human for the salvation of the human race. This, in a nutshell, is the incarnation Christology of several New Testament authors."

The Great Angel Returns

So what sort of preexistent divine being was Jesus?

Here is where it gets complicated. Please bear with me.

You will remember that, at least by some theories, there were originally two Gods in Israel: El, the high God, and Yahweh, God of Israel alone, sometimes known as the Angel of God or the Angel of the Lord.

Eventually, however, the Jews decided that Yahweh was not an angel. He was the high God himself. El and Yahweh were the same.

But the Great Angel did not go away. He continued to survive in Judaism for centuries afterward. He was sometimes known as the Son of Man.

The first usage of the expression "the Son of Man" in this sense appears in the book of Daniel, written in the second century BC: "I saw in the night visions, and, behold, one like the Son of Man came with the clouds of heaven, and came to the Ancient of days, and they brought him near before him" (Daniel 7:13). In this passage, the "Ancient of days" would be equivalent to God, and the Son of Man, to the Great Angel.

Sometimes the Son of Man was called Metatron, a name that looks more Greek than Hebrew. That may be because it is. One theory says this name comes from the Greek *metà toû thrónou*—the angel "with the throne" of God.

Metatron, the Great Angel, was known in other ways too, depending upon which text you look at. Here is a list of some names for him:

The Angel of the Lord
The Son of Man
The Son of God
The second God (*deúteros theós* in Greek)
The Name of God
The Logos = The Word
Wisdom

These names aren't totally equivalent. Some texts use them slightly differently. Most texts use only some or one of them.

It would take a long and highly technical treatise to go through all of these terms and explain where they occur and how they connect to one another. That's impossible here. For our purposes it's best to take them as kind of a basket of names for more or less the same concept. It would be hard to overstate the importance of this concept to early Christianity.

Here it is: there is a kind of subordinate God, through whom the high God relates to the universe, and through whom he created the universe. This subordinate God is actually an angel.

Here is one text that sheds some light on the subject. It's from a pseudepigraphical work called *1 Enoch*:

> And at that time that the Son of Man was named, in the pres-
> ence of the Lord of Spirits
> And his name before the Head of Days.
> And before the suns and the "signs" [i.e., constellations] were
> created
> Before the stars of the heaven were made,
> His name was named before the Lord of spirits.

There are two figures here: One is the Lord of Spirits, the Head of Days (or Ancient of Days), the high God, the Father. The other is the Son of Man (just as in the verse from Daniel). You will notice that the last line emphasizes his "name." This is important.

The ancient Hebrews saw a much closer connection between the word and the thing than we do. In fact, they used the same word for both: *davar*. This fact meant that God's name was, in some way, equivalent to God himself. (To this day pious Jews sometimes refer to God as *ha-Shem*, "the Name.")

The Name is a *hypostasis*. We've come across this term already. It is an attribute (usually of God) that takes on a life of its own and becomes a kind of independent entity, even a person.

It's even in the Bible. In Exodus the Lord says to the children of Israel, "Behold, I send an Angel before thee, to keep thee in the way, and to bring thee into the place which I have prepared. Beware of him, and obey his voice, and provoke him not: for he will not pardon your transgressions: *for my name is in him*" (Exodus 23:20–21; my emphasis).

Now we know who the Son of Man is. He is the Great Angel, the personification of the Name. Why was he called the Son of Man? Here's one answer: many of these texts are not just the results of imagination or theologizing. They sometimes represent real visionary experience. We have almost no idea of how this kind of experience was produced. But in it the angels often had the form of men.

The texts say this over and over. Here's a well-known example, from the famous throne vision of Ezekiel: "And above the firmament . . . was the likeness of a throne, as was the appearance of a sapphire stone: and upon the likeness of the throne was the likeness of the appearance of a man above upon it" (Ezekiel 1:26).

But there's more. Metatron may have been called the "Son of Man" partly because he originally *was* a man. Enoch, to be specific. Antediluvian patriarch, great-grandfather of Noah, after living 365 years, "Enoch walked with God: and he was not; for God took him" (Genesis 5:24).

That is all the Bible has to say about Enoch.

But Jewish mysticism had much more to say. Enoch not only was taken to heaven, but was elevated to the highest of all positions—in fact he became Metatron, the Great Angel.

Below is a verse from a mystical text known as *3 Enoch*, which tells of a rabbi's journey into the heavenly realms. (The date of *3 Enoch* isn't known. The best guesses are between the second and sixth centuries AD, but it incorporates traditions that are much older.) In it Metatron says:

> I am Enoch, the son of Jared. When the generation of the Flood sinned and turned to evil deeds, . . . the Holy One, blessed be He, took me from their midst to be a witness against them in the heavenly height.

To sum all of this up: Judaism at the time of Christ, and long before, had a notion of the Great Angel, the hypostasis of the divine Name. At some point he was identified with the patriarch Enoch, who had ascended to heaven and become the angel Metatron. Hence Metatron was called the Son of Man.

Christianity took this idea over. The early Christians decided that Jesus was the Son of Man, the Great Angel, who had come down to earth. He had degraded himself to take on fleshly form in order to deliver us from our sins. God rewarded him by exalting him to a still higher level than he had had before.

This is what the passage above from Philippians is trying to say. Here is another example, from the epistle of the Hebrews:

> God, who at sundry times and in divers manners spake in time past unto the fathers by the prophets, hath in these last days spoken to us by his Son, whom he hath appointed heir to all things, *by whom also he made the worlds*: who being the brightness of his glory, and the express image of his person, and upholding all things by the word of power, when he had by himself purged our sins, sat down on the right hand of the Majesty on high: being made so much better than the angels, as he hath [been allotted] *a more excellent name* than they (Hebrews 1:1–4; my emphasis).

The bracketed passage indicates my own addition to the King James translation. That's because the King James Version fails to translate one word in the Greek: *keklēronómēken*, "has been allotted." To say that Jesus was "allotted" his excellent name created some discomfort in light of later belief, so the word was left out from the translation. Most versions of the Bible, even the most reputable and up-to-date ones, do similar things with passages like these.

In any event, the Great Angel starts with a very high status. In fact, God made the creation through him. But he chose to come down to earth and offer himself up for our sins, so God elevated him to a still higher standing, to God's right hand. He is thus no longer below God, but is literally on the same level.

This passage also says that God made the worlds through the Great Angel. You may be reminded of the opening of the Gospel of John: "All things were made by him"—the Logos, the Word (John 1:3).

You'll also have noticed that I put the Logos, the Word, on the same list as the Great Angel and the Son of Man. That's because the name Logos was also applied to the Great Angel. The first man to do this was the Jewish theologian Philo of Alexandria. Philo lived at the time of Jesus (Philo's dates are c.15 BC–c.AD 50), although he never mentions Jesus and apparently doesn't know of him.

But Philo does know of the Logos:

> And even if there be not as yet any one who is worthy to be called a son of God, nevertheless let him labour earnestly to be adorned according to his first-born word, *the eldest of his angels, as the great archangel of many names*; for he is called, the authority, and *the name of God, and the Word*, and man according to God's image, and he who sees Israel.

There you have it. The "great archangel" is "the name of God" and "the Word."

Word here is a translation of the Greek *lógos*. *Lógos* is an extremely common word in Greek. And it does mean *word*.

Sort of.

In fact when I think back to any Greek text I've read, *word* is almost never the best translation for *lógos*. It's often best translated as *speech, argument, reason*, even *true story*. But its meaning goes much further still.

It's no small feat to say what *lógos* meant over the course of a thousand years of ancient Greek philosophy. But here is the main idea: *lógos* is the *structuring principle of consciousness*. Or, if you like, *consciousness as a structuring principle*.

What on earth do I mean by this?

To understand, simply take a look at your surroundings. Whether they're familiar or not, you can easily identify objects and people: a table, a chair, that man over there, and so on. Your mind is picking them out from a background of colors, sounds, and other impressions. By picking them out, your mind is organizing them. They are no longer an ocean of random sense data. They are an organized and coherent world. Moment by moment, the *lógos* in you is creating the world.

It's no coincidence that the root behind *lógos* is the verb *légō*, which originally meant "to pick up" or "pick out."

By the time of Philo, Greek philosophers had devoted a lot of attention to this idea. In his day, the Stoics were one of the dominant philosophical schools. They said that this *lógos*, this structuring principle of consciousness, was the basis not only of our experience but of all existence. This idea was extremely influential.

Philo wanted to connect traditional Jewish teachings with Greek philosophy. So he identified this *lógos* with the Name, the Great Angel.

One man who was probably familiar with Philo's thought was the evangelist John. That was how he came to write "In the beginning was the *lógos*, and the *lógos* was with God, and the *lógos* was God" (John 1:1).

Philo identified the Logos with the Great Angel. We see in Philippians that the Great Angel was identified with Jesus. John the evangelist made the obvious connection. The Logos = the Great Angel, incarnated in Jesus. Elsewhere Philo has the Word say:

> And I stood in the midst, between the Lord and you, neither being uncreate [*sic*] as God, nor yet created, but being in the midst between these two extremities, like a hostage, as it were, to both parties: a hostage to the Creator, as a pledge and security that the whole race would never fly off and revolt entirely ...; and to the creature, to lead it to entertain a confident hope that the merciful God would not overlook his own work.

It's easy to see here the origins of Jesus's later role as mediator between God and man. But he is not God. He still remains subordinate to God.

The accompanying diagram shows these relations in a rough schematic form.

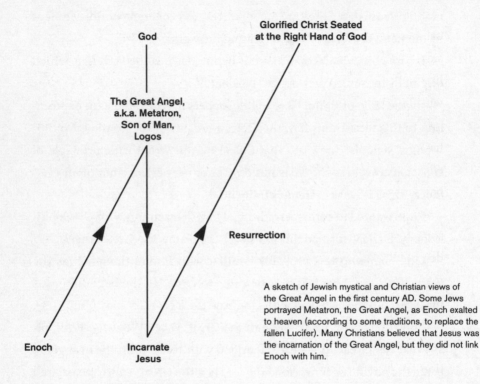

A sketch of Jewish mystical and Christian views of the Great Angel in the first century AD. Some Jews portrayed Metatron, the Great Angel, as Enoch exalted to heaven (according to some traditions, to replace the fallen Lucifer). Many Christians believed that Jesus was the incarnation of the Great Angel, but they did not link Enoch with him.

Metatron Dethroned

If this Great Angel was so important, you may be asking why you haven't heard of him before.

Here's one reason. At one point the Jewish sages decided that Metatron had gotten too big for his britches. So they dethroned him.

We find out about this in *3 Enoch*. It is a striking and revealing passage.

At one point a heretical rabbi ascends to heaven in a mystical vision. He sees Metatron on his throne and exclaims, "There are indeed two powers of heaven!" Then the Holy One—God himself—dethrones Metatron. The angel Anapiel comes and, Metatron says, "struck me with sixty lashes of fire and made me stand to my feet."

The passage suggests why Metatron was dethroned. The rabbi is called Acher (the "other one")—a contemptuous epithet: the Jews considered him an archheretic. His real name was Elisha ben Abuya, and he lived around the turn of the second century AD. Although it's not clear what kind of heretic he became, most likely he converted to Christianity.

If this is true, it tells us a great deal. The idea of "two powers of heaven" had been in Judaism for centuries. But the Christians turned it to great effect: there was the Father, and there was the Son, sitting at the right hand of the Father. They identified this Son with Jesus.

At some point the rabbis decided to rid themselves of this troublesome second god, who was leading mystics to heresy. Metatron was demoted in the heavenly hierarchy. He was taken off his throne and made to stand on his feet. Dethroning Metatron was a way of putting a distance between Judaism and Christian doctrines.

Obviously I don't mean that Metatron was actually deposed in the celestial realms (of which, if they exist, we can have very little conception). Rather I mean that the rabbis of the second century AD had become uncomfortable about some theological claims that were being made about him and decided to downplay his role.

Nevertheless, Metatron is still mentioned in later Judaism, mostly in the Kabbalah, which preserves many of the most ancient and profound Jewish teachings. He is also still identified with Enoch, who was, according to the Kabbalah, the first fully realized man.

Metatron vanished from Christianity because Christianity identified him with Jesus. It would continue to exalt the status of Jesus throughout the first to the fourth centuries. We've already seen how Jesus was placed on the right hand of God—made equal to God. The next step was to say that not only was he equal to God, but he had *always* been equal to God.

Thus the doctrine of the Trinity was born.

It was decreed as the official doctrine of the Catholic church at the Council of Nicaea in 325. Those, including a bishop named Arius, who held that Jesus was originally a created being were denounced as heretics. Arius's views were probably closer to the beliefs of the New Testament authors than were those of the side that won.

Paul himself would have probably agreed more with Arius. It's sobering to think that if Paul, the fount of all Christian theology, had been at the Council of Nicaea, he would probably have been thrown out as a heretic too. But history is full of many such ironies.

Nevertheless, the doctrine of the Trinity was not merely the fabrication of some fourth-century bishops. The sacred ternary is a universal motif. It is found almost everywhere, under different names. There is the Hindu trinity of Brahma, Vishnu, and Shiva, also the three primordial elements, *rajas* (force), *tamas* (inertia), and *sattva* (equilibrium). Chinese thought calls this ternary "heaven," "earth," and "man." Jewish mysticism uses the three letters in the name of Yahweh—*yod* (Y), *heh* (H), and *waw* (W)—to express the same idea. And the ancient Slavs had Tribog ("Three-God"), a three-headed deity. It would be an oversimplification to say that all these trinities are talking about exactly the same thing. Nevertheless, the sacred ternary is a genuine, profound, and universal teaching. The Christian Trinity is merely one way of approaching it.

One final question: Clearly some of Jesus's earliest followers saw him as the Great Angel, the Son of Man. But was that how he saw himself?

At times he speaks of himself that way. To take one example, "Foxes have holes, and birds of the air have nests; but the Son of man hath not where to lay his head" (Luke 9:58).

But to repeat a now-familiar point, the final answer depends on the authenticity of verses whose authenticity is by no means clear—that is, on whether Jesus really did say something like this or whether these words were put in his mouth later on by the Christian church.

Mainstream scholars tend to regard Jesus's Son of Man statements as authentic. An entry in *The Oxford Companion to the Bible* says, "It is . . . reasonable to suppose that the usage of the expression in the Gospels originates in the way in which Jesus spoke of himself." Why? Partly because the later Christian church didn't quite know who the Son of Man was. You will almost never see this name used in liturgies. Present-day theologians often seem clueless about it as well.

The later church was not likely to make up this title for him because the church no longer knew what it meant. For this reason, scholars tend to think that the Son of Man comes from the earliest years of Christianity, probably from Christ himself.

Jesus, then, may have himself believed he was the incarnation of the Great Angel, the Son of Man, and hinted as much to his disciples. He also seems to have identified this Son of Man with the Messiah.

What, in fact, was the relation of the Son of Man to the Messiah? Were they the same? If not, what was the difference?

The answer I am about to give is highly speculative. But I find it very attractive, because, if true, it would tie together a number of otherwise baffling facts. I am taking it for the most part from Margaret Barker's book *The Great Angel*.

To start with, let's turn to 1 Chronicles 29:20: "And David said to all the congregation, Now bless the Lord [Yahweh] your God. And all the congregation blessed the Lord God of their fathers, and bowed down their heads, and worshipped the Lord, and the king." It would seem that in some way the king was worshipped along with, or even as, Yahweh.

This is one of several hints that the king of Israel in the monarchic period was reverenced as a kind of embodiment of Yahweh. (Canaanite kings were often revered as incarnations of their nations' gods.) At any rate he was a "son" of Yahweh: "And [Yahweh] said to me [David], Solomon thy son, he shall build thy house and courts: for I have chosen him to be my son, and I will be his father" (1 Chronicles 28:6).

So Yahweh was the father, and the king, the anointed one (this is the literal meaning of *Messiah*), was his son. If Yahweh at this time (the monarchical period) was still identified with the Great Angel, then the anointed one, the king, was his son, and in a way his embodiment. This was particularly true of the house of David, with its special relationship with Yahweh, as in Jeremiah 33:7: "For thus saith the LORD [Yahweh]; David shall never want a man to sit upon the throne of the house of Israel."

This fact, like many other aspects of preexilic Israelite faith, was covered over by radical monotheists such as the Deuteronomist and Second Isaiah. But it may have persisted in Jewish belief even up to the time of Christ. (Judaism in that era was almost as diverse as Christianity is today.)

Possibly, then, Jesus, as a descendant of David, was considered to be not only the Messiah, but a kind of incarnation of the Great Angel, just as the old Davidic kings were of Yahweh. To put it in rough schematic form:

The Davidic kings = incarnations of Yahweh, the Great Angel.

Jesus, the descendant of David = an incarnation of the Son of Man, the Great Angel.

Some of Jesus's followers—certainly many of those who wrote the New Testament—seemed to see him this way. He may have believed something like this himself.

If so, he saw his role in a spiritual sense; he was not interested in the political liberation of the Jews. But the priests were able to use these beliefs to frame him as an agitator and hang him by them.

A strange consequence of this reasoning: if Metatron was the Son of Man, and this Son of Man was originally Enoch, Jesus may have been regarded as a reincarnation of Enoch. A fascinating possibility—but one that is, to my knowledge, unexplored by scholarship.

How God Became God

All of this, I realize, is an enormous amount of detail. If it's any consolation, I've never seen this material set out clearly anywhere else.

Let me summarize what I've said up to now. I will add some dates to make things clearer. Remember that they are very approximate.

1200 BC: Yahweh, the God of Israel, is a hypostasis, a personification, of the creative powers of El, the high god of the Canaanites—*Yahweh ts'v'ot*—"he who causes the hosts to be." He is often if not always pictured as the Great Angel, the Angel of God.

600 BC–AD 1: The Jews come to identify Yahweh with El. Yahweh is no longer the Great Angel. Yahweh *is* El.

The Great Angel doesn't go away, however. He survives in Judaism, this time as the hypostasis of the Name Yahweh. He is identified with the patriarch Enoch, who was taken into heaven. He is also known as Metatron, the Son of Man, and the Logos.

AD 30–100: Some Christians—maybe even Christ himself—say that Jesus Christ is the Great Angel, the Son of Man, who incarnated as a flesh-and-blood man. Before he became a man, he was the highest and greatest angel. After he came down and paid for the sins of humanity, God rewarded him by elevating him still higher. After Jesus was resurrected, God set him on God's own right side, and made him virtually equal to God. This is what Paul is saying and what the Gospel of John is saying.

AD 100–325: Christianity discards the idea of Jesus as the Great Angel, the Son of Man. It no longer even remembers what the Son of Man originally meant. It decrees that Jesus is the Second Person of the Trinity, eternally uncreated, equal to God himself.

AD 150: The Jews, objecting to the use Christianity has made of the Great Angel, demote—literally dethrone—him. He survives, as Metatron, in Jewish legend and in the Kabbalah.

To restate a now perhaps obvious point: *the early Christians did not believe that Jesus was God.* But they— or some of them anyway—believed he was the Great Angel incarnated in human form. He may have believed this himself.

Not all of the early Christians thought of Jesus this way. The Ebionites believed that Jesus was simply a man. There were also the Gnostics, whose views differed from those described above in some important but subtle ways. (Marcion is often classed among the Gnostics.) No doubt there were other Christian groups about which we know nothing. But these are the views of the early Christians whose writings made up the New Testament.

These few paragraphs above sum up how God became God. Not the God of others, perhaps, but of our civilization. This is *our* God. He is the God of our thrownness, whether or not we choose to believe in him.

The Mother of God

Let's now turn to Mary, the mother of Jesus, who is in many ways as popular as Jesus himself.

If you read the Gospels on their own, Mary is a marginal figure. She is prominent in Luke's Nativity account, but fades into the background afterward. Sometimes Jesus is rude to her. In one scene (Matthew 12:46–50; Mark 3:31–35; Luke 8:19–21), she and his brothers come to see him. Jesus's answer is, in effect, "Let them wait." At the marriage feast of Cana, she tells him that the party is out of wine. His reply is curt: "Woman, what have I to do with thee? mine hour is not yet come" (John 2:4).

Only on the cross (and this only in John's Gospel: John 19:26–27) does Jesus take some thought for her, commending her to the care of the beloved disciple. (According to ancient tradition, John, the disciple, obeyed and took her to settle in Ephesus in Asia Minor.)

In the early centuries of Christianity, Mary was honored and revered, but had no special status. Only in the fourth century did she become more than a mere side figure. At this time Christianity was taking over the Roman Empire.

Writers often say that Christianity had many competitors for the religious allegiance of the empire, and this is true. Some have said its chief rival was Mithraism, a Persian-inspired mystery religion with seven degrees of initiation.

This isn't really true. Mithraism never captured the popular imagination. It was a cult that, for whatever reason, was mostly popular in the Roman legions. The great rival to Christianity was something quite different.

It was the cult of Isis, the mother goddess of Egypt. Worship of Isis bloomed throughout the Roman Empire in the early centuries AD.

Why? If you're familiar with Greek and Roman myth, you'll realize that its goddesses are not particularly warm or motherly. Hera comes across as jealous and vindictive, while Artemis and Athena are emphatically virgins. Aphrodite may offer the sum of all sexual delights, but she's not very motherly either.

There was Cybele, the Great Mother, imported from Asia Minor, but the Romans always felt ambivalent toward her. Her castrate priests and the weird, shrieking cries of her devotees always seemed strange and alien. For centuries Roman citizens were forbidden to become her priests.

And yet people experience love first and foremost as mother's love. It's natural to think of God's love in this way too. A society that worshipped gods and goddesses equally might well find itself in search of a mother goddess.

Isis fit the bill perfectly. She's most familiar from the Egyptian myth of Osiris, in which she is Osiris's wife and sister. When Osiris's jealous brother Seth kills him, dismembers him, and scatters his parts all over Egypt, it is Isis who reassembles the parts and brings Osiris back to life as lord of the dead. Isis is also the mother of Horus, vanquisher of Seth and avenger of Osiris.

So Isis is the personification of love and care and healing. She is often pictured with her child Horus in much the same way as the Virgin Mary would later be shown with the baby Jesus.

After the fourth century BC, the cult of Isis became a proselytizing religion, spreading far beyond Egyptian borders. Her missionaries were her priests. Some of their characteristics are recognizable today, because the Catholic church took them over. Scholar R. E. Witt says that the priest "sprinkled blest water in the temple of Isis. He resembled the minister of Mithras and of Christ inasmuch as he performed the rite of baptism. Wearing now a black cassock and now a linen surplice he held fixed daily services. . . . He was a man set apart as holy."

Although Isis would always retain her Egyptian flavor, she became increasingly Hellenized. There are statues of her that are more or less identical to those of Greek goddesses. They are identified as Isis only because they hold her symbols, the *sistrum*—a small percussion instrument—and the water jar.

The ancient city of Pompeii lies in southern Italy just outside of Naples. It was buried in a volcanic eruption in AD 79 and unearthed only in recent centuries. More than any other site, Pompeii tells us what it was like to live in the Roman Empire. Its ruins show that Isis was highly popular. Pompeii has an Iseum, a temple of Isis, in the center of town. Private houses have murals and frescoes that depict her, sometimes in a holy, sometimes in an erotic guise.

If you want to catch a glimpse of Isis's religion, you can read *The Golden Ass* of Lucius Apuleius, a second-century novel in which the narrator is turned into an ass by magic. He is only restored to his human state by the mercy of Isis. Finally he is initiated into her cult. (Apuleius himself is thought to have been an initiate of Isis, so his description of this rite may be one of the very few direct glimpses we have of ancient mystery religions.)

In this atmosphere, Mary became increasingly exalted too, perhaps as a way of counteracting Isis's appeal. Images of Mary in art begin to appear in the third century. In the fourth century, as Christianity made its bid for the allegiance of the whole Roman world, the cult of Mary came even more into the ascendant.

This trend culminated in the church's proclamation of the Virgin as *theotókos*, the Mother of God, in 431. It may be no coincidence that all the pagan temples had been closed relatively recently (the first closing was ordered by the emperor Theodosius I in 391; other antipagan measures continued to follow). Perhaps the bishops and emperors knew that people would continue to worship the Great Mother whether they were supposed to or not. The solution was to make her a Christian.

The transference of allegiance from Isis to Mary is easy to understand, given the aggressive proselytizing of the Christian faith. Some of this was no doubt due to a shrewd clergy making a bid for Isis's devotees. But much of it was very likely unconscious. The Great Mother has always been worshipped, as whore, as life giver, and in countless other guises. Christianity chose to see her as a virgin.

To this day the allure of the Virgin Mary in Catholicism far outstrips that of God the Father, possibly even that of Jesus himself. The Marian apparitions at Lourdes, Fatima, and Medjugorje are famous. Of the many others, some can be bizarre or comical. In 2000, residents of an apartment complex in Houston began to venerate a puddle of spilled ice cream that, they believed, had congealed into an image of the Virgin.

The Woman at the Empty Tomb

Another woman connected to Jesus is far more mysterious still: Mary Magdalene.

If you follow the popular conceptions about Mary Magdalene, you will think she was the woman taken in adultery whom Jesus forgave and who was the sister of Martha who listened to Jesus while Martha was working in the kitchen and who poured out an expensive jar of ointment on Jesus's feet and who may have been married to him besides.

This is quite a package.

But as a matter of fact, there is no reason to associate Mary Magdalene with the woman taken in adultery or the woman who poured the ointment on Jesus's feet or the sister of the industrious Martha. The Gospels do not connect these figures at all.

Just to make one thing clear at the outset: The name *Mary* in the Gospels is the English rendition of the Greek *María*. This in turn is the equivalent of the Hebrew *Miriam*. Miriam, in the Old Testament, was Moses's sister. The name was very common among Jewish women in Jesus's day. Several Marys surround Jesus, including his mother; the mother of James and John; the sister of Martha and Lazarus; and the wife of Cleophas.

Because we know most of these as names only, it's impossible to say much about them. But let's focus on Mary Magdalene.

The Gospels in the New Testament say only two things specifically about Mary Magdalene: (1) that she had had seven devils cast out of her (Luke 8:2), and (2) that, according to all four Gospels, she was the one who first discovered that Jesus's tomb was empty.

That's it.

For the sake of argument, say you are a scholar who tends toward the skeptical side. You may well doubt the story about the empty tomb. You may also doubt that there is anything in the idea of casting out devils.

In that case you might conclude that we know nothing whatsoever about Mary Magdalene apart from her name.

Nevertheless, the figure of Mary Magdalene has grown much more prominent over the last generation—especially in alternative forms of Christianity. So it's worth looking at some of the traditions that have caused her to be seen afresh.

The Wife of Jesus?

There's an increasingly popular belief that Mary Magdalene was actually the wife of Jesus. Let's look at the evidence for this.

The *Gospel of Thomas*, as we've seen, may go back to the mid–first century. There is a Mary who appears at the end of it.

> Simon Peter said to them, "let Mary leave us, for women are not worthy of life."
>
> Jesus said, "I myself shall lead her in order to make her male, so that she too may become a living spirit resembling you males. For every woman who shall make herself male will enter the kingdom of heaven."

It would seem that being "male" has an esoteric meaning. Sometimes in mystical literature "to be male" means to remember one's inner dimensions in order to be able to "marry" one's internal energies (seen as female). It may have a meaning like that here.

In any event, the Mary in this passage is often identified with Mary Magdalene. But as a matter of fact she isn't *called* Mary Magdalene, and there were lots of Marys around Jesus. So even this connection is highly speculative. Nor does the text imply any kind of sexual or romantic connection between Jesus and Mary.

Everything else about Jesus's relationship with Mary Magdalene either is legend or is taken from Gospels that were written much later.

To take one example, let's turn to the Gnostic *Gospel of Philip*, dated to the second or third century. It includes this tantalizing passage: "And the companion of the [. . .] Mary Magdalene. [. . . loved] her more than [all] the disciples, [and used to] kiss her often on her [. . .]. The rest of the [disciples . . .]. They said to him: 'Why do you love her more than all of us?' The savior answered and said to them: 'Why do I not love you like her?'"

Note that this passage is fragmentary. Everything in square brackets was added by the translator.

As a result, there are more questions than answers here. "Companion"? What does "companion" mean? It's certainly not the same as a wife. And what exactly did Jesus kiss her *on*? Her mouth? Possibly. But unless men have changed enormously since ancient times, they don't go around ostentatiously kissing their wives in public. They are more likely to kiss their girlfriends, leading one to suspect that this is what "companion" may have meant.

Actually the passage goes on in quite a different direction. Jesus says:

> When a blind man and one who sees are both together in darkness, they are no different from one another. When the light comes, then he who sees will see the light, and he who is blind will remain in darkness. . . . The superiority of man is not obvious to the eye, but lies in what is hidden from view.

The context thus suggests that Jesus is pointing to some kind of spiritual superiority in Mary Magdalene rather than a romantic interest.

Nevertheless, this passage has led some to claim that Jesus had some kind of sexual or romantic relationship with Mary Magdalene. Some even argue that she was his wife, a theory reinforced by a newly discovered papyrus fragment, of disputed authenticity but possibly dating to eighth-century Egypt. This fragment has the words "Jesus said to his wife . . ." The text breaks off, so we don't know who his wife was supposed to have been or what he is supposed to have said.

By all accounts, both this papyrus fragment, recently dubbed "The Gospel of Jesus's Wife," even if it is genuine, and the *Gospel of Philip* date to much later than the time of Christ. While this evidence suggests that there was some *belief* that Jesus had a wife, who could have been Mary Magdalene, no one can say he actually *did*. The evidence shows nothing more than that there was a later tradition to this effect. It could be handing down an authentic piece of fact, but the best we can say is that we simply don't know. Much the same is true of practically everything we learn about Jesus from the apocryphal Gospels.

Scholars generally doubt that Jesus was married, to Mary Magdalene or anyone else. Here is their reasoning: If he *had* been married, surely there would have been more references to it than there are. But with the exception of one late and dubious text, no one ever says that Jesus was married.

Admittedly, the absence of evidence is not the evidence of absence. In other words, the fact that something isn't mentioned doesn't prove that it wasn't there. But in a case like this, where Jesus was venerated so soon after his death, if he had been married, his wife would have been worthy of some veneration too. And at least the fact would have been mentioned or recorded somehow—especially when Jesus's family was held in such high esteem by the Christian community in the years after his death.

If, on the other hand, Jesus was celibate, it would provide another link to the Essenes, who (unlike other Jews) were mostly celibate. Although, as I've said, Jesus's teachings are at odds with what we know of Essene doctrine, he could conceivably have taken a vow of celibacy when he was connected with the sect and kept it even after he left. But that is highly speculative.

If you want to hang on to the idea that Mary Magdalene was Jesus's wife, you would have to make an argument like this: The apocryphal Gospels that mention Mary Magdalene the most were those connected with Gnostic teachings. The *Gospel of Philip* is one of these. Another is a long and convoluted mystical treatise called the *Pistis Sophia* ("Faith-Wisdom"). There is even a fragmentary *Gospel of Mary*, dating from the second century, that is Gnostic as well.

From this evidence you might conclude that Mary Magdalene was one of Jesus's closest disciples, maybe even his wife, and that she was given certain hidden esoteric teachings that later came to be called Gnostic.

The leaders of what would become the Catholic church—particularly

Peter, whom the Gnostic Gospels often portray as an opponent of Mary—did not approve of these teachings. As Mary Magdalene's line grew more and more into the Gnostic tradition, her memory was shunted aside in the Catholic church. In later centuries, she was even associated with the woman taken in adultery (John 8:1–11) to the point where *magdalen* came to mean "repentant whore."

Of course this argument too is highly speculative. Furthermore, Mary Magdalene could have passed on Gnostic teachings from Jesus without having been romantically involved with him in any way.

Mary Magdalene in Legend

Beyond even the apocryphal Gospels, a huge amount of lore about Mary Magdalene has come to the surface over the past generation. The trend took off with a book published in 1982: *Holy Blood, Holy Grail* by Michael Baigent, Richard Leigh, and Henry Lincoln. The authors set out an elaborate and fantastic argument saying that Jesus and Mary Magdalene not only were married, but had offspring. They were the ancestors of the Merovingian dynasty, which ruled France from AD c.457 to 752. The "holy grail" (*sangreal* in Old French) did not actually refer to the cup used at the Last Supper, as is usually believed. Instead it referred to the sacred Merovingian bloodline (*sang real* = "royal blood"; hence the "holy blood" of the title). Although the Merovingians lost the throne, their bloodline continues to the present day.

In 2003 this legend was injected into the veins of mass culture with Dan Brown's novel *The Da Vinci Code*, which more than hinted that the legend was fact.

But even at the time when *The Da Vinci Code* was published, the theory in *Holy Blood, Holy Grail* had been refuted often and in detail. The story of the hoax is a bizarre one, involving a far-right French monarchist named Pierre Plantard and a mysterious society that he supposedly represented called the Priory of Sion. (I have discussed this at some length in my book *Forbidden Faith: The Secret History of Gnosticism*.) The French scholar Jean Markale is no doubt right when he calls it "a story sewn from whole cloth by failed would-be writers, country squires boasting their Merovingian ancestry, and some crackpots of stage and screen."

It's probably true that *Holy Blood, Holy Grail*'s version of the Jesus–Mary Magdalene legend was cooked up by some French crackpots. But the legend did not start, nor does it stop, with them.

In fact I have encountered similar legends from quite independent sources. In a 1998 interview, the British occultist R. J. Stewart told me that according to Robert de Boron, a medieval author who wrote about the Grail, Joseph of Arimathea

> brought the vessel [i.e., the Grail] and two cruets, one containing the blood and one containing the sweat of Jesus—sometimes thought to be a euphemism for seed, for semen. And one of the "secret" things that was taught in the English occult lodges—which is now quite widespread, but I heard this in the 1960s, when no one had publicized anything like it—was that the Grail was embodied in a son and a daughter of Jesus by Mary Magdalene. These were the "vessels," one of blood and one of seed, and Joseph brought these two children to Cornwall and Glastonbury.

And it is true that according to a much better-known tradition, Joseph of Arimathea went to Britain after the death of Christ and founded a church at Glastonbury in Somersetshire in southwestern England. Partly for this reason, Glastonbury has become a major New Age center in Britain.

Other lore abounds regarding Mary Magdalene. Rosamonde Miller, a Gnostic bishop living in California's Silicon Valley, claims that in the south of France she was initiated into an Order of Mary Magdalene that goes back to Mary herself. This order was maintained in secret for centuries. It admitted women only. Miller has said that she has been authorized to make the order public and to admit men, which she has done.

Many of the Mary Magdalene legends are centered around the south of France, where, tradition says, she settled in later years (just as John and Christ's mother were said to have settled in Ephesus, and Joseph of Arimathea in Britain).

I don't know of any direct connection among any of these legends or these groups. It's probably true, at the very least, that the groups themselves exist and that the legends have circulated. Whether they go back anywhere nearly as far as the first century is impossible to say.

At the very least, these legends show that the spirit of Mary Magdalene still exercises its own unique allure. In the last generation or so, her reputation has shifted among the mainstream public. She is now seen, more and more, not as a repentant whore or a shadowy side figure, but as a powerful and authoritative figure whom Jesus himself held in high regard. Women who are not inspired by the docile Virgin are looking to this reimagined Mary Magdalene as a role model.

Is this legitimate? Certainly. As long as you remember one thing: the relationship of individuals to their role models is an interactive one. You shape yourself according to your role model, but you also shape your role model according to your image of yourself.

Part Four

15.

Practical Mysticism

IN ROBERT LOUIS Stevenson's *Treasure Island*, the mutinous crew tries to take over the ship that brought them to the island. One of them, named Dick, had been well brought up "before he came to sea and fell among bad companions." He has a Bible. His companions tear a page out to put a black spot on it as a summons to their leader, Long John Silver.

"Where might you have got the paper?" says Long John when he gets it. "Why, hillo! Look here, now; this ain't lucky! You've gone and cut this out of a Bible. What fool's cut a Bible? . . . A Bible with a bit cut out! . . . It don't bind no more'n a ballad-book."

The Bible "with a bit cut out" keeps being mentioned throughout the last part of the novel. It is a portent that the mutiny is doomed.

After all the scrutiny, it seems that we're left with a Bible that has had much more than a bit cut out. If you took a Bible and cut out the parts that turn out to be factually problematic or questionable, the book would fall apart in your hands.

Is this a bad omen?

I mean for our civilization.

In all likelihood the tatters won't be replaced—not in respect to its literal sense. The historical-critical method, as it's sometimes called, has gone too far to turn back. Nor should it. It has taught us a great deal.

You might want to believe that someday soon they will turn up evidence of the children of Israel's journey across the desert or Moses's two tablets or the great palaces of David and Solomon. They may. Only a fool says that something will *never* happen.

But the trend isn't looking good for the Bible's literal truth. At Harvard in 1976, I could take a course from one of the preeminent biblical scholars of his time and hear a lecture about the foreign policy of David and Solomon. It would be hard to give the same lecture today, at any rate outside of a fundamentalist college.

So the belief in the literal truth of the Bible has eroded a great deal and continues to erode. This trend shows no sign whatsoever of reversing.

At this point someone usually makes a rejoinder: "Well, the Bible wasn't *meant* to be literally true."

Really? So in what kind of way was it meant to be true? For millennia, the Christian church held up the Bible to the world as the fountain of truth, literal and spiritual. Even up to a few years ago, the stories of David and Solomon were taken to be historical accounts. Now, it seems, they are little more than romantic historical novels.

The Imaginary and the Historical

Actually, there have always been those who knew that the Bible was not to be taken literally. Even in the third century, Origen—who was by far the most learned of all the church fathers—wrote:

> Very many mistakes have been made because the right method of examining the holy texts has not been discovered by the greater number of readers . . . because it is their habit to follow the bare letter. . . .

Scripture interweaves the imaginary with the historical, sometimes introducing what is utterly impossible, sometimes what is possible but never occurred.... not even [the Gospels and the writings of the apostles] are purely historical....

And who is so silly as to imagine that God, like a husbandman, planted a garden in Eden eastward, and put in it a tree of life, which could be seen and felt?

Ultimately no one can say how the original texts of the Bible were *meant* to be taken. In order to know that, you would have to know something about the authors and the immediate contexts in which these books were written. Because we know practically nothing about any of the authors—except Paul—we cannot see into their motives.

All the same, there is a long tradition of alternative interpretations of Scripture. It goes back at least as far as Philo of Alexandria, who wrote elaborate allegorical explanations of the Bible. Origen is part of this tradition as well. Origen said there were three levels of meaning to Scripture: (1) the literal meaning, for the simple; (2) the moral level, for those who have made some spiritual progress; (3) the spiritual meaning, for those who are "perfect" in the sense of Paul's statement: "Howbeit we speak wisdom among them that are perfect: yet not the wisdom of this world, nor of the princes of this world, that come to nought: But we speak the wisdom of God in a mystery, even the hidden wisdom, which God ordained before the world unto our glory" (1 Corinthians 2:6–7).

Spirit, Soul, and Body

There is another dimension to Origen's threefold interpretation of Scripture: it corresponds to the human makeup as seen in early Christianity. As he puts it, "For just as man consists of a body, soul and spirit, so in the same does the scripture, which has been prepared by God to be given for man's salvation."

The early Christians did not believe that a human being consisted merely of a body and soul: they believed that the human constitution was threefold, with a *body, soul,* and *spirit*: "I pray God your whole spirit and soul and body be preserved blameless unto the coming of our Lord Jesus Christ" (1 Thessalonians 5:23). And then there is Hebrews 4:12: "For the word of God is quick, and powerful, and sharper than any twoedged sword, piercing even to the dividing asunder of soul and spirit."

This teaching has been almost completely lost in the Christianity of today. If you ask the typical clergyman about the difference between the soul and the spirit, you will usually get a vague and confused answer. But this distinction is very important.

It's not all that hard to explain.

You will find it easier to understand if you start with the knowledge that this structure is not the human being as perceived externally, as a collection of nerves and veins and bones. It is the human structure as we experience it, as we live it from the inside.

The body is fairly self-explanatory. In this sense it is the sum total of external, sensory experience, which is what you perceive through your body.

The soul is also fairly easy to grasp, once you realize that in the New Testament the word translated as "soul" is *psuché*—the source of our word *psyche*. Actually *psyche* is a better translation than *soul*. You can get into all sorts of arguments about whether you have a soul or not, what it is, whether it is immortal, and so on. But you have a psyche. Nobody can dispute that. It is the sum total of the thoughts and images that make up your inner experience, both conscious and unconscious. It is what psychology studies or is supposed to study. It has its own organic structure, like the physical body, although this structure is still not well understood.

From this point of view, then, you can say that the physical body is the sum total of your experience of the world through the senses. The soul or psyche is the sum total of the world of your inner experience.

That's it. All your life, all your experience, fits into one or another of these categories (sometimes both). There is nothing left.

Except something I mentioned earlier when I was discussing the kingdom of heaven. It may be the most important thing in this book, so I will repeat it here.

There is something in you that *is conscious*, that *is aware*. It is not your body, nor is it even your thoughts and feelings, because you can step back inwardly and observe all these things as if from a distance (this is the point of many meditative practices). Here are some names for it from around the world: the Atman, the Self, Buddha nature, "I am that I am." The ancient Greek philosophers called it *nous*, which means something roughly like "mind" or "consciousness." The early Christians called it *pneuma*, or spirit.

So you could say that the spirit is the kingdom of heaven. Everyone has it—you would not exist without it—but for the vast majority of people it is submerged, forgotten, and unseen—because of course it is *that which sees*. They know, but *they do not know that they know*. In the language of Christ's parable, in most people this "I" is a seed that has fallen on stony ground or has been eaten up by birds.

These truths have been expressed in many contexts and many ways. If you have some understanding of them, not only the Gospels but much of the world's mystical literature will suddenly seem much clearer.

So there are three parts: body, psyche, and spirit. The early Christians believed that one of these three parts was dominant in every person. Those whose chief reality is bodily experience—what they can see and feel and eat and drink—are what Paul calls the "carnal" people. "Carnal" in the sense of "fleshly," or being oriented to the flesh.

You have known people who are ruled by their stomachs or their genitals. They are fairly easy to spot, and there are a lot of them. These are the carnal people. They will only understand the Bible—if they care about it at all—as a collection of stories, historical or not.

The next level consists of what the early Christians called the *psuchikoí*—"psychic" people. This is not what we understand today by the word *psychic*. It simply means people who have some sense of an inner life. They are a little bit more enlightened, and so they can understand the Bible as a collection of edifying moral tales.

The third level has to do with the "perfect." In the passage from 1 Corinthians I quoted above, Paul says, "We speak wisdom among the perfect." Despite what Paul says, they are not "perfect." Nobody is ever perfect, now or then, not even Paul. The Greek word here—*téleios*—does mean "perfect," but it also means things like "mature" or "accomplished." Sometimes it was used to refer to the initiates of the mystery cults. Paul is using it to speak of those who are initiated into the hidden wisdom.

What exactly was this hidden wisdom?

Part of it consisted of some of the things that I've been explaining here.

The "perfect"—also called *pneumatikoí*, the "spiritual"—are those who have had this conscious "I" awakened at least to some degree. Unlike the "carnal" and "psychic" or "psychological" people, they are oriented toward the spirit. In a sense, they have created a spiritual body in themselves.

You will remember that Paul did not believe in the resurrection of the physical body. He wrote: "It is sown a natural body; it is raised a spiritual body. There is a natural body, and there is a spiritual body" (1 Corinthians 15:46).

In Greek, "spiritual body" is *sôma pneumatikón*. "Natural body" doesn't mean what the English translations suggest it does. The Greek phrase is *sôma psuchikón*—"psychic body," or, if you like, "psychological body."

So this is what Paul is really saying: "It is sown a psychological body; it is raised a spiritual body. There is a psychological body, and there is a spiritual body."

Only the "spiritual body"—that is, the spirit—is truly immortal. The soul, the "psychic body," is not. It is merely a "seed" for the spiritual body. This is Paul's teaching. Christian dogma changed it later.

Levels of Meaning

To talk more specifically about the deeper levels of scripture, it's useful to remember that according to the inner Christian tradition, the events in the Bible sometimes refer to things that happen within the seeker as she progresses. The story of Christ's Nativity may not be literally true, but it is at least partly about a new birth within the seeker. Paul may have had a similar idea in mind when he wrote: "My little children, of whom I travail in birth until Christ be formed in you . . ." (Galatians 4:19).

Another aspect of the Bible's inner meaning: its characters represents aspects of human nature that all of us possess. Each of us has an inner scribe, a Pharisee, a hypocrite—a part of the self that constantly seeks to justify ourselves while putting down others. Christ's criticisms of the scribes and Pharisees apply not only to the religious hypocrites of his day but to the hypocrite within each of us.

Finally, many of the objects in the Bible also have a symbolic meaning that relates to inner development. *Water* refers to the psyche. *Wine* represents the level of the spirit. When Christ changes water into wine, he is symbolically taking the level of the psyche and raising it to that of the spirit.

The Exodus from Egypt is another example. It is about liberation from the bondage in "Egypt"—servitude to the material world.

One text that illustrates this idea is *The Life of Moses*, written by the church father Gregory of Nyssa in the fourth century. The first part is a straightforward account of Moses's life, taken from the Bible. The second part is intended "to lay bare the hidden meaning of the history," which has to do with the growth of the new self through spiritual awakening. The birth of Moses (like that of Christ in the Gospels) is the birth of this new self. This distresses the "tyrant"—Pharaoh—who represents the old, false self, the ego, and seeks to destroy the new life. To save it, the parents of the new self put it in an "ark" and set it adrift on the "waters": the stream of life. Gregory writes:

Whenever life demands that the sober and provident rational thoughts which are the parents of the male child launch their good child on the billows of this life, they make him safe in an ark so that when he is given to the stream he will not be drowned. The ark, constructed out of various boards, would be education in the different disciplines, which holds what it carries above the waves of life.

Similarly, Pharaoh's daughter, who rescues the infant Moses, symbolizes "profane education." Since, as we've seen, Egypt often represents the profane world, the daughter of the ruler of this world symbolizes the knowledge of this world.

Notice how the passage above is like the interpretation of Noah's ark I gave in chapter 3. While the two accounts are not saying the precisely same thing, they resemble each other strongly: the contents of the ark are the new self, the ark is the vehicle that fosters and preserves it, and the waters symbolize the exterior life.

This perspective has immense value for anyone today who still wants to gain wisdom from the Bible without being forced to accept its literal truth. Like most of the church fathers, Gregory of Nyssa accepted the literal truth of the story of Moses. It is much harder for us to do so today. As we've seen, there is little or no evidence for it.

But rather than discard the story entirely, this "hidden meaning" enables us to see its deeper and more universal truth. If the story of the Exodus were factually true, it would just be another piece of history like all the others. As a picture of spiritual regeneration, it loses none of its power and never can.

Curiously, this type of interpretation is more prominent in exegesis of the Quran—even in regard to many of the same figures. Islamic scholar Seyyed Hossein Nasr writes: "Quranic sacred history is seen more as events within the human soul rather than as just historical events in the world. All human beings possess within their being, for example, the qualities of Moses and those of Pharaoh, the beauty of Joseph and the conniving of his brothers; this sacred history is a means of teachings Muslims about their own souls."

In any event, the meaning of Scripture is multivalent. It is not like a code you can crack to get a hidden message. Sacred texts are objects of contemplation that reveal many layers of meaning. The Western mystical traditions—the Kabbalah and esoteric Christianity—explore and uncover these layers of meaning. But never finally or definitively. There is always further to go.

Two Creation Stories

To look at the inner meaning from another angle, let's turn to the beginning of the Bible: the creation account at the beginning of Genesis. You'll remember that I had put off discussing this earlier. Now is the time to take it up.

Scholars often say that there are really two Genesis creation stories. The first starts with the beginning of Genesis 1 and ends at Genesis 2:4: "These are the generations of the heavens and of the earth when they were created." The second picks up immediately afterward: "In the day that the Lord God made the earth and the heavens . . ."

You may also remember the Documentary Hypothesis, which says that the Pentateuch—the first five books of the Bible—is composed of a number of earlier texts woven together.

According to this hypothesis, the first Genesis creation story comes from P, the Priestly source. The second comes from J, the Yahwist. The first refers to the Creator as Elohim, usually translated "God." The second refers to him as Yahweh, usually translated as "the Lord." This fact helps explain why scholars think the texts come from two sources.

But what about the Redactor—the man who put these texts together in their present form? What was he thinking? Did he just have a bunch of texts that he had to cut and paste to create some kind of passable whole? Could that have been his sole motive?

The Kabbalah explains this discrepancy in the creation accounts in an unusual and profound way. If you look through the first, Priestly account in most translations, you will see that it uses the word *create* a great deal. In Hebrew, this word is *bara'*.

The Yahwist, the author of the second account, does not use the word for *create*. He uses a different word: *form*. "And the Lord God *formed* man out of the dust of the ground" (Genesis 2:7; my emphasis here and below). This is a translation of a different Hebrew verb: *yatzar*. You see it again in Genesis 2:19: "And out of the ground the Lord God *formed* every beast of the field, and every fowl of the air."

To the Kabbalist, these facts are extremely significant.

Because these words represent different levels of reality.

The Four Worlds

In the Kabbalah, there are four levels of reality, commonly called the Four Worlds. The physical world, the world known through the senses, is called *Assiyah*, from the verb *'asah*, "to make." Assiyah is the world of the body. The whole universe as known to science is at this level. Science does not know, and cannot know, about the other three levels. It is not designed to study them.

The next higher level is *Yetzirah*, the world of "formation." It is the world of thoughts, images, and concepts. It is the world we see *without* using the senses, by using the mind's eye—consciously, by imagination, or unconsciously, in dreams. It is the realm of the psyche.

The third level is *Beriah*, the world of "creation." It is a realm of primordial spirit, the realm of the archangels, according to traditional teaching. A human being has access to this level only extremely rarely—sometimes as a result of intense spiritual practice, sometimes as a spontaneous glimpse of revelation.

The fourth level is *Atzilut*, from the Hebrew *'atzal*, "to stand near." It is the realm that "stands near" the Divine. It is part of God—the part of himself that he wishes to make manifest in the universe. Practically no one experiences this level, except the holiest individuals of all. Even they can only stand to experience it indirectly, which is why Moses in Exodus sees only the back side of God. And no one can experience it for long and remain in this body. The physical body was not, so to speak, made to stand the power of its vibration. Hence "no man hath seen God at any time" (John 1:18).

Let's backtrack for a moment to sum up the structure of the Four Worlds, from top to bottom:

Atzilut	God; the Divine
Beriah	Creation
Yetzirah	Formation
Assiyah	Making

Let me just add one thing to this table: their equivalents in the human structure as seen in early Christianity.

Atzilut	God; the Divine	God
Beriah	Creation	Spirit
Yetzirah	Formation	Soul; Psyche
Assiyah	Making	Body

Thus the system in Genesis and the early Christian system correlate perfectly. They are essentially the same.

The Meaning of the Fall

Now that you know this, you can see why Genesis is written the way it is. The first account uses the word *create, bara'*. It is about Beriah (which comes from the same root), the realm of creation proper.

The second creation account uses *yatzar, to form*. It is about the realm of Yetzirah, formation.

Assiyah, the physical world, is not mentioned until the very end. The Genesis story takes place in the world of Yetzirah, esoterically known as *Eden*. The Garden of Eden was and is not in this physical world. This physical world is the world of *exile* from Eden.

How can we tell? Consider the Tree of Knowledge of Good and Evil. Its forbidden fruit is thought of as actual fruit, as sex, as any number of things. But its identity is much more obvious: the fruit is literally *the knowledge of good and evil*. God forbids the couple to eat of it, because they will die. But the serpent says that they will be as gods, knowing good and evil. Who is telling the truth?

Consider the consequences of eating the fruit:

Unto the woman [God] said, I will greatly multiply thy sorrow and thy conception; in sorrow thou shalt bring forth children; and thy desire shall be to thy husband, and he shall rule over thee.

And unto Adam he said, . . . cursed is the ground for thy sake; in sorrow shalt thou eat of it all the days of thy life; . . . In the sweat of thy face shalt thou eat bread, till thou return to the ground. (Genesis 3:16–17, 19)

The result is this: man and woman will know good and evil through life on earth. Here it hurts to have babies and people have to work hard for a living. The man and woman are punished by being given what they asked for.

This too is part of our thrownness. Each of us inevitably and certainly comes to know good and evil by experiencing them in life. The portions allotted to each one vary wildly, for reasons that we do not fully understand. But however lucky or however wretched, everyone will taste of good and evil to some degree.

Still not convinced? Look, then, at what God does next. "Unto Adam also and to his wife did the Lord God *make* coats of skin, and clothed them" (Genesis 3:21; my emphasis). Here the verb *'asah*, "make," is used. We are finally talking about Assiyah, the physical realm.

As for the coats of skin, you're wearing one right now. You are wearing one even if you are stark naked. These coats of skin are the physical body.

In the end both God and the serpent are telling the truth. The man and woman *do* become as gods, knowing—experiencing—good and evil. And "they shall surely die." Death too is inevitable. Moreover, the esoteric tradition often reverses the meaning of *life* and *death*. Death, paradoxically, means life on this material plane.

You can take all of this much further, but this at least gives an idea of what Genesis may be saying on deeper levels, and why it is not only true but profoundly true, although none of these events ever happened on earth.

Esotericism

Obviously there is much more to say about the creation account and its esoteric dimensions. But even with the little we have seen, it's clear how absurd the arguments about creationism are—the claims that the world is only six thousand years old, that everything was made in six days, and so on. The opening of Genesis is not talking about the physical world and says virtually nothing about it at all.

So then, if Genesis wasn't meant to be taken as an account of physical creation, why have so many people insisted that it is?

This bring us to the problem of esotericism. The word *esoteric* has many meanings, but it's derived from Greek roots meaning "further in." You have to go further into these teachings and texts (and into yourself) in order to understand them in any kind of complete sense.

This knowledge, at least ideally, is not kept hidden from ordinary people. But as you can see even from the little I've said, these ideas are not that easy to grasp. Even the difference between Assiyah, the physical world, and Yetzirah, the realm of the psyche, is not so clear. This confusion shows up in certain philosophers—and cognitive scientists—today. They keep trying to reduce Yetzirah (psychological inner experience) to Assiyah (merely physical, neurochemical reactions and so on).

The traditional approach, used in times when people were mostly uneducated, was to allow the general run of people to believe in the stories literally. But if someone showed unusual aptitude—including, possibly, a tendency to doubt the literal truth—he would be taken aside and shown the deeper mysteries.

This is at least the way it was supposed to work. But problems can arise. The biggest one comes when religion—whether it is Christianity or anything else—comes to have real political and social power.

At that point the leadership changes. The leaders are no longer those who are the most spiritually advanced or learned, who understand the inner meaning. Leadership means power, and it is sought by those who crave power. They eventually become the heads of the institutions. They are not interested in the deeper knowledge, and they generally don't like to know that it's there. It represents a source of power that they can't control.

So the deeper spiritual meaning is pushed more and more aside, as are those who have some grasp of this meaning. Under certain circumstances they are persecuted and killed.

This scenario doesn't play itself out everywhere or at all times. But by all appearances it is exactly what happened with Christianity over the last two thousand years.

Jacob's Ladder

This Four Worlds system—is there any sign that the biblical authors knew of it?

Yes. The Old Testament has a huge number of references that make sense only in terms of the Kabbalah, which is often seen as the oral tradition informing the Bible. In fact it's a moot point whether the Kabbalah was based on the Bible or whether the Bible was based on the Kabbalah.

To take one simple example, the Kabbalistic system, encompassing the Four Worlds, is sometimes pictured as a ladder of lights ascending from the earth to heaven. It's often called Jacob's ladder, from this passage: "And [Jacob] dreamed, and behold a ladder set up on the earth, and the top of it reached to heaven: and behold the angels of God ascending and descending on it" (Genesis 28:12).

There are many more, but explaining them would require me to explain the Kabbalistic system here. For a concise description of it, you can read chapter 4 of my book *Hidden Wisdom: A Guide to the Western Inner Traditions*.

As for the New Testament, take this verse, in which Paul writes: "I knew a man in Christ above fourteen years ago, (whether in the body, I cannot tell; or whether out of the body, I cannot tell: God knoweth;) such an one caught up to the third heaven" (2 Corinthians 12:2).

The Kabbalistic system of the Four Worlds makes Paul's statement easy to understand. There is one world—the familiar physical one—that is earthly. The other three—Yetzirah, Beriah, and Atzilut, in ascending order—are *not* earthly. They are seen as three "heavens." Paul is saying that this man was taken up to the world of Atzilut, the divine realm. This is a very high level of ascent. Many scholars believe that Paul is talking about himself here. If so, he is being modest. He avoids saying directly that he's had this experience.

Skimming the Ocean

This system of invisible worlds and ladders climbed by angels seems terribly otherworldly, terribly irrelevant to the hard realities that confront us on every side. So it could hardly have any meaning or value for our needs today.

Don't be too sure. Say there are some people who study the ocean. They devote a great deal of time and energy to it. Except they study only the *surface* of the ocean. They aren't interested in understanding anything about the ocean as it is beneath. In fact they don't even believe there *is* anything below the surface. If they're faced with evidence of life in those depths—say when a fish or some seaweed washes ashore—they deny it exists. They claim the evidence is faked, or that the people who saw these things were just imagining them.

How much about the ocean can we expect oceanographers of this sort to understand?

It's useful—necessary—to understand what's going on in the ocean. But if you believe that nothing is happening beneath the surface, you won't be able to make even the most remotely plausible guesses about it or take even minimally successful actions. What you believe will be little more than guesswork combined with superstition—and a great deal of denial.

This is precisely the situation of today's educated West in regard to the unseen worlds.

So there may be some practical value in exploring these realms. In fact this is exactly what the wise people of all times and places have been trying to tell us.

Does everyone have to do this exploration? No, probably not. Not everyone has to have a profound understanding of the ocean either. But we are better off if *somebody* does. We are better off even if some will admit that they know nothing but are at least willing to learn about it.

The Individual Versus the Collective

Even so—all these obscure words for invisible heavens and talk about spiritual bodies versus psychic bodies—how otherworldly it all sounds! How far from our problems today—environmental destruction, climate change, inequality, poverty, a greed that is choking our nation, and our world, to death!

Such criticism has some weight to it. Let's see if there is some practical application for all these mystical ideas.

Nearly all of today's difficulties—as well as those that humanity has faced throughout its history—can be traced to one, single, fundamental, often unnoticed problem: a distorted relation between the individual and the collective, that is, humanity.

The problem is easiest to see from extreme examples: sociopaths. There are not many sociopaths, but there are certainly some. Figures from the Web put them at between 1 and 3 percent of the population. Sociopaths are often defined as people without a conscience. They are incapable of sympathy or empathy. Nor do they feel affection.

The sociopath has no sense of connection with other people. Emotionally, he is completely isolated from everyone else. He lives for himself alone. And he does not mind. Other people are only things to be used instrumentally.

To put it in terms that I've used already, the sociopath has no connection with the "I that is we." He is so dissociated that he doesn't even feel the need for it.

It is grim to consider that a large number of the most powerful people in the world are very likely sociopaths.

Most of us are not so isolated. We are capable of human relations. But there is still some sense of isolation—often a profound one. This is especially true in America, where loneliness and isolation are among the central issues of our culture. Practically every major work of American literature is about this theme, whether you're talking about crazy Ahab on the *Pequod*, Huck Finn on his raft down the Mississippi, or Jay Gatsby, friendless in his ostentatious mansion.

We also feel this isolation to be painful. You feel pain as a result of some lack—you feel the anguish of starvation, for example, from a lack of food. The pain of our isolation means that we have a need that is not being met. Again to use my language, there is a need for a connection with the "I that is we," but this connection is not felt, or not felt strongly enough.

It would seem that the healthiest way of experiencing this connection with others can be seen as a series of concentric circles: your family, community, nation, religion, humanity, all of life.

But are we to experience this connection with others *only* in the context of a small group, a family or tribe or religion, or are we going to extend this sense of connection to all humanity?

Here is one place where the dysfunction can set in.

Someone longs to be part of a greater whole. He casts about desperately for something to be part of. He may choose this greater whole rather arbitrarily. You live in a certain city, and that city has a sports team, so you feel part of the community by being a fan of the team.

Sports fandom is mostly innocent. People get real pleasure out of watching sports, and the thrill of having your team win usually balances out the disappointment of having them lose. Even when the team doesn't win very often, fans share some fellow feeling in commiserating about how bad it is.

Of course there is nothing wrong with being a sports fan—at least up to this point. But it often seems as if being a fan requires not only loving your own team, but hating the rival team. Often the second part is more fun than the first.

Sometimes it can get out of hand. In the Byzantine Empire—the eastern half of the Roman Empire that went on for a thousand years after the fall of Rome itself—chariot racing was popular. There were two teams, the blues and the greens. The fans of these teams started to band together, and they started to fight. There were riots. There were even points at which the factions nearly brought the empire down.

So you can see how this sense of belonging to something greater than yourself can turn destructive. The Byzantine chariot factions are a comparatively rare example of this happening with sports fans. But you can find many examples with political parties, sects, religions, nations, and so on. Human history is largely the history of such conflicts.

At some point the sense of these widening concentric circles—family, society, humanity—comes to a halt. It can be arrested at any point. Some people consider the whole world outside their own families as enemies to be feared and fought. Others feel that way about their villages, nations, religions.

In these cases the need for connection to a larger whole is dysfunctional. It stops before it's supposed to. It leads to hatred, violence, and atrocity.

It can be awkward to use the expression *supposed to*, and it is doubly so here. Because it would be easy to mistake my meaning. I am not really saying that you are *supposed to* have this sense of a larger connection as a kind of moral duty—at least not entirely. I'm saying that this sense of an "I that is we" is a genuine, organic need. The human affinity for connection is *supposed to* work a certain way, just as your heart is supposed to work a certain way. If this sense of connection is arrested, or if it doesn't develop properly, the human apparatus doesn't work right. Much as a child may not develop right if she doesn't get enough protein.

The sociopath is thus an extreme example of a condition that most of us suffer from to one degree or another.

This sheds a completely different light on thorny issues such as morality and self-interest. At the core, the "I" that is in you is the same "I" that is in me, and indeed in all creation. That is, ultimately your self-interest and mine are identical. If you understand this to some degree, consciously or not, you are healthy. If you don't, you're not.

This health expresses itself in such things as love, compassion, and empathy. I would go further. I would say it is the source of all true love, compassion, and empathy. All other forms of human relations are merely transactions.

If I'm right about these things, it explains something else. We now know why—for a normal person at any rate—it feels good to do kind things and to help others. It feels good for the same reason that sex feels good or sleep feels good. These are all the satisfactions of real organic needs.

Now it's a bit more clear why being a kind person is, in a very deep sense, healthy for you.

If people could function normally in this sense, with a proper orientation toward the larger Self that is the human race and indeed the universe, most of the problems of the present would vanish. They would be seen simply as technical problems. And humanity has gotten very good at solving technical problems. It's often said that there is enough money, resources, and know-how to end the environmental crisis and provide everyone on earth with a decent standard of living. But the will is not there. The will is not there because not enough people are connected to "the I that is we."

I doubt that there is any genuine or lasting way of dealing with the human predicament apart from this. In the end, it may or may not be expressed in the language of Christianity. That in itself does not matter.

But then I heard once of a remark by a twentieth-century Russian Orthodox saint (I don't remember his name) saying that Christianity is still in its infancy.

Coda

AT THIS POINT you may find yourself asking again about me, the author, and what I believe. In a way I've said very little about what I believe. In another way I've said very little else.

I've described my theological views in my other books, especially *Inner Christianity, Conscious Love,* and *The Dice Game of Shiva.* So I won't go into them here.

But since so much of this book has been about Christianity, you may be curious to know what I think about Jesus Christ. This question is particularly important to some Christians, who believe that unless you agree that Jesus was the Second Person of the Trinity, fully equal to God, you will, regrettably, be damned.

I don't believe this myself. As I've said, the early Christians themselves did not believe this and would not have agreed with, or possibly understood, the later dogma of the Trinity.

I do think that Jesus believed he was the Messiah, at least on the grounds that he was a descendant of David. Did he also think he was the Son of Man, the Great Angel? To all appearances, he thought so. But whether he really described himself as such—rather than having had all these claims put in his mouth by later believers—is impossible to say.

I see things this way: Throughout history there have been countless numbers of men and women who are, in some indeterminable way, far above the level of ordinary mortals in spiritual sanctity and power. Even the ones of whom we have some reliable information are mysterious. They never completely say who they are. They give ambiguous messages, no doubt because any clear message would, from a higher perspective, be inaccurate. Their disciples wonder about them and make up stories and, as we have seen, theologies after they have gone. I believe that all this holds true for Jesus: the elaborate theologies and Christologies are all speculations. They can be enlightening from a certain point of view—but not if they lead to bigotry and fanaticism.

For me the most important thread is the concept of the cosmic Christ, the body of Christ that Paul talks about and that the Catholic church still speaks of.

There is the Cosmic Man. He is all of us. And even though I use the word *he*, he is androgynous. Each of us, man or woman, is a cell in his body. This is the source of our unity as human beings, of our connection to the "I that is we."

For some reason, this Cosmic Man wished to experience—that is, to *know*—good and evil. He fell from Eden. This was not an event that happened in the physical world. The Fall did not happen on earth, in a pleasant garden in Armenia six thousand years ago. It was a cosmic event. It gave rise to the physical world.

As a result of the Fall, the Cosmic Man shattered into countless pieces. Each of these pieces is an individual self clothed in a body. Although we experience these selves as our primary realities, they are not. From a higher point of view they are illusory.

Everything we know about the physical world is experienced through these coats of flesh—or, if you prefer, through the filtering mechanism of the nervous system. Thus sensory experience—everything from the feel of your hand on your desk to the most intricate types of submolecular research—can tell us little or nothing about how this Fall came about.

We can know about it only through myth. The myth of the Fall is not literally true. It is merely one way of expressing a situation that goes much further and deeper than conventional reality.

Other religions have other ways of describing it. They are, in all probability, no less or more accurate than this one. Each gives a perspective—a useful perspective—on this situation. I am using this one because, again, it is the myth of Christianity, the myth of our thrownness.

To continue: After the Fall, this cosmic Adam remained a unity, even if he no longer experienced himself as such. At a certain point it was time to remember that unity and to begin to return to it. If the claims of Christianity are correct, then the coming of Christ may have been the turning point in that reversal. The Jesuit theologian Pierre Teilhard de Chardin expresses a similar view in works such as *The Phenomenon of Man*.

A Course in Miracles claims to be channeled from Jesus himself—another thing that cannot be proved one way or the other—but it is certainly the most powerful expression of inner Christianity in the twentieth century. It says this about him:

> The name of *Jesus* is the name of one who was but a man but saw the face of Christ in all his brothers and remembered God. So he became identified with *Christ*, a man no longer but at one with God. . . . In his complete identification with the Christ—the perfect Son of God, His one creation and His happiness, forever like Himself and one with Him—Jesus became what all of us must be. . . . Is he the Christ? O yes, along with you.

In this case Christ's coming would have been a momentous event in the history of the world, and it was experienced as such. Those who were close to it felt its power, but they did not understand it entirely (just as we don't entirely understand it). They understood it in the religious language of their time—as blood sacrifice, as ransom paid to Satan, and so on. It was the best they could do, but there is no reason for us to stop at their limits.

At some remote point this Cosmic Man, the Son of God, the body of Christ—or Adam Kadmon, or Purusha, or Gayomart, as he is known in other traditions—will be restored to his original unity. Whether this will take place on history's time line is moot. And it will probably not bring about the fiery judgment imagined by Daniel and Revelation. *A Course in Miracles* says, "The world will end in laughter, because it is a place of tears."

There is a teaching known as *universalism*. It teaches that in the end everyone will be saved, with no exceptions. Origen believed in it, or in a version of it. People who believe in it sometimes point to a line from Paul: "For as in Adam all die, even so in Christ shall all be made alive" (1 Corinthians 15:22).

Maybe this all sounds a bit too anthropocentric. The Cosmic Man caused the Fall? Our entire universe in its present form exists because of a *human* decision, a *human* error?

No, that doesn't seem likely. But we are bound to see it that way. We know that humanity is not the center of the universe. But humanity is the center of *our* universe, because we are human. Protagoras's statement that man is the measure of all things is true. Of course. It has to be that way, because we are doing the measuring, and we are human. But it is not an absolute or final stance. The visionary science fiction writer Philip K. Dick gave the idea a different spin: "We—all creatures—are the immortal man, and . . . that 'immortal man' is not a man at all but living information." Mahayana Buddhism speaks of the cosmic regeneration as "the liberation of all sentient beings."

I doubt this event will come anytime in the course of my own life or of the lives of anyone living as I write this. That is, if time has any meaning at all in this context.

Coda

———

LOOKING BACK ON the terrain this book has covered, I find myself somewhat dumbfounded.

Of course I had some idea of what I was going to say when I started this book. By and large it has turned out according to the plan I had for it. But I didn't realize how much what is believed about Christianity and its origins differs from what actually happened.

Strange, especially, that the Great Angel keeps resurfacing. I knew of him before I started writing this book, but I had no idea that he would keep cropping up in so many places and in so many ways. He started as Yahweh, the God of Israel alone. Eventually he was merged with El, the one, high God. Even so, the idea of the Great Angel survived in later Judaism. Christians believed that he was incarnated in Jesus. Yet again he was exalted to equality with God.

The same process took place twice.

It may take some time for me to fully digest the implications of this. But I think that part of the answer lies in the metaphor that I started with: groundwater. The groundwater erupts, and it always erupts in a particular place and time. People cannot help seeing that groundwater in the context of that time and place. They somehow confound the two.

To put it theologically, the location—the immanent God—becomes identified with the groundwater, the transcendent God. Yahweh becomes El; the Great Angel becomes the Second Person of the Trinity. In a way it is a mistake, but it is a mistake that cannot help but happen.

There is probably only one way out. The Gospels may allude to it. Jesus, dying on the cross, cries out, "My God, my God, why hast thou forsaken me?" (Mark 15:34).

This may be the ultimate sacrifice we are called upon to make—that of *my* God.

Further Reading

No one person could read everything that has been written about biblical history and scholarship.

All the same, there are not many books that try to discuss this scholarship in a broad and accessible way. Most are highly technical and are intended for university-level and graduate students. (That's why I wrote this book.) Here are some of the most intelligent and accessible ones.

The Hebrew Bible

Israel Finkelstein and Neil Asher Silberman. *The Bible Unearthed: Archaeology's New Vision of Ancient Israel and the Origin of Its Secret Texts*. New York: Simon & Schuster, 2001.

Probably the best place to start if you want to find out about the implications of archaeology for the Bible. Finkelstein and Silberman's *David and Solomon* (New York: Free Press, 2006) focuses on the period of the united monarchy.

William G. Dever. *Did God Have a Wife? Archaeology and Folk Religion in Ancient Israel.* Grand Rapids, Mich.: Eerdmans, 2005.

Dever is one of the world's most renowned archaeologists specializing in the biblical period. His works are written for university-level students, but are reasonably accessible. This one focuses on Asherah in biblical times and her relationship to Yahweh.

Other works of Dever's include *What Did the Biblical Writers Know and When Did They Know It?* (Eerdmans, 2001) and *Who Were the Early Israelites and Where Did They Come From?* (Eerdmans, 2003).

Raphael Patai. *The Hebrew Goddess.* Detroit: Wayne State University Press, 1999.

A groundbreaking study of the feminine forms of the divine in the Jewish tradition.

Joseph Gaer. *The Lore of the Old Testament.* New York: Grosset & Dunlap, 1966 (1951).

This is an old book, but one that holds up quite well. It's quite enjoyable. A good place to dip into the legends and lore of the Bible. Its equally enjoyable companion volume is *The Lore of the New Testament* (New York: Grosset & Dunlap, 1966 [1952]).

Margaret Barker. *The Great Angel: A Study of Israel's Second God.* Louisville, Ky.: Westminster John Knox, 1992.

Not really for beginners, this brilliant and innovative book nevertheless gives the best picture of the Great Angel in biblical times and thought.

Simon Goldhill. *The Temple of Jerusalem.* Cambridge, Mass.: Harvard University Press, 2005.

A brief, learned, and engaging work on the history of the Temple.

The New Testament

Raymond E. Brown. *An Introduction to the New Testament*. New York: Doubleday, 1996.

Brown, a Catholic priest and professor, was one of the most respected New Testament scholars of his generation. This book is more for reference than for reading, but it is invaluable to have on hand to help you sort your way through the background of the New Testament.

Bart D. Ehrman. *Did Jesus Exist? The Historical Argument for Jesus of Nazareth*. San Francisco: Harper One, 2012.

This book and its sequel, *How Jesus Became God: The Exaltation of a Jewish Preacher from Galilee* (San Francisco: Harper One, 2014), are masterful accounts of Christology for the general reader.

Albert Schweitzer. *The Mysticism of Paul the Apostle*, trans. William Montgomery. Baltimore: Johns Hopkins University Press, 1998.

First published in 1930 by the great theologian and humanitarian, this too is not a book for beginners. In fact it is quite difficult. But it is one of very few works that I know of on the apostle Paul that are worth reading.

Elaine Pagels. *The Gnostic Gospels*. New York: Vintage, 1989 [1979].

This extremely successful book is both sharp and readable. It's especially valuable for its insights on how the apostolic tradition was formed.

Kabbalah

The best way to approach the inner meaning of the Bible is to learn something about the Kabbalah, which has tremendously influenced both Judaism and Christianity. Kabbalistic ideas help explain an enormous amount that is arcane and baffling in the biblical text.

Halevi, Z'ev ben Shimon. *Kabbalah: Tradition of Hidden Knowledge.* London: Thames & Hudson, 1979.

The British Kabbalist Warren Kenton, who writes under the name Z'ev ben Shimon Halevi, is one of today's most distinguished and accomplished teachers of Kabbalah in the world. (Full disclosure: he is a good friend of mine.) He has written a number of books. This lavishly illustrated picture book is probably the best one to start with.

Another, less heavily illustrated, is *Introduction to the Cabala* (York Beach, Maine: Samuel Weiser, 1972). *A Kabbalistic Universe* (Samuel Weiser, 1977) presents a discussion of Genesis like the one I described in chapter 15. *Kabbalah and Exodus* (Samuel Weiser, 1980) provides a detailed account of the inner meaning of the second book in the Bible.

Esoteric Christianity

Richard Smoley. *Inner Christianity: A Guide to the Esoteric Tradition.* Boston: Shambhala, 2002.

The tradition of inner, or esoteric, Christianity has been submerged for many centuries. For this reason it can be hard to get a handle on. I wrote this work a number of years ago to provide an accessible starting point. It contains references to many of the most useful texts in the tradition.

Another book I wrote (with Jay Kinney) is *Hidden Wisdom: A Guide to the Western Inner Traditions* (Wheaton, Ill.: Quest Books, 2006). This one is more about the Western mystical traditions in general. There are chapters on Kabbalah, esoteric Christianity, and Gnosticism among other subjects.

Notes

Introduction

xx   *John Dart quote.* John Dart, "Biblical Research Findings for the Public," Society for Biblical Literature Web site; www.sbl-site.org/publications/article.aspx?articleId=567; accessed Dec. 10, 2014.

xx   *"In Search of Moses."* David Van Biema, "In Search of Moses," *Time*, Dec. 14, 1998; http://content.time.com/time/world/article/0,8599,2053940,00.html; accessed Nov. 2, 2015.

xx   *"How Moses Shaped America."* Bruce Feiler, "How Moses Shaped America," *Time*, Oct. 12, 2009; http://content.time.com/time/magazine/article/0,9171,1927303,00.html; accessed Nov. 2, 2015.

xxii   *Spong quote.* John Shelby Spong, "Gospel of John: What Everyone Should Know About the Fourth Gospel," *Huffington Post*, June 11, 2013; www.huffingtonpost.com/john-shelby-spong/gospel-of-john-what-everyone-knows-about-the-fourth-gospel_b_3422026.html; accessed Jan. 15, 2015.

xxiii   *Jesus eaten by dogs.* John Dominic Crossan, "The Dogs Beneath the Cross," chapter 6 in *Jesus: A Revolutionary Biography* (San Francisco: Harper One,

1994); quoted in Bart D. Ehrman, *How Jesus Became God: The Exaltation of a Jewish Preacher from Galilee* (San Francisco: Harper One, 2014), chapter 4.

xxvi *Hezekiah's seal.* Will Helpern, "Biblical King's Seal Discovered in Dump Site," CNN, Dec. 3, 2015; http://www.cnn.com/2015/12/03/middleeast/king-hezekiah-royal-seal/index.html; accessed Dec. 3, 2015.

xxvii *Moses's name.* Baruch Halpern, "The Exodus from Egypt: Myth or Reality?" chapter 3 in Hershel Shanks, ed., *The Rise of Ancient Israel* (Washington, D.C.: Biblical Archaeology Society, 1992).

xxviii *Schweitzer quote.* Albert Schweitzer, *The Quest of the Historical Jesus,* trans. William Montgomery (New York: Macmillan, 1961 [1906]), 399.

Chapter 1: Groundwater: The Problem of God

3 *Big Bang.* "Carolina's Laura Mersini-Houghton Shows That Black Holes Do Not Exist," University of North Carolina at Chapel Hill website; http://uncnews.unc.edu/2014/09/23/carolinas-laura-mersini-houghton-shows-black-holes-exist/; accessed Mar. 1, 2015.

5 *"Everybody knows..."* Thornton Wilder, *Our Town,* act 3. Emphasis Wilder's.

7 *"The gate was opened..."* Quoted in Richard M. Bucke, *Cosmic Consciousness: A Study in the Evolution of the Human Mind* (New York: Arkana, 1991 [1901]), 182.

8 *"I continued forward..."* Eben Alexander, *Proof of Heaven: A Neurosurgeon's Journey into the Afterlife* (New York: Simon & Schuster, 2012), 46–48.

10 *"Imagine that..."* In P. D. Ouspensky, *In Search of the Miraculous: Fragments of a Forgotten Teaching* (New York: Harcourt, Brace, 1949), 96.

Chapter 2: The Defective Scripture: What We Now Know About the Bible

13 *The "limp leather Bible."* Harold Bloom, *The American Religion: The Emergence of the Post-Christian Nation* (New York: Simon & Schuster, 1992), 57.

19   *"Had Moses not..."* Hayim Nahman Bialik and Yehoshua Hana Ravnitzky, *The Book of Legends: Sefer Ha-Aggadah,* trans. William G. Braude (New York: Schocken, 1992), 152; Babylonian Talmud, Sanhedrin 21b.

21   *"It is not possible..."* Irenaeus 3.11.8. In Irenaeus, *Against the Heresies, Book 3,* Dominic J. Unger, trans. (New York: Newman, 2012), 56.

22   *"These are fountains..."* Athanasius, *Thirty-Ninth Festal Letter:* www.ccel .org/ccel/schaff/npnf204.xxv.iii.iii.xxv.html; accessed Oct. 20, 2014.

25   *"A scribal lapse."* Frank Moore Cross, "Light on the Bible from the Dead Sea Caves," in Hershel Shanks, ed., *Understanding the Dead Sea Scrolls* (New York: Random House, 1992), 161.

26   *"No king is punished..."* Giovanni Pico della Mirandola, *Neuf-cent conclusions philosophiques, cabalistiques, et théologiques,* ed. Bertrand Schefer (Paris: Allia, 1999), 46. My translation.

29   *"You are my Son..."* Bart D. Ehrman, *The Orthodox Corruption of Scripture: The Effect of Early Christological Controversies on the Text of the New Testament* (New York: Oxford University Press, 1993), 62–67.

Chapter 3: The Haze of Legend: From the Flood to the Judges

36   *The Flood myth.* E. J. Michael Witzel, *The Origin of the World's Mythologies* (New York: Oxford University Press, 2012), 355.

36   *"There have been..."* Plato, *Timaeus* 22c; my translation.

37   *The Flood as retribution.* Witzel, *Origin of the World's Mythologies,* 355.

39   *"Ships, arks, and cradles..."* Geoffrey Hodson, "The Hidden Wisdom in Christian Scriptures," in *Sharing the Light: Further Writings of Geoffrey Hodson,* vol. 3, ed. John and Elizabeth Sell (Quezon City, Philippines: Theosophical Publishing House, 2014), 389.

40   *Middle Bronze Age names.* Halpern, in Shanks, *Rise of Ancient Israel,* chapter 3.

41   *Yaqub-Har.* Shanks, *Rise of Ancient Israel,* chapter 3.

42   *"Canaan has been plundered..."* Quoted in ibid., chapter 1.

45   *Baruch Halpern.* Ibid., chapter 3.

46 *Circumcision and the Egyptians.* Herodotus, 2.104; Flavius Josephus, *Against Apion*, 1.22.

48 *Milkom* ... Hershel Shanks, *Frank Moore Cross: Interviews with a Bible Scholar* (Washington, D.C.: Biblical Archaeology Society, 1994), chapter 3.

Chapter 4: Monarchy, United and Divided: From Saul to the Fall of Israel

51 *Saul's reign.* Israel Finkelstein and Neil Asher Silberman, *David and Solomon* (New York: Free Press, 2006), 64–65.

51 *The extent of Saul's kingdom.* Ibid., 67.

53 *"In no other part..."* Robert Draper, "Kings of Controversy," *National Geographic*, Dec. 2010; http://ngm.nationalgeographic.com/print/2010/12/david-and-solomon/draper-text; accessed Nov. 5, 2014.

54 *Plaster overlaid on stone.* Shanks, *Frank Moore Cross*, chapter 4.

54 *Sheshonq's route.* Finkelstein and Silberman, *David and Solomon*, 72.

55 *Omri.* Israel Finkelstein and Neil Asher Silberman, *The Bible Unearthed: Archaeology's New Vision of Ancient Israel and the Origin of Its Secret Texts* (New York: Simon & Schuster, 2001), 178.

58 *"Land of the Red Jews."* Joseph Gaer, *The Lore of the Old Testament* (New York: Grosset & Dunlap, 1966 [1951]), 283.

Chapter 5: Who Was Yahweh?

61 *Causative imperfect form.* Frank Moore Cross, *Canaanite Myth and Hebrew Epic: Essays in the Religion of the History of Israel* (Cambridge, Mass.: Harvard University Press, 1973), 65.

62 *"Hosts."* Ibid., 66–71.

62 *"A cultic name of 'El..."* Ibid., 71.

63 *Teman.* P. Kyle McCarter, Jr., "The Origins of Israelite Religion," in Shanks, *Rise of Ancient Israel*, chapter 4.

65 *"Yahweh remained standing..."* E. A. Speiser, ed. and trans., *The Anchor Bible: Genesis* (Garden City, N.Y.: Doubleday, 1964), 134.

68 *Atirat-yammi.* Cross, *Canaanite Myth and Hebrew Epic*, 15, 37, 66–67.

68 *"It appears that..."* Raphael Patai, *The Hebrew Goddess*, 3d ed. (Detroit: Wayne State University Press, 1999), 50.

69 *Saul M. Olyan.* Quoted in Dever, *Did God Have a Wife? Archaeology and Folk Religion in Ancient Israel* (Grand Rapids, Mich.: Eerdmans, 2005), 201.

69 *"[Y]ahweh of Teiman..."* William G. Dever, *Did God Have a Wife?*, 162. Bracketed insertions are Dever's.

70 *Asherah with a tree.* Dever, *Did God Have a Wife?*, 225–28.

72 *The worship of the goddess.* Margaret Barker, *The Great Angel: A Study of Israel's Second God* (Louisville, Ky.: Westminster John Knox, 1992), 51.

72 *The estrangement of the Shekhinah.* Gershom Scholem, *On the Kabbalah and Its Symbolism*, trans. Ralph Manheim (New York: Schocken, 1965), 107–8. Italics are Scholem's.

Chapter 6: Fall and Return: The Exile and Its Aftermath

76 *Jeremiah and the Scythians.* J. M. Powys Smith, *The Prophets and Their Times*, 2d ed. (Chicago: University of Chicago Press, 1941), 143–45.

78 *"Hebrew is a spoken tongue..."* Bialik and Ravnitzsky, *Book of Legends*, 376; Esther *Rabbah* 4:12.

80 *"The holy originally..."* Paul Tillich, *The Essential Tillich*, ed. F. Forrester Church (New York: Macmillan, 1987), 21.

86 *The book of Daniel.* See W. Sibley Towner, "The Book of Daniel," in Bruce M. Metzger and Michael D. Coogan, eds., *The Oxford Companion to the Bible* (New York: Oxford University Press, 1993), 151.

87 *Resurrection in the Hebrew Bible.* See James H. Charlesworth, ed., *The Old Testament Pseudepigrapha* (Peabody, Mass.: Hendrickson, 2013 [1983]), 1:xxxiii.

87 *The "Laurasian mythos."* Witzel, *Origin of the World's Mythologies*, 422.

87 *"Laurasian mythology..."* Ibid., 181.

88 *"The end of the world..."* Ibid.

88 *Man is the measure...* Protagoras, fragment 801b DK; *The Internet Encyclopedia of Philosophy*; www.iep.utm.edu/protagor/; accessed Dec. 17, 2015.

Chapter 7: Jesus in His Context

94 *"Gnaeus Pompey..."* Tacitus, *Histories*, 5.9; my translation.

94 *The restoration of the republic. The Oxford Classical Dictionary*, 3d ed., Simon Hornblower and Antony Spawforth, eds. (Oxford: Oxford University Press, 1996), 217.

95 *"The outside of the building..."* Flavius Josephus, *The Jewish War*, 5.5.6; translation by Simon Goldhill. In Simon Goldhill, *The Temple of Jerusalem* (Cambridge, Mass.: Harvard University Press, 2005), 71.

95 *"We are not at liberty..."* Flavius Josephus, *Against Apion*, 2:7, 8. Quoted in Patai, *Hebrew Goddess*, 82.

96 *"When Israel used to make..."* This is from the Talmudic treatise B. Yoma 54a, quoted in Patai, *Hebrew Goddess*, 84. Bracketed insertions are Patai's.

96 *Eighteen thousand people.* Peter Richardson, *Herod: King of the Jews and Friend of the Romans* (Columbia: University of South Carolina Press, 1996), 185–86.

97 *"Around this time..."* Flavius Josephus, *Antiquities of the Jews*, 18.3.3. My translation.

97 *"[Ananus] assembled..."* Ibid., 20.9.1, my translation.

99 *"How is it that..."* Samuel Beckett, *Waiting for Godot* (New York: Grove, 1954), 9.

101 *Pontius Pilate and Jesus.* Tacitus, *Annals*, 15:44.

101 *The Jesus Seminar.* Robert W. Funk, Roy W. Hoover, and the Jesus Seminar, ed. and trans., *The Five Gospels: What Did Jesus Really Say?* (San Francisco: Harper San Francisco, 1993), 34.

102 *"Eighty-two percent..."* Ibid., 5.

102 *"Methodological skepticism."* Ibid., 37.

104 *"Like the cowboy hero . . ."* Ibid., 32–33.

105 *"The Jesus story . . ."* Timothy Freke and Peter Gandy, *The Jesus Mysteries: Was the "Original Jesus" a Pagan God?* (New York: Three Rivers, 1999), 9.

106 *"What, for example . . . ?" and "What we know about Jesus . . ."* Bart D. Ehrman, *Did Jesus Exist? The Historical Argument for Jesus of Nazareth* (San Francisco: Harper One, 2012), 26–27.

Chapter 8: The Life of Jesus: Origins

110 *The Nativity accounts.* John Dominic Crossan, *The Historical Jesus: The Life of a Mediterranean Jewish Peasant* (San Francisco: Harper San Francisco, 1991), 371.

111 *"The only common features . . ."* Ibid.

111 *The conjunction of Jupiter, Saturn, and Mars.* Charlesworth, *Old Testament Pseudepigrapha*, 1:479n.

111 *Quirinius.* See the entry "Quirinius," *The Oxford Classical Dictionary*, 2d ed., N. G. L. Hammond and H. H. Scullard, eds. (Oxford: Oxford University Press, 1970), 908.

113 *Eusebius.* Eusebius, *Ecclesiastical History*, 1.7.

115 *"In their anxiety . . ."* Flavius Josephus, *The Jewish War*, 2.8.6; in Josephus, *The Destruction of the Jews*, trans. G. A. Williamson (London: Folio Society, 1971), 263. See also Joan E. Taylor, *The Essenes, the Scrolls, and the Dead Sea* (New York: Oxford University Press, 2012), 188.

115 *"Some of them claim . . ."* Josephus, *Jewish War*, 2.8.12; *Destruction of the Jews*, 265.

115 *The prophecy about Herod.* Richardson, *Herod*, 257; Josephus, *Antiquities*, 15.10.5.

115 *The Essenes' property on the Dead Sea.* Taylor, *The Essenes, the Scrolls, and the Dead Sea*, 270.

116 *The purpose of the Essene community.* Ibid., 303.

116 *"Every word . . ."* Josephus, *Jewish War*, 2.8.6; *Destruction of the Jews*, 262.

116 *"Teaching the same doctrine . . ."* Josephus, *Jewish War*, 2.8.11; *Destruction of the Jews*, 264.

117 *Relieving themselves on the Sabbath.* Josephus, *Jewish War*, 2.8.9; *Destruction of the Jews*, 263.

118 *Herodians.* Taylor, *The Essenes, the Scrolls, and the Dead Sea*, 130.

119 *Literacy.* Christopher John Farley, "Was Jesus Illiterate? Author Reza Aslan Thinks So." *The Wall Street Journal,* Aug. 1, 2013; http://blogs.wsj.com/speakeasy/2013/08/01/was-jesus-illiterate-author-reza-aslan-thinks-so/; accessed Dec. 17, 2015.

121 *"There is not one Moral Virtue . . ."* William Blake, *The Complete Poetry and Prose of William Blake*, ed. David V. Erdman, rev. ed. (Berkeley: University of California Press, 1982), 875.

122 *Jesus and Sepphoris.* Craig A. Evans, ed., *The Routledge Encyclopedia of the Historical Jesus* (New York: Routledge, 2010), 296.

122 *Diogenes masturbating.* Diogenes Laertius, 6.46; in R. Bracht Branham and Marie-Odile Goulet-Cazé, eds., *The Cynics: The Cynic Movement in Antiquity and Its Legacy* (Berkeley: University of California Press, 2000), 226.

Chapter 9: What Jesus Taught

125 *"The Pharisees are routinely . . ."* Funk, Hoover, and the Jesus Seminar, *The Five Gospels*, 547.

126 *"The notion that . . ."* Reza Aslan, *Zealot: The Life and Times of Jesus of Nazareth* (New York: Random House, 2014), introduction.

129 *Wikipedia.* "Kingship and kingdom of God"; http://en.wikipedia.org/wiki/Kingship_and_kingdom_of_God; accessed Jan. 3, 2015.

130 *"To carry out the will of the Father . . ."* Catechism of the Catholic Church, §541. Quoted material within the passage is taken from *Lumen gentium*, the Dogmatic Constitution of the Church, promulgated by Pope Paul VI in 1964.

130 *The "ecclesiastical" interpretation.* Pope Benedict XVI, *Jesus of Nazareth: From the Baptism in the Jordan to the Transfiguration* (New York: Doubleday, 2007), 50.

130 *"God's sovereignty over history."* Reinhold Niebuhr, *The Nature and Destiny of Man: A Christian Interpretation* (Louisville, Ky.: Westminster John Knox, n.d. [1943]), 2:35.

131 *"Seat yourself, then . . ."* In *The Philokalia: The Complete Text,* trans. G. E. H. Palmer, Philip Sherrard, and Kallistos Ware (London: Faber & Faber, 1995), 4:205–6. Here I have modified the authors' translation of one word from "intellect" to "consciousness." The word in question is *nous,* which does not mean "intellect" in its present-day sense. It actually means "consciousness" or "mind," as we see from its derivatives in modern English, such as "noetic." On this point see *Philokalia,* 4:432.

133 *"Those who pray . . ."* Quoted in Pope Benedict XVI, *Jesus of Nazareth,* 50.

134 *"This Self is the Lord . . ."* Brihadaranyaka Upanishad, 5, 6; in *The Ten Principal Upanishads,* trans. W. B. Yeats and Shree Purohit Swami (New York: Macmillan, 1937), 135, 137.

135 *"Natural selection favors . . ."* Drew Westen, *The Political Brain: The Role of Emotion in Deciding the Fate of the Nation* (New York: Public Affairs, 2008), 72. Emphasis Westen's.

137 *"Regard rather than affection."* Henry George Liddell and Robert Scott, *A Greek-English Lexicon,* ed. Henry Stuart Jones (Oxford, UK: Oxford at the Clarendon Press, 1968), s.v. *agapáo.*

139 *The date of Mark.* For a succinct summary of the argument, see Morna D. Hooker, "The Gospel according to Mark," in *The Oxford Companion to the Bible,* 493.

142 *Jesus's ethical statements.* Walter Schmithals, *The Theology of the First Christians,* trans. O. C. Dean Jr. (Louisville, Ky.: Westminster John Knox, 1997), 9.

Chapter 10: The Life of Jesus: The Public Career

145 *"Mark, who had been Peter's interpreter..."* Quoted in Eusebius, 3.39; Eusebius, *History of the Church*, trans. G. A. Williamson (London: Penguin, 1989), 103–4.

146 *"John called to baptism..."* Josephus, *Antiquities* 18.5.2; my translation.

150 *The Mandaeans.* Edmondo Lupieri, *The Mandaeans: The Last Gnostics,* trans. Charles Hindley (Grand Rapids, Mich.: Eerdmans, 2002).

150 *The Mandaeans today.* "Sabian Mandaeans," World Directory of Minorities and Religious Peoples Web site; www.minorityrights.org/5746/iraq/sabian-mandaeans.html; accessed Jan. 15, 2015.

151 *Paulus.* For this discussion I am relying on Schweitzer, *The Quest of the Historical Jesus,* 52–55.

152 *"A serious enquirer..."* C. H. Dodd, *The Interpretation of the Fourth Gospel* (Cambridge, UK: Cambridge University Press, 1953), 332.

153 *Mosquito and ammonia.* Charles Tart, *Waking Up: Overcoming the Obstacles to Human Potential* (Boston: Shambhala, 1986), 6, 100.

154 *"Consensus trance induction..."* Ibid., 91.

154 *Zombies in Haitian law.* Barbara Bavis, "Does the Haitian Criminal Code Outlaw Making Zombies?," Library of Congress website, Oct. 31, 2014; http://blogs.loc.gov/law/2014/10/does-the-haitian-criminal-code-outlaw-making-zombies/; accessed Dec. 17, 2015. For more on zombies, see Wade Davis, *The Serpent and the Rainbow: A Harvard Scientist's Astonishing Journey into the Secret Society of Haitian Voodoo, Zombis [sic] and Magic* (New York: Simon & Schuster, 1985).

156 *The Jesus Seminar on Mark 8:27–30.* Funk, Hoover, and the Jesus Seminar, *The Five Gospels,* 75.

157 *"It is impossible to derive..."* Charlesworth, *Old Testament Pseudepigrapha,* 1:xxxi.

163 *"My view now..."* Ehrman, *How Jesus Became God,* chapter 4.

164 *"One night when I am nine . . ."* Dan Wakefield, *How Do We Know When It's God?: A Spiritual Memoir* (Boston: Little, Brown, 1999), chapter 1.

Chapter 11: The Birth of the Church

167 *Abgar.* Eusebius, 1.13; Josephus, *Destruction of the Jews*, 30–34.

167 *Tiberius.* Eusebius, 2.2; Josephus, *Destruction of the Jews*, 38–39.

167 *John at Ephesus.* Eusebius, 3.20, 23; Josephus, *Destruction of the Jews*, 82, 83. Cf. Jerome, *De viris illustribus*, 9.

168 *"John the apostle . . ."* Eusebius, 3.28; Josephus, *Destruction of the Jews*, 92.

172 *Theopedia:* www.theopedia.com; accessed Dec. 22, 2015.

174 *"James, who is called . . ."* Jerome, *De viris illustribus* 2; www.newadvent .org/fathers/2708.htm; accessed Nov. 3, 2015.

174 *"The disciples said . . ."* *Gospel of Thomas* 12, in James M. Robinson, ed., *The Nag Hammadi Library*, 3d ed. (San Francisco: Harper San Francisco, 1990), 127

174 *"After the apostles . . ."* Jerome, *De viris illustribus* 2; www.newadvent.org/ fathers/2708.htm; accessed Nov. 3, 2015.

175 *"The Lord . . ."* Ibid.

175 *The martyrdom of James.* Eusebius, 2.23; in Josephus, *Destruction of the Jews*, 60.

176 *"Herod [the Great] . . ."* Eusebius, 1.7; in Josephus, *Destruction of the Jews*, 22.

177 *"Practise no magic . . ."* *Didache*, 2; in Maxwell Staniforth, trans., *Early Christian Writings* (London: Penguin, 1987), 191.

177 *"If anyone comes . . ."* *Didache*, 11; in ibid., 195.

178 *"Even in the same . . ."* Gregory J. Riley, *One Jesus, Many Christs: How Jesus Inspired Not One True Christianity, but Many* (San Francisco: Harper San Francisco, 1997), 4.

179 *"My twin . . ."* *The Book of Thomas the Contender*, in Robinson, ed., *Nag Hammadi Library*, 201.

180 *"And he [Jesus] ..."* Gospel of Thomas, 13, in ibid., 128.

181 *"Cremated remains..."* "What Does the Church Teach about Cremation?," Catholic Cemeteries of the Archdiocese of Washington Web site; www.ccaw .org/about_cremation.html; accessed Jan. 26, 2015.

182 *"New Testament accounts..."* Elaine Pagels, *The Gnostic Gospels* (New York: Vintage, 1989 [1979]), 6.

Chapter 12: Paul: The Great Apostle

184 *"No one has ever understood..."* In Albert Schweitzer, *The Mysticism of Paul the Apostle,* trans. William Montgomery (Baltimore: Johns Hopkins University Press, 1998), 38.

187 *Marcion "did little more than..."* Quoted in *The Anchor Bible: Galatians,* J. Louis Martyn, ed. and trans. (New York: Doubleday, 1997), 370.

189 *"The Divine justice..."* Anselm of Canterbury, *Cur Deus Homo,* chapter 24; in *St. Anselm: Basic Writings,* trans. S. N. Deane, 2d ed. (La Salle, Ill.: Open Court, 1962), 235.

190 *"The permissibility..."* Arthur O. Lovejoy, *The Great Chain of Being: A Study of the History of an Idea* (New York: Harper & Row, 1960 [1936]), 83.

Chapter 13: Revelation: The Overthrow of the Wicked Angels

199 *"Muddled fantasy-thinking."* Dodd, *Interpretation of the Fourth Gospel,* 215n.

199 *"All, great, genuine..."* Boris Pasternak, *Doctor Zhivago,* trans. Max Hayward and Manya Harari (New York: Pantheon, 1958), 90.

201 *The date of Revelation.* Irenaeus, 5.30.3; in Eusebius, 3.18.

201 *The persecution under Domitian.* For a summary of the arguments, see Brown, *Introduction to the New Testament,* 805–9.

202 *Nancy Reagan.* Kitty Kelley, *Nancy Reagan: The Unauthorized Biography* (New York: Simon & Schuster, 1991), chapter 24.

202 *"Proof that Ronald Reagan..."* www.datehookup.com/Thread-107446 .htm; accessed Feb. 1, 2015.

202 *"On the 10th Anniversary ..."* "Barack Hussein Obama: Occult Gematria and Numerology"; http://obama793.com/2014/11/10/the-devils-number -666-and-its-connection-with-barack-obama/; accessed Feb. 1, 2015.

202 *"Final warning ..."* "%100 Proof Pope Francis I Antichrist 666 Obama Mark of the Beast"; www.youtube.com/watch?v=s_K-OsxiNqQ; accessed Feb. 1, 2015.

204 *"The Revelation is ..."* Boris Mouravieff, *Gnosis: Study and Commentaries on the Esoteric Tradition of Eastern Orthodoxy,* trans. S. A. Wissa (Newburyport, Mass.: Praxis Institute Press, 1989), 1:180.

206 *Seven zones.* See for example, the *Corpus Hermeticum,* 1:24–28.

209 *"The Secret Revelation of John ..."* Gilles Quispel, *The Secret Book of Revelation* (New York: McGraw-Hill, 1979), 130.

209 *James M. Pryse.* Pryse, *The Apocalypse Unsealed, Being an Esoteric Interpretation of the Initiation of Iôannês* (Los Angeles: James M. Pryse, 1931), 35, 36.

210 *"Other books ... similar lines."* See, for example, Omraam Mikhael Aïvanhov, *The Book of Revelations* [sic]: *A Commentary,* rev. ed. (N.p.: Prosveta, 2000), and Zachary F. Lansdowne, *The Revelation of St. John: The Path to Soul Initiation* (York Beach, Maine: Weiser, 2006). More titles can be found in Richard Smoley, "The Esoteric Revelation," *Quest* 102(4) (Fall 2014): 138.

Chapter 14: The Master and Two Marys

212 "The absolute God ..." Emanuel Swedenborg, *True Christianity,* trans. Jonathan S. Rose (West Chester, Pa.: Swedenborg Foundation, 2006), 1:149, §26. Emphasis in the original.

213 *"Paul, a slave ..."* Ehrman, *How Jesus Became God,* chapter 6.

213 *"There are more examples ..."* For a full discussion, see ibid., chapter 6.

215 *"Jesus was thought of ..."* Ibid., chapter 7.

216 *Metatron.* See Gershom Scholem, *Kabbalah* (New York: Dorset, 1974), 377–81.

217 *"And at that time..."* 1 Enoch 48:1–4. Quoted in Moshe Idel, *Ben: Sonship in Jewish Mysticism* (London: Continuum, 2007), 21.

218 *"I am Enoch..."* 3 Enoch 4:1; in Charlesworth, *Old Testament Pseudepigrapha*, 1:238.

220 *"And even if there be..."* Philo, *On the Confusion of Tongues*, 28; in C. D. Yonge, trans., *The Works of Philo* (Peabody, Mass.: Hendrickson, 1993), 247. My emphasis.

220 *Lógos.* For some insights along these lines, see Martin Heidegger, *Early Greek Thinking*, trans. David Farrell Krell and Frank Capuzzi (New York: Harper & Row, 1975), chapter 2. See also my book *The Dice Game of Shiva: How Consciousness Creates the Universe* (Novato, Calif.: New World Library, 2009), chapter 2.

221 *"And I stood in the midst..."* Philo, *Who Is the Heir of Divine Things?*, 42; in Yonge, *Works of Philo*, 293.

223 *"Struck me with sixty lashes..."* 3 Enoch 16:5, in Charlesworth, *Old Testament Pseudepigrapha*, 1:268.

224 *Tribog.* Boris Mouravieff, *Beliefs of the Pre-Christian Slavs: Parallels with Early Christianity* (Newburyport, Mass: Praxis Institute Press, 1997), 9; https://books.google.com/books?id=gmKGVkEAD_UC&pg=PA9&lpg=PA9&dq=Tribog+Slavs&source=bl&ots=jISA6seWVL&sig=IYNDaR6ozwxCo3XPpvjK-1a0Yto&hl=en&sa=X&ved=0ahUKEwiRusiyxfDJAhVDXh4KHQ88COkQ6AEIIDAA#v=onepage&q=Tribog%20Slavs&f=false; accessed Dec. 29, 2015.

224 *The sacred ternary.* For a full discussion of this theme, see René Guénon, *The Great Triad*, trans. Peter Kingsley (Cambridge, UK: Quinta Essentia, 1991).

225 *"It is...reasonable..."* Mogen Müller, "The Son of Man," in *The Oxford Companion to the Bible*, 712.

225 *The Great Angel and the Messiah.* Barker, *The Great Angel*, 36–38.

230 *"Sprinkled blest water..."* R. E. Witt, *Isis in the Graeco-Roman World* (Ithaca, N.Y.: Cornell University Press, 1971), 22.

231 *A puddle of spilled ice cream.* Megan K. Stack, "Faithful See Virgin of Gua-
dalupe in Spilled Ice Cream in Houston," *Amarillo Globe-News* website,
Jan. 14, 2000; http://amarillo.com/stories/2000/01/14/tex_see.shtml;
accessed Nov. 8, 2014.

233 *"Simon Peter said ..."* Gospel of *Thomas,* 114, in Robinson, ed., *Nag Hammadi Library,* 138.

233 *"To be male."* Annick de Souzenelle, *Le symbolisme du corps humain: De
l'arbre de vie au schéma Corporel,* 3d ed. (St.-Jean-de-Braye, France: Dan-
gles, 1984), 149.

233 *"And the companion of ..."* The Gospel of Philip, 63–64, in Robinson, ed.,
Nag Hammadi Library, 148.

236 *Refuting* Holy Blood, Holy Grail. See, for example, Robert Richardson,
"The Priory of Sion Hoax," *Gnosis* 51 (Spring 1999): 49–55.

237 *"A story sewn from whole cloth ..."* Jean Markale, *The Church of Mary Magdalene: The Sacred Feminine and the Treasure of Rennes-le-Château,* trans.
Jon Graham (Rochester, Vt.: Inner Traditions, 2004), 13.

237 *"Brought the vessel ..."* Richard Smoley, "The Mystery of Regeneration:
The *Gnosis* Interview with R. J. Stewart," *Gnosis* 51 (Spring 1999): 26.

237 *Order of Mary Magdalene.* Gnostic Sanctuary website; www.gnosticsanc
tuary.org/lineage.html; accessed Jan. 2, 2016.

Chapter 15: Practical Mysticism

241 Treasure Island. Robert Louis Stevenson, *Treasure Island,* chapter 29.

242 *"Very many mistakes ..."* From *The Philokalia of Origen,* 1.8, 16–17, trans.
George Lewis; www.tertullian.org/fathers/origen_philocalia_02_text.htm;
accessed Mar. 1, 2015. Cf. Origen, *On First Principles,* trans. G. W. Butterworth
(New York: Harper & Row, 1966), 4.3.1.

243 *Three levels of meaning.* Origen, *On First Principles,* 4.2.4, 275–76.

243 *"For just as man ..."* Ibid., 276.

245 Pneuma *and* nous. Dodd, *Interpretation of the Fourth Gospel,* 27.

247 *Exodus.* Z'ev ben Shimon Halevi, *Kabbalah and Exodus* (London: Rider, 1980).

247 *"To lay bare . . ."* Gregory of Nyssa, *The Life of Moses*, Abraham J. Malherbe and Everett Ferguson, trans. (New York: Paulist, 1978), 2:5, p. 56.

248 *"Whenever life demands . . ."* Gregory, *The Life of Moses*, 2.7, p. 56.

248 *"Quaranic sacred history . . ."* Seyyed Hossein Nasr, ed., *The Study Quran: A New Translation and Commentary* (San Francisco: Harper One, 2015), xxvii.

250 *The Four Worlds.* See Richard Smoley and Jay Kinney, *Hidden Wisdom: A Guide to the Western Inner Traditions*, 2d ed. (Wheaton, Ill.: Quest, 2006), 87–88.

252 *Eden and Yetzirah.* See Z'ev ben Shimon Halevi, *A Kabbalistic Universe* (London: Rider, 1977), 67.

259 *Chariot factions.* See, for example, Mike Dash, "Blue Versus Green: Rocking the Byzantine Empire," Smithsonian.com, Mar. 2, 2012; www.smithso nianmag.com/history/blue-versus-green-rocking-the-byzantine-empire -113325928/?no-ist; accessed Nov. 3, 2015.

Coda

263 *"The name of Jesus . . ."* *A Course in Miracles: Manual for Teachers* (Tiburon, Calif.: Foundation for Inner Peace, 1975), 83.

264 *"The world will end . . ."* Ibid., 36.

264 *"We—all creatures . . ."* Philip K. Dick, *The Exegesis of Philip K. Dick*, ed. Pamela Jackson and Jonathan Lethem (Boston: Houghton Mifflin, 2011), 446.